The Internet and the Mass Media

The Internet and the Mass Media

Lucy Küng, Robert G. Picard and Ruth Towse

Los Angeles | London | New Delhi
Singapore | Washington DC

SAGE Publications Ltd
1 Oliver's Yard
55 City Road
London EC1Y 1SP

SAGE Publications Inc.
2455 Teller Road
Thousand Oaks, California 91320

SAGE Publications India Pvt Ltd
B 1/I 1 Mohan Cooperative Industrial Area
Mathura Road
New Delhi 110 044

SAGE Publications Asia-Pacific Pte Ltd
33 Pekin Street #02-01
Far East Square
Singapore 048763

Library of Congress Control Number: 2007932677

British Library Cataloguing in Publication data

A catalogue record for this book is available from
the British Library

ISBN 978-1-4129-4734-3
ISBN 978-1-4129-4735-0 (pbk)

FSC
Mixed Sources
Product group from well-managed
forests and other controlled sources
Cert no. SGS-COC-2953
www.fsc.org
© 1996 Forest Stewardship Council

Typeset by CEPHA Imaging Pvt. Ltd., Bangalore, India
Printed in Great Britain by CPI Antony Rowe, Chippenham, Wiltshire
Printed on paper from sustainable resources

CONTENTS

List of figures and tables   vii
List of contributors   viii
Preface   xiii

1   Introduction   1
    Lucy Küng, Robert G. Picard and Ruth Towse

2   Theoretical perspectives on the impact of the Internet on the
    mass media industries   17
    Lucy Küng, Robert G. Picard and Ruth Towse

3   The impact of the Internet on media technology, platforms and
    innovation   45
    Anders Henten and Reza Tadayoni

4   The impact of the Internet on media content   65
    Richard van der Wurff

5   The impact of the Internet on users   86
    Piet Bakker and Charo Sádaba

6   The impact of the Internet on media policy, regulation and
    copyright law   102
    Des Freedman, Anders Henten, Ruth Towse and Roger Wallis

7   The impact of the Internet on media organisation strategies and
    structures   125
    *Lucy Küng, Nikos Leandros, Robert G. Picard, Roland Schroeder
    and Richard van der Wurff*

8   The impact of the Internet on business models in the media
    industries – a sector-by-sector analysis   149
    Marko Ala-Fossi, Piet Bakker, Hanna-Kaisa Ellonen, Lucy Küng,
    Stephen Lax, Charo Sádaba and Richard van der Wurff

9   Conclusions   170
    Lucy Küng, Robert G. Picard and Ruth Towse

Index   178

LIST OF FIGURES AND TABLES

Figures

2.1 '3-C' model of convergence 37
3.1 Media and communication technologies/applications: timeline 46
7.1 Value chain in the movie industry 143

Tables

1.1 Households with access to the Internet as a percentage of all households 6
4.1 Selected Web size indicators 71
4.2 Websites and documents accessible via Yahoo! Directory (on 10/01/06) 75
5.1 Percentage of European 16–24 year olds intending to use their mobile/PDA/Blackberry to ... 91
5.2 World Internet usage and population 92
5.3 Time spent (in minutes) on different media in six countries, 2001–2006 97

LIST OF CONTRIBUTORS

Marko Ala-Fossi is senior lecturer in radio at the Department of Journalism and Mass Communication, University of Tampere, Finland. Prior to his academic career, he has worked for YLE (Finnish Broadcasting Company) as a radio journalist, producer, training advisor and market analyst (1989–2004). He holds a PhD (2005) from the University of Tampere on the quality cultures in Finnish and US commercial radio. Besides different forms of local, commercial and digital radio content and production cultures, his research interests also include political economy and social shaping of the new media delivery technologies.

Piet Bakker studied political science at the University of Amsterdam. He worked as a journalist for several newspapers, magazines and radio stations, and was a teacher at the School for Journalism in Utrecht. He also organised workshops for newspaper publishers and worked as a consultant on newspaper innovation. Since 1985, he works at the Department of Communications at the University of Amsterdam/Amsterdam School of Communications Research (ASCoR) as an associate professor, and since 2007, he is also professor of cross media content at Hogeschool Utrecht. He has edited and published books and articles on reading habits, media history, local journalism, the Internet, Dutch media, international news, investigative journalism, the music industry and free newspapers. He teaches mass communication and journalism at undergraduate and MA levels.

Hanna-Kaisa Ellonen is senior lecturer in knowledge management at the School of Business, Lappeenranta University of Technology (LUT). She holds an MSc degree in economics and business administration from Helsinki School of Economics, and a DSc(Econ) from LUT. Her doctoral dissertation was about the impact of the Internet in magazine publishing. Her research interests are in the areas of media management, the Internet and technological change. Her work has been published in the *International Journal of Innovation and Technology Management, International Journal of Technology Marketing* and *International Journal of Web-Based Communities*.

Des Freedman is senior lecturer in communications and cultural studies in the Department of Media and Communications, Goldsmiths, University of London. He is the author of *The Television Policies of the Labour Party, 1951–2001* (Frank Cass, 2003), *The Politics of Media Policy* (forthcoming, Polity) and co-editor of *War and the Media: Reporting Conflict 24/7* (Sage, 2003).

Anders Henten is associate professor at Center for Communication, Media and Information Technologies at Copenhagen Institute of Technology, Aalborg University in Denmark. He is a graduate in communications and international development studies from Roskilde University and holds a PhD from the Technical University of Denmark. His main areas of research are regulation of telecommunications, information and communication technology innovation, service innovation and internationalisation, socio-economic implications of information and communication technologies including e-commerce and business models. Anders Henten has worked professionally in the areas of communications economy and policy for 20 years. He has participated in numerous research projects financed by the European Union, the Nordic Council of Ministers, Danish Research Councils and Ministries, and in consultancies financed by World Bank, UNCTAD, ITU, etc. He has published in over 200 academic publications.

Lucy Küng is associate professor at the Media Management Transformation Centre at Jönköping International Business School and a member of the executive board of the Swiss Broadcasting Corporation, SRG. Her research focusses on strategic change in the media sectors, particularly the impact of 'soft' factors such as culture, cognition, leadership and creativity on performance. She holds a PhD and Habilitation from the University of St. Gallen, where she was director of the Competence Centre for the Media and Communication Industries, an international research consortium/think tank examining strategic, management and organisational challenges facing the media industry. She is the author of *Inside the BBC and CNN: Managing Media Organisations* (Routledge, 2000) and *Strategic Management in the Media Industry* (Sage, 2007), as well as numerous academic articles and conference papers. She is a Research Fellow at Ashridge, and holds or has held many advisory positions in the field of media management, including being the Swiss Representative for EU COST Action 20 on 'The impact of the Internet on the Mass Media in Europe' (since 2001), Founding Board Member of the European Media Management Association (since 2005), Visiting Fellow in New Media at the BBC (2001–2002) and Member of UK Government Foresight Taskforce 'The Future and Development of Information Relationships' (2000–2001).

Stephen Lax is lecturer in communications technology at the Institute of Communications Studies, University of Leeds. His research interests are in the social role of communications technologies. He is a member of the Digital Radio Cultures in Europe research group, and is on the steering committee of the UK Radio Studies Network. He is author of *Beyond the Horizon: Communications Technologies Past Present and Future* (University of Luton Press, 1997) and *Media and Communication Technologies* (forthcoming, Palgrave), and editor of *Access Denied in the Information Age* (Palgrave, 2001).

Nikos Leandros is assistant professor at Panteion University of Social and Political Sciences, where he teaches Media Economics and Economics of Culture, at both undergraduate and postgraduate levels. He holds a BSc degree in Applied Economics from University of East London, an MSc in Economics and a PhD from Salford University. He has worked as lecturer at Salford University, at the Economic Research Division of the Bank of Greece and was Director of the Research and Documentation Observatory of the National Book Center. He teaches at the National Centre for Public Administration and Local Government. Nikos Leandros has published extensively in leading academic journals, and he is the author of a number of books and monographs, including *Print Media in Greece. Economic and Technological Perspectives* (1992), *The Political Economy of Mass Media* (2000) and *The Internet: Development and Change* (2005). He is the editor of *The Impact of Internet on the Mass Media in Europe* (2006). His current research interests include new media, information society, ICTs, e-Business and the new economy and cultural management.

Robert G. Picard is director of the Media Management Transformation Centre at Jönköping International Business School. His research focusses on economic structures of media markets, media industries and firms, demand for media products and services, business models and strategies of media operations, productivity of media firms, financial performance and government policies affecting economic aspects of media. His research has involved newspapers, advertising, broadcasting and new media. Picard is the author and editor of 20 books, editor of the *Journal of Media Business Studies* and is the founding editor of the *Journal of Media Economics*. Picard has been a fellow at the Shorenstein Center at the John F. Kennedy School of Government at Harvard University, has consulted and carried out assignments for governments in North America and Europe and for international organisations including the European Commission, UNESCO and the World Intellectual Property Organisation. He has been a consultant for leading media companies in North America, Europe, Asia, Africa and Latin America.

Charo Sádaba is associate professor of interactive marketing and head of the Media Management Department at the School of Communication of the University of Navarra (Spain). She lectures Interactive Marketing and New Advertising Media for undergraduate students and New Media in the MSc in Corporate Communications at the University of Navarra. She acted as Vice-Chair for the A20 COST Action, a European research network on the Impact of the Internet on the mass media, where she coordinated the Television and Film Working Group. Her research focusses on the commercial uses of the new interactive media platforms, and on the special relationship between youth and information technologies.

Roland Schroeder is professor of media management at the University of Applied Science Business and Information Technology School in Iserlohn, Germany. His research focus is on new media developments, network economy and comparative media systems. He is also the managing director of the Erich Brost Institute for Journalism in Europe at Dortmund University.

Reza Tadayoni is associate professor at Center for Communication, Media and Information Technologies at Copenhagen Institute of Technology, Aalborg University. He holds an MScEE from Danish Technical University (DT), specialised in broadband communication, and holds a PhD from DTU, with the title 'Technological, political and economic changes and their implications for the evolution of broadcasting services'. Between 1991 and 1997, he participated in several Danish and European research and development projects within the field of communication technologies partly at DTU and partly as an R&D engineer. From 1997 to the beginning of 2008, he worked as a part of scientific staff at DTU, first at Center for Tele-Information and later Center for Information and Communication Technologies. In this period, he has been involved in a variety of research and education projects. His main research focus is on media convergence, and he has published a number of scientific papers and research reports.

Ruth Towse is professor of economics of creative industries at Erasmus University Rotterdam, the Netherlands, and at Bournemouth University, UK. She specialises in cultural economics and the economics of copyright. She has published widely on both fields in academic journals and books and has also edited several collections of papers and original contributions, notably *A Handbook of Cultural Economics* (2003). Her most recent publication (2006) is, 'Copyright and artists: a view from cultural economics' *Journal of Economic Surveys*, 20, 4; 567–585. Ruth Towse was joint editor of the *Journal of Cultural Economics* from 1993 to 2002, and is president of the Association for Cultural Economics International (2006–8). She was president of the Society for Economic Research in Copyright Issues from 2004–6, and is one of The

Netherlands' national representatives on the COST A20 programme. She has consulted for Arts Council of England, Welsh Arts Council, Industry Canada, World Intellectual Property Organisation (WIPO) and Spanish Authors' Society.

Richard van der Wurff is senior researcher at The Amsterdam School of Communications Research. His research interests include the relationship between media competition and performance, and the impact of the Internet on publishing. He teaches on media economics, strategic management of media organisations and Internet regulation. He has published in the *Journal of Media Economics*, the *European Journal of Communication*, the *Journal of Broadcasting and Electronic Media* and *New Media & Society*. He has edited a book on media and open societies (Het Spinhuis, 2000, with Jan van Cuilenburg), and *Print and Online Newspapers in Europe* (Het Spinhuis, 2005, with Edmund Lauf). He coordinated the newspaper working group of COST A20, and is a member of the International Advisory Board of *New Media & Society*.

Roger Wallis is professor of multimedia at the Royal Institute of Technology in Sweden. As a composer, he is also an elected board member of the Swedish Music Copyright Society, and an executive chairman of the Swedish Society of Popular Music Composers. He is a member of the Programme Committee of the annual eChallenges conference (EU supported) and the Advisory Board to the Swedish Ministry of Enterprise on matters of IT strategy and policy. Dr. Wallis holds an MA from Cambridge in Natural Sciences and Industrial Management and a PhD from Gothenburg University on the changing structure of the international music industry. He is the author of numerous books, chapters and articles on the media industry and the digital environment, and recently concluded an EU-funded study of policy implications of the music industry's response to digital technology (www.musiclesssons.se). His research interests include the IPR/copyright regime, creativity, trust, integrity and responsibility in the Internet world, e-commerce and new partnerships and consumer acceptance of new media delivery technologies.

PREFACE

In 2000, 50 academics, all with sufficient expertise to have been nominated by their European government agencies, gathered in a small, stuffy room in Brussels to be initiated to the ins and outs of the European Science Foundation's Committee on Science and Technology (COST) procedures and, specifically, to formally start the COST A20 Project, the 'Impact of the Internet on the Mass Media'. For many of us, this did not seem a propitious beginning, but to the surprise of many, it developed into a most fruitful co-operative venture. Through it, a group of people from different countries were able to meet and, perhaps of equal importance, people from different disciplines met regularly to exchange intellectual viewpoints on what was clearly a very difficult topic to analyse. Every time we met over a five-year period, things 'on the ground' had changed and had to be interpreted. It has been a unique experience and challenge for all concerned.

From the outset, it had been planned by Professor Colin Sparks, the moving force behind this initiative, that there would be three Working Groups: (1) newspapers and print media, (2) television and film and (3) music and radio. This last group began to find itself mainly discussing questions on changing technologies for music distribution and the associated business models alongside the regulatory regime, particularly copyright law, and realised that these were issues that affected all media in some degree or the other and, moreover, could be expected to impact on all media eventually as the Internet developed and spread. Hence, the Cross Media Group was formed, and the authors of this book took part in its activities. We have met in various locations in Europe over the period of the COST A20 Action and got to know and value each others' ideas and insights. What we all agreed on is that there is no one way to study the impact of the Internet on the mass media, and that whatever we produce will, in one sense, not be contemporaneous by the time it is published. Nevertheless, we also concluded that we did have a lot to say about how independent academic observers approach the question and try to cut through the hype that has surrounded this subject to find long-term trends. This book is the outcome of these deliberations. It has been written by many of the people involved in the Cross Media Group, who have co-operated magnificently with the editors to ensure its successful production. We felt (and still feel) that our research can be put to the service of teaching students and informing policy-makers everywhere. Accordingly, we hope this book will be read in the spirit in which it is intended – as a statement of our interpretation of the results of our researches as they stand at the present time.

We would like to acknowledge our great debt to Colin Sparks, chairman of the COST A20 Action, who lead the whole project through good times and bad, and also to the officials responsible for the project at the European Science Foundation for financing our meetings.

Finally, we would like to thank everyone who has contributed to this book – directly and indirectly – for their ideas, hard work and support. Some firm friendships as well as academic connections have been formed through its conception and realisation.

1

INTRODUCTION

Lucy Küng, Robert G. Picard and Ruth Towse

Aims, objectives and audience

The Internet has established itself with remarkable, perhaps unprecedented, speed as an integral part of everyday life for many people all over the world, at work and in the home. This book offers a comprehensive analysis of the impact of the Internet on the production and consumption of the mass media. It explores and discusses the changes this evolving communications platform is bringing about in the media and mediated content industries, and the implications of those changes. The book is written by a group of experts who have been involved in research and analysis of these issues over a period of five years.

During this period, perceptions and experience of the Internet have changed considerably. To take the example of the music industry, five years ago P2P and MP3 had only just become established. At that point, the music industry perceived file-sharing as something likely to precipitate a crisis for the industry – customers would be reluctant ever to pay for music again, artists would not get paid, the industry would not survive and so forth. Now online licence fees are growing faster than sales revenue streams. In the meantime, copyright law has been changed to counteract the effects of the Internet.

Five years ago, it was predicted that electronic books would displace paper book sales but barely anything has materialised in that sector (yet). Indeed there are dozens of examples to be found that illustrate the effect of the Internet on the mass media, but examples quickly date: what is attempted in this book is an overview not so much of the outcomes of the use of the Internet but more of how social scientists set about analysing the processes involved in the adoption of, adaptation to and acceptance of the Internet in the context of the media industries.

When technological changes take place, they are exciting, they are destructive, they are confusing and they alter the status quo. Young people adopt them faster than old people, richer people and countries have access to them before poorer people and countries. There are many dimensions to these changes and they have to be considered from many points of view – as economic, political and social opportunities and threats. These changes impact on the whole of society both within a country and in the international context. They have had a particularly significant effect impact on the media, affecting consumers and producers, users and non-users and influencing the content of and access to information, the ways it is produced and how the firms within the industries adapt strategically and re-orientate themselves. Governments have to respond to these changes, perhaps without understanding them fully, since information about emergent developments and consumer responses to them is inevitably incomplete. Although the Internet itself is not regulated, the media industries are and governments have had to realign regulations and law to the new platform.

The authors of this book are social scientists from all over Europe, doing research in the field of media industries, who specialise in a range of disciplines – media and business economics, communications, cultural economics, cultural studies, media management, media technology, political science and sociology – and who share an interest in the impact of the Internet on the mass media. This interest is both 'academic', in the sense that we want to know the what, why and how of its impact, but we also share a concern to provide a basis from which to objectively assess policy. Each of the disciplines represented by the researchers who have contributed to this book offers a different perspective on the developments under review. We are not, however, concerned with attributing the analysis to any particular one. Some of the topics covered in the book fall naturally into one field or another, but the main point is that they all have a contribution to make: how media firms have reacted to the Internet can be looked at by analysing the change in content and how users (viewers, listeners, buyers) respond, how firms have changed their business practices in terms of organisation, business models, management and strategies, and by reacting to the external environment, including regulation. This is a short book, and it is not intended to provide all the answers, as much as to set an agenda for how to go about looking for them. This is important as there has been inordinate hype and over-excitement about the power of the Internet and related technologies to change our lives.

The book draws together what the authors have jointly concluded about the impact of the Internet on the media industries. Given their varied backgrounds, the book's standpoint is simultaneously multi-lens, interdisciplinary and cross-national. By approaching a common topic and single sector from a number of different theoretical and geographical standpoints, it generates comprehensive and universal insights, and thus provides scholars, policymakers, media practitioners and social observers with a strong explanatory and interpretive overview of how the Internet and mobile media has affected, and is affecting, media, and the implications of those effects. Thus, the aim of the book is to present, as far as is possible, a contemporaneous account of these researches arising out of objective academic investigation.

What is the Internet?

One of the points that will be frequently made throughout this book is that the Internet is a catch-all phrase for a number of technological developments that relate to economic and social changes. At the time the Internet was developing, other changes were taking place in the world of media industries that also influenced the eventual outcome, central among these are the World Wide Web and digitalisation, as well as the development of cable and satellite television and of coaxial cable enabling broadband delivery. An account of the historical development of the Internet is to be found in Chapter 3.

It is also important to make the distinction between the terms 'digital' and 'Internet' because in common usage these are often falsely used interchangeably. The term 'digital' refers to a technology that stores data in binary form. This can be information allowing the storage of text, photography, graphics, video and audio. The term 'Internet' refers to a distribution system for information. Data transmitted through the Internet and other distribution systems including telephones, television, radio and computers can be either analogue or digital, depending on the architecture of the system.

'Digitalisation' means mathematically reducing all types of information (video, still pictures, audio, text, conversations, games or graphics) into binary form. Once in this format, it can be understood, manipulated and stored by computers, transmitted by networks in perfect fidelity to the original and used immediately by another party on the network or stored for later use. In recent years, information has been increasingly converted into digital formats, from consumer entertainment products to corporate knowledge to money supply. Once information is digitised, new possibilities for new products and services result. Different forms of information – pictures, sound, text – can be combined to produce new multimedia products. When combined with the Internet, such complex information products can be compressed, stored, transmitted and retrieved instantly from any point on the globe, irrespective of physical distance.

The Internet refers to a telephony-based system that links computers and computer networks worldwide to permit distribution of data, e-mail, messages and visual and audio materials to individuals, groups of individuals and the public. What has driven many of the developments of the last ten years has been the development of the World Wide Web. 'World Wide Web' is a term indicating an Internet-based system accessed using browsers to access information, graphics, photography, video and audio materials made available to specific individuals or the public.

For many observers, it is digitalisation, rather than the Internet, which is the true enabler of convergence. 'Convergence' is one of the developments of particular interest to media scholars; however, the term can be understood in a number of different ways. In this book, convergence is understood as the technologically driven fusing of the content (that is, media), computing (information technology) and communications (telecoms and broadcast distribution) industries (Chakravarthy, 1997; Bradley and Nolan, 1988). Another use of the term convergence, this time at industry level, is 'corporate convergence', whereby companies from one sector acquire or start new ones in another of the converging industries. However, it should be noted that other scholars have defined convergence in relation to the delivery platforms used for media products, or in terms of the convergence of the devices used to 'receive' or use media products.

Previous technological advancements in the media and communications industries prior to digitalisation tended to mimic and optimise existing processes or products without altering the underlying concepts: thus, early television programmes were radio shows with pictures, and the word-processor offered enhancements to electronic typewriters. Digitalisation differs from these because it allows the development of fundamentally new products, services and processes. One might conclude, therefore, that digitalisation has had a more profound impact on economic and social change than the Internet itself.

'Cross-currents' from other changes in the world of media

As is so often the case with research in the social sciences, laboratory conditions do not exist, and it is almost impossible to isolate changes due to one cause or another that is not connected with the phenomenon being investigated. At the time of the development of the Internet, other changes were taking place in the world of media industries, which set up their own influence on the eventual outcome. Besides digitalisation, the development of cable and satellite television and of coaxial cable enabling broadband delivery strongly influenced the structure of the television broadcasting industry. These developments triggered off the discussion about the role of public service broadcasters and the use of taxes to finance them. On the other hand, developments in home copying equipment for time-shifting television programmes that enabled eliminating the advertisements raised doubts about the role of advertising as a source of finance for television. The main aims of this book are to try to eliminate these cross-currents and to ascribe correctly to the Internet what its impact has been.

Facts about the Internet

Because the Internet is not owned or regulated, there is no responsible body that can provide information about it. In the early stages, it was hard to find reliable data on the features of the Internet of the sort that are of interest to social scientists. This state of affairs has now changed radically, with various public and private bodies collecting Internet data for a range of purposes: governments collect statistics on 'connectivity' to monitor their IT policies, international data are collected for purposes of inter-country comparison and trade and private firms are supplying market research and business information to organisations, which they make public. However, it is still difficult to establish trends over more than a few years relating to its use and content. Further, a substantial element of content such as pornography, gambling and pirated media products cannot be easily researched, because data concerning this type of activity are hard to collect. For some purposes, therefore, we have to resort to indirect measures of the scope and growth of the Internet.

In terms of sheer numbers, the most Internet users in 2007 were to be found in Asia (389 million), followed by Europe (313 million), North America (232 million), Latin America (89 million), Middle East (19 million) and Australia/Oceania (19 million). However, when these figures are standardised according to the size of population, the picture concerning the penetration of the Internet, that is, users in a country expressed as a percentage of its population, change. Then we find North America (69 per cent), Australia/Oceania (54 per cent), Europe (39 per cent), Latin America (16 per cent), Asia (11 per cent), Middle East (10 per cent) and Africa (4 per cent), according to www.internetworldstats.com (January 11, 2007).

Looking at figures on the growth of Internet penetration for a selection of Organisation for Economic Co-operation and Development (OECD) countries, Table 1.1 shows how uneven the development has been. Some countries (Australia, Canada, South Korea and USA) already had over 40 per cent of households with access to the Internet in 2000, whereas others (France, Germany, Italy, UK) had less than 20 per cent. Some 'slow starters', especially Germany, have reached very high penetration, while others (Italy) have grown only modestly. The highest flier of all is South Korea, with a head start in 2000 and nearly 93 per cent penetration by 2005. The relatively high figures for the Netherlands reflect that country's determined effort to develop IT.

Table 1.1 Households with access to the Internet as a percentage of all households

Country/year	2000	2001/2	2003	2004	2005
Australia	41.5	42	53	56	
Canada	42.3	49.9	56.9	59.8	
Finland	30	39.5	47.4	50.9	54.1
France	11.9	18.1	31	33.6	
Germany	16.4	36	60	61.6	84.4
Italy	18.8		32.1	34.1	38.6
Japan			53.6	55.8	57
Korea	49.8	63.2	68.8	86	92.7
Netherlands	41		60.5		78.3
Spain		40	27.5	33.6	35.5
UK	19		55.1	55.9	60.2
USA	41.5	50.3	54.6		

Source: OECD Key ICT indicators

Similar country differences can be seen in access to broadband: in 2006, the average penetration was 15 per cent of all households for all OECD countries, and this figure had doubled since 2003. Germany, Spain and Italy were below that average, with Finland, Netherlands and South Korea being over 25 per cent (1 in 4 households). The growth of access to broadband is an indicator of greater potential use of the Internet for uses such as downloading images and films.

Growth in the number of Internet hosts worldwide is an indicator of the expansion of the Internet: in 1990, there were 0.3 million Internet hosts and in 1995, 6.6 million; by 2000, there were 93.0 million and by 2006, 439.2 million Internet hosts. The Internet Domain Survey, http://www.isc.org/index.pl?/ops/ds/ provides data on the percentage of domain names worldwide: dot com 75.9 per cent, dot net 11.2 per cent, dot org 6.7 per cent, dot info 4.0 per cent, dot biz 2.0 per cent and dot edu 11.6 per cent. (Zooknic, Domain Name Counts http://www.zooknic.com/Domains/counts.html).

To assess the economic significance of the Internet, we have to resort to several indirect indicators. In 2006, worldwide e-commerce was estimated to be US$7 trillion, with the bulk being wholesale sales. In the US, according the the US Census Bureau, e-commerce represented 2 per cent of total retail sales and 17 per cent of total wholesale sales; in terms of content, personals/dating, business/investment and entertainment/lifestyle represented 65 per cent of the dollars spent. In Europe, the numbers were about 1 per cent for retail and 7 per cent for total wholesale sales; France, Germany and UK account for 70 per cent of European online sales.

Initially, debate raged concerning how Internet activities would be financed. It is still the case that a great deal of Internet traffic is funded by non-commercial users. However, as with other media platforms, advertising has established itself as a source of finance. Internet advertising expenditures were US$18.3 billion globally in 2005 and increasing at a rate above 30 per cent each year, with North America accounting for 62 per cent of expenditures and Europe for 22 per cent (according to *World Advertising Trends*, 2006). The leading countries by expenditures are USA, UK, Japan, France, Australia, Germany, Canada, South Korea, Sweden and Italy. As this book shows, these trends are of considerable importance to the media industries.

What are the media industries?

'Media' is a term that refers to technologies (print, radio, television, sound recording and such like) through which content created for groups of consumers is moved and organised. Firms in the media industries act as packagers of materials that utilise those technologies. Thus, radio stations, magazines, television broadcasters, Internet content aggregators and mobile content services are media firms. By their very nature, media affect the forms of content that can be conveyed through them. Content industries are closely related to media because they create material that can be conveyed through media. 'Content industries' is a term that is often used to characterise those industries whose primary activities are the creation of original content material for use in media, information and communication products. These include industries creating motion pictures, television and radio programming, games, music, books, magazines, newspapers and other non-personal content. Enterprises in the content industries also include firms for which creating media content may not be the primary goal. Thus, for example, a symphony orchestra or theatre group whose primary activity is live performance may record those performances as audio or video recordings and make them available for sale or for downloading over the Internet. The recordings are thus the content, and such activities are included within the content industries. Similarly, museums and other collectors of art, graphics, etc., become content producers when they produce images of their art for use by consumers. The distinction between the production of content and the medium by which it is delivered is, therefore, crucial. Internet content is the subject of Chapter 4 of this book. How it is used is analysed and discussed in Chapter 5.

Another aspect of the media industries is 'cross-media'. The term 'cross-media' refers to communication (or media) products that are designed and intended for use in more than one medium, or on more than one media platform. The term also covers the organisational activities involved in coordinating and moving content into more than one medium. Cross-media activities are typically regulated by the state in situations where large corporations dominate the production and distribution of information, such as news, that is regarded as vital for societal health. Chapter 6 discusses these issues in relation to the Internet.

An aspect of the media industries that has to be taken into account, especially in generalising across many countries, is that, in most, the media industries are privately owned, for-profit enterprises. Even before digitalisation, the economic and political environment in which they functioned was changing (or had only recently changed). The way media organisations adapt is discussed in detail in Chapter 7 of this book. However, especially in the smaller countries, there are also subsidised areas, such as film production or popular music in the national or even a regional language, meaning that there can be a clash between the goals of preserving cultural diversity and pluralism, and free-trade objectives. Even in those countries in which private enterprise is the adopted model, the industries are regulated by national law on aspects such as cultural diversity provision, respect for minorities, decency laws and such like, as well as by policy on cultural content in the European Union (EU) and elsewhere, for example, Canada (see Chapter 6).

A name for the Internet era?

One issue that has yet to be agreed upon by social scientists is what we should call this new era, if such it is, that is characterised by the spread of the Internet. Is the term 'Information Society' used by the EU and many other governmental organisations worldwide the most appropriate and what are the alternatives? Despite the focus on the Internet as the driver of these changes, the term 'Internet era' has not been adopted to characterise the advent of a new age. However, several other terms are frequently used: 'knowledge economy', 'knowledge society', 'digital economy', 'information economy' and 'information society', 'information age', 'network economy' and 'network society', 'new economy' and so on. These terms (which are discussed in greater depth in Chapter 2) all relate to wider developments than the Internet alone, but it is clear that the Internet has played an important part in them. They also apparently make a significant distinction between 'knowledge' and 'information', though that distinction is far from clear, even in dictionaries, and has been much debated by philosophers and others. 'Knowledge' is typically defined in terms of intellectual perception of information, facts, ideas and so on, while 'information' is defined as 'the communication of facts and knowledge'. On the fact of it, therefore, these terms are not particularly helpful, and we need to delve beneath the surface for any deeper meaning.

Besides its contribution to national income and output, the Internet has also enabled the globalisation of international trade. Globalisation is understood in this context as the emergence of global markets, a phenomenon which is closely linked both to the development of the media and communications industries, in particular the information goods they produce and the revolution in production and distribution they have precipitated. Indeed, in some respects, globalisation can be viewed as the development of one large global network for trade and business. Markets are globalising too, as customers become increasingly accustomed, on the one hand, to sourcing goods from all over the world, and on the other, demanding access to the same brands and goods from any point on the globe. Organisations active in these markets must compete across geographic divides and meet the needs of customers, wherever they are, this in turn has created a highly competitive environment which has forced the pace for the development and adoption of digital technologies. These trends affect firms' management and business models as well as labour markets everywhere and have had structural effects on the economies of both developed and developing countries.

Theoretical perspectives employed in this book

This book uses three major theoretical perspectives as focal points from which to examine and analyse the developments taking place in the media industries that are ascribed to the Internet: economic perspectives, regulatory perspectives and managerial/strategic/organisational perspectives. The reason for this is that the changes taking place in the media and content industries as a result of the Internet are extremely complex with many different dimensions. The employment of a single theoretical lens, while allowing a clearer focus, would not accommodate the richness and subtlety of developments, nor provide an adequate tool for analysing and discussing their implications. Thus, for example, new business models that are currently emerging in many sectors of the media industry can be viewed as primarily driven by the emergence of the Internet and other technological developments as industry by industry in Chapter 8. But these new business models also reflect the business strategies adopted by organisations in response to technological change. And the scope of those strategies is determined to a large extent by the policy and regulatory framework that regulators have established in response to technological change. The three perspectives adopted are outlined below with a full analysis in Chapter 2.

Economic perspectives

Studying how the Internet has affected the media industries requires that economic perspectives be used to answer questions regarding industry structure, consolidation and concentration, demand for the original media products and materials online, financing available for media operations, company costs and organisational decisions, quality and diversity of content. Economic questions are at the heart of industry and market studies, company studies and policy studies regarding the Internet and new media. Economic analysis is important because economic and financial pressures affect choices about the kinds of media and means of communications available in society, the kinds of content in the media, the way media organisations behave and operate, the implications of these factors on culture, politics and society as a whole, and the roles of media and information in economic and social development. The perspectives used to understand developments come from theoretical economics, political economy and business economics and offer ways of understanding what is changed because of the development of the Internet and how the business dynamics of the media industries have been affected.

Entrepreneurship is recognised as the driver of industrial change, especially in industries dominated by private ownership. Entrepreneurship drives innovation motivated by the desire for profit and the result in economic growth. That is the essence of the capitalist economy. Moreover, by its nature, innovation is messy, fraught with uncertainty and costly. Many investments do not pay off and many inventions are not successfully exploited by their inventors but by other entrepreneurs who are better able to do so. An example in the media industries is supplying track-by-track titles over the Internet: this is not done by the sound recording industry but by companies like iTunes that recognised the demand and met it.

Over the last ten years, basic questions concerning the 'Internet economy' have been asked: is it very different from its predecessors? What is its likely economic organisation (or industrial structure)? What type of regulation is required? Do we need a new kind of economic analysis to analyse a 'new economy'? On balance, it is fair to say that economists do not believe any revolution in modes of either thinking or trading are required. Production and consumption, supply and demand, incentives and rewards, costs and prices are all features of the economy with or without the Internet. Firms that adapt to technological changes will succeed and those that do not will fail, but that is the order of capitalism. Markets are markets online or offline. Price discrimination might be much more common but as long as customers can be made to pay and producers can turn in a profit, markets will go on working. It may well be asked if this is not a complacent outlook: are there not some vital areas of change with the potential to radically alter the way economists think about these questions? The possible prevalence of public goods, for example – that is, products that are non-rival (meaning that there is no diminution of consumption for one user no matter how many other consumers there are) and non-excludable (meaning that they cannot be 'privatised' and the whole potential revenue captured by a producer) – raises some doubts about this complacency. The excessive cost and difficulty of controlling illegal downloading of music, which threatens to become a de facto public good, are a case study in this respect.

Regulatory perspectives

Regulation of the media sector is achieved in several different ways. First, like any other sector of the economy, the media industries are subject to anti-monopoly legislation/competition law (in the US called antitrust). The European Union (as well as the constituent individual nation states) has become active in controlling merger activity and firm growth in this as in other areas of economic endeavour; the treatment of Microsoft is a case in point. Some of the media industries, namely, press and broadcasting, are subject to more specific ownership rules that relate to both concentration or integration within one industry (such as newspapers or television broadcasting) and to cross-media ownership rules (ownership of both newspapers and TV stations) that are designed to protect or promote diversity of content and points of view. In addition, broadcasting is specifically regulated under the terms of the licence it must acquire from the government and required to comply with rules on content in addition to laws on decency, defamation, etc. The impact of Internet on content diversity and on ownership in media industries is a much discussed topic as is the separate question whether the Internet should be specifically regulated, and if so how and by what regulatory body. There are many difficult issues here: media industries typically require individual regulatory regimes but the Internet carries a mixture of content from all these industries; moreover, the Internet is global and evasion of regulation within one country is obviously extremely easy. Only an international regulatory body could take on such a task using international law and sanctions.

Another strand of regulation is specifically targeted on the media industries in some countries, particularly throughout Europe, and is concerned with promoting European cultural diversity. Its aim is to promote and protect European cultural identity and to prevent excessive 'invasion' of non-European programmes and films. Other countries have similar rules and they are much disputed, especially by the USA, in trade negotiations in the World Trade Organization (WTO) and General Agreement on Trade in Services (GATS).

A second means of regulation is intellectual property (IP) law, mainly copyright law, and in many ways this has become a universal regulatory force. Copyright law (while still national law) has become increasingly globalised over the last decade through international treaties setting minimum standards for rights and their enforcement (and subject to sanctions in the case of the WTO's treaties). Copyright law has become progressively stronger as its scope and duration have been increased as well as the penalties for non-compliance. This global agenda reflects the globalisation of the media industries themselves and to a considerable extent has been set by US interests. It requires conformity on the part of the EU, which in turn sets the agenda for national copyright legislation within its boundaries. The development of digitisation and the Internet have caused copyright law to be updated to take in the effects of the new technologies, something that has become increasingly controversial.

Management perspectives

The field of research covered by management complements the other two perspectives outlined above by focussing on media organisations and their host industry sectors. The methodologies employed are drawn from theories of management, strategy and organisational change. Taken together, these bodies of knowledge provide insights into the relationship between media organisations and their strategic environments, and the activities they must undertake to align organisations and their available resources with changes in its environment.

That environment is unstable and complex, due in large part to the emergence of the Internet as a new media platform, but also as a result of inter-related changes in regulatory and policy frameworks, and in consumer behaviour and lifestyle. This perspective provides insights into the impact of these environmental changes on strategies, for example, on business models and product portfolios, on organisational structures – looking where Internet-based activities are housed, and on life inside media firms – in terms of changes to job design, work processes, employment patterns, organisational culture and so on.

Organisation of the book

The book is organised as follows: Chapter 2 (Theoretical perspectives on the impact of the Internet on the mass media industries, by Lucy Küng, Robert G. Picard and Ruth Towse) reviews the concepts and theories that are used by researchers to understand the phenomenon of the Internet. The first of these are economic theories which are applied to the understand the impact of the Internet as a technological innovation that has had an impact on the wider economy, market structures, value chains, business strategies and company structures and operations.

The second set of theories concern policy and regulation which are used to analyse and understand what policy measures might be necessary as a result of the emergence of the Internet and, as indicated above, these include competition law (antitrust), copyright law and media regulation.

The third set of theories comprises approaches from the discipline of management. One focus is on theories exploring the inter-relationship between scientific advance and organsations, and particularly the implications of technological change for incumbent organisations. Concepts discussed include theories of organisational technology, the dominant design and technology transitions. Another focus is a range of concepts from the general management and business press, which were viewed as likely to transform industrial structures and society, and which received much attention during the first Internet era. These include convergence, the network, Internet or new economy, the knowledge economy/society and the information economy/society.

Chapter 3 (The impact of the Internet on media technology, platforms and innovation, by Anders Henten and Reza Tadayoni) examines the Internet as a production and distribution tool for video, audio and text media. From a production perspective, the Internet enables changes in the production flows and structures of the media and content industries, for example, the presentation of media products on different communication platforms. On the distribution side, the Internet creates new distribution possibilities for the media and content industries, as well as the potential for interactivity, and also the self-organised distribution and exchange of material, as in peer-to-peer communications and blogs.

Digitalisation is one of the fundamental technological developments in the communication and media areas. The transformation from analogue to digital is potentially a radical change within the broadcast sector, but this chapter's focus is on digitalisation as the technological driving force for convergence (and divergence) and the synergies obtained between the Internet evolution and media developments. This applies to video as well as audio and text-based media.

Chapter 3 includes a brief historical account of the development of the Internet. The purpose is to avoid conceptualising the Internet as a fixed and finite 'entity'. The Internet has developed over time with different implications for the media, and it will keep on developing technologically with new consequences for media developments. This can be important when pointing at future implications for the media. Chapter 3, therefore, examines the different technologies which are part of what we understand as the Internet today, with an emphasis on the Internet Protocol (IP) as the basis for the Internet as a network as well as for managed IP networks.

Chapter 4 (The impact of the Internet on media content, by Richard van der Wurff) analyses the impact of the Internet on content. It starts from the dual observation that the Internet minimises the costs of content reproduction and distribution, but not of content production. Changes in content follow from the opportunities that these changes in cost structure create, and from the way in which different types of actors use these opportunities in ways they see fit. The chapter discusses several 'impacts' of the Internet on content; with existing content being increasingly made available via the Internet, it results not only in a tremendous increase in the amount of available content, but also in fragmentation of content and audiences, and this creates opportunities for companies that organise access to content, especially for those that serve large numbers of users. Compared with the amount of existing information that is for the first time or additionally distributed via the Internet, a relatively small amount of content is specifically developed for the Internet. That type of content illustrates the different ways in which Internet content might develop in the near future. Traditional offline content in response borrows design items from Internet webpages, such as the use of hyperlinks (or pointers) and frames. Finally, the changes in available content raise considerable regulatory questions, in particular on the protection of minors and necessary guarantees for diversity.

Chapter 5 (The impact of the Internet on users, by Piet Bakker and Charo Sádaba) takes as a starting point the 'user-perspective' – how technologies are used in their social context. The focus is on the use of the Internet and the impact this technology has had on audiences in different countries. The authors concentrate on the ownership and use of computers with Internet connection, and other devices related to the Internet, including mobile phones, game computers, satellite television, mobile music players and digital cameras. The issues included in Chapter 5 are: penetration and consumption and how these change over time; differences between groups; connectivity to the Internet and how households are connected; applications, uses and time spent, and in particular, what young people are doing. A more qualitative analysis considers what the results are of these changes of media use: why these technologies attract so much of audiences' interest, time and money; the impact on societal change; whether there is fragmentation or individualisation; what the consequences are for other media consumption and new interactive forms of those media; what the impact is on language and/or frontiers on the Internet and consequently on culture. Finally, the chapter deals with questions of control, the way people work with media (actors in content creation) and future media use.

Chapter 6 (The impact of the Internet on media policy, regulation and copyright law, by Des Freedman, Anders Henten, Ruth Towse and Roger Wallis) discusses how, for some time now, the Internet has been the spectre haunting the corridors of media policy-making and regulation in Europe, ever-present and ominous, but perhaps more disturbing in theory than in reality. The Internet has had an uneven impact on actual policy development and has affected some industries (for example, music) far more than others (for example, television). Chapter 6 distinguishes between the rhetorical and the material impact of the Internet, between the ways in which it has been used prescriptively to justify particular policy and regulatory positions and how it has forced specific media industries to respond to the challenges posed by the growth of broadband. In particular, the chapter examines how the Internet has affected policy and regulatory initiatives concerning media pluralism, cultural diversity, intellectual property rights, competition issues and the emergence of new digital platforms. The chapter attempts to capture the complex dynamics of the Internet's impact on European media policy and regulation.

Chapter 7 (The impact of the Internet on media organisation strategies and structures, by Lucy Küng, Nikos Leandros, Robert G. Picard, Roland Schroeder and Richard van der Wurff) explores the effect of the Internet on the media organisations, specifically from the perspective of the inter-related issues of strategy, structure, processes and business models. In order to do this, it draws two important distinctions. The first is between incumbent and new organisations. To respond to a development such as the Internet, incumbent firms face a challenge that is an order of magnitude greater than those of start-up firms. They must not only develop an appropriate response to a changing strategic environment, but implement this despite the hurdles presented by 'legacy' systems and processes. As this book explores the impact of the Internet on the existing mass media, the focus is inevitably on its effect on the established media firm.

The second, and related, distinction is between the first and second Internet eras. The first Internet era was one of hype and hyperbole, where Internet-related businesses carried extraordinarily high stock market valuations, and the established mass media industries found themselves under intense pressure to move into the Internet arena, and with it into a very new type of strategic arena, an unpredictable emergent context. This chapter reviews the established media firms' responses to the first Internet era, and explores the surprising failures of the largest companies' strategies. It explores the nature of the strategic environment of the second Internet era, and discusses typical strategic responses to it, particularly competition and cross-media strategies. Survival in a complex and uncertain environment involves changes to a firm's core processes. A key tool employed by actors and observers of the media industry to understand the impact of the Internet on industry processes has been the value chain. Chapter 7 reviews the transformations taking place in firm value chains including disintermediation or unbundling, fragmentation, extension and non-linear or reverse value chain arrangements, as well as exploring how the Internet has affected journalistic work processes. That the Internet is changing the structure of media firms is indisputable, but the ongoing changes display a wide variation; the chapter reviews these, in particular, developments such as alliances, networks, mergers and acquisitions, spin-offs, new media investment funds and the location of Internet activities by established media firms.

Chapter 8 (The impact of the Internet on business models in the media industries – a sector-by-sector analysis, by Marko Ala-Fossi, Piet Bakker, Hanna-Kaisa Ellonen, Lucy Küng, Stephen Lax, Charo Sádaba and Richard van der Wurff) provides a segment-by-segment overview of the new medium's effect on the various constituent sectors of the media industries. It complements the theoretical approach taken in Chapter 7 by giving numerous examples of business models that have been applied in the media in response to the threats and opportunities offered by the Internet. Each section has been contributed by an expert in that sector medium and, therefore, represents the state of the art at the time of writing.

Chapter 9 (Conclusions, by Lucy Küng, Robert G. Picard and Ruth Towse) summarises the main findings of the research and considers what future research is needed. At the turn of the Millennium, the starting point of the research, it was widely believed that the Internet would profoundly change the way mass media are produced and consumed. It has certainly done so in the music industry and may soon also impact on the film industry, but it has not so far had much effect on books publishing and television broadcasting. However, it has changed the editorial and marketing processes of all these products.

What we see now with the value of some limited hindsight is that the Internet became emblematic of and has come to stand for a whole range of issues which each have an impact on the media as well as on other industries. In a wider sense, the Internet is only one aspect of a reorientation of thinking in social sciences about our economy and society and the role of the mass media. It is obvious that there are many technological, economic, social and managerial changes already underway now, and that they will persist into the future. We do not attempt to foresee that future, but instead we have provided a framework from which to assess its meaning for the economy and for society.

References

Bradley, S. P. and Nolan, R.L. (Eds.) (1998). *Sense and Respond: Capturing value in the network era*. Boston: Harvard Business School Press.

Carlaw, K., Oxley, L., Walker, P., Thorns, D. and Nuth, M. (2006). 'Beyond the Hype: Intellectual Property and the Knowledge Society/Knowledge Economy'. *Journal of Economic Surveys*, 20 (4), 633–90.

Chakravarthy, B. (1997). 'A New Strategy Framework for Coping with Turbulence'. *Sloan Management Review*, Winter 1997: 69–82.

World Advertising Trends (2006). Ozon, UK: World Advertising Research Center.

2

THEORETICAL PERSPECTIVES ON THE IMPACT OF THE INTERNET ON THE MASS MEDIA INDUSTRIES

Lucy Küng, Robert G. Picard and Ruth Towse

Introduction

This chapter reviews concepts from a number of academic disciplines and research streams that provide background perspectives about and insights into the changes the established media industries are experiencing as a result of the emergence of the Internet. These fall into four main groups: economic theories, regulatory theories, management theories and general business concepts.

The goal of this chapter, therefore, is to provide a theoretical foundation for understanding the analysis that follows in subsequent chapters. The theoretical perspectives chosen may seem broad, but the selection is not eclectic. All have been screened for relevance to the topic of this book and each provides analytical tools and conceptual frameworks that allow the impact of the Internet on the mass media industries to be analysed and assessed. No attempt is made to synthesise the various lenses into an over-arching framework. Rather, they are viewed as complementary, each yielding additional dimensions and insights. Multi-lens approaches of this type have been shown to yield richer and deeper understanding of complex phenomena.

Economic theories

Many contemporary developments in media businesses and the Internet are strongly influenced by economic forces and economic theories and conceptual approaches are central in understanding the impetus for those developments and how those developments affect media on and offline.

These economic factors affect the fundamental aspects of value chains, business strategies and company structures and operations. Changes in information and communication technologies have thus altered costs, functions, structures and operations, value chains and markets of traditional media industries, and presented opportunities for traditional and new media to provide products and services in ways not technically or economically possible previously. This section introduces some of the most relevant economic theories and approaches because they are fundamental to comprehending how the Internet has affected traditional media and to understanding the subsequent chapters of this book.

Economics utilises a variety of approaches to the analysis of innovation and to its impact on the wider economy as well as on specific sectors and businesses. In general, economists have resisted the idea that the Internet is a revolutionary technology and have seen it as evolutionary and, therefore, capable of being analysed with established economic theories. However, it also happened that prior to the development of the Internet the role of information in economic theory had become more prominent, and interest in Schumpeter's theory of dynamic competition had increased (Schumpeter, 1983). This theory emphasised the role of technological progress in a process of competition and economic development he labelled 'creative destruction', by which unfit firms that do not adapt to new technologies go out of business. Moreover, even before the effect of digitalisation on copyright had become apparent, an economic analysis of copying and copyright law had begun to be developed in relation to previous technologies, such as photocopying and VCRs, both within economic theory and in the field of law and economics. Thus economics as a discipline was well prepared to deal with the newer developments with a menu of possible economic approaches.

Nevertheless, the 'traditional' neoclassical theory of the firm has continued to be used to analyse the so-called 'information economy' by some analysts, notably Shapiro and Varian (1999); their book *Information Rules* combined the use of neoclassical economic concepts, such as economies of scale and scope and price discrimination, with those of business economics, such as product bundling, and it also introduced notions like network economics. In later work, Varian (2005) has emphasised the role of business models as a protection against losses due to copying rather than copyright and other intellectual property rights (IPRs). These economic theories, therefore, are relevant not only to understanding the structure of the media industries but also to analysing regulation by competition law and the role of IPRs.

Neoclassical approaches

The term neoclassical economics is used to denote the theory of how individual rational economic agents make decisions about production and consumption in response to prices. Business firms face a range of technological possibilities for the use of resources and the profit-seeking entrepreneur chooses a combination of resources or factors of production based on their relative prices and the expected revenues from the sale of the product. Consumers decide what combination of products will give them the most satisfaction considering the relative prices and their incomes. Neoclassical economics, therefore, concentrates on the workings of markets in response to price and from these basic models, has developed detailed microeconomic analysis as well as welfare economics that apply to a whole society; these theories are used to support a wide range of applications and policy implications.

The neoclassical industrial organisation model is a well established framework for analysing the structures, conduct and performance of industries and markets and it has been applied widely to many sectors, including media (Busterna, 1988; Wirth & Bloch, 1995). The model asserts that the elements of market structure influence the behaviour of firms, and ultimately the performance of those firms and the performance of the market in serving social needs (Scherer & Ross, 1990). Market structures are affected by factors such as economies of scale in production and economies of scope in consumption, the number of and concentration of buyers and sellers, the extent of vertical and horizontal integration, cost structures for operations, barriers to entry or mobility, amount of product differentiation, costs for switching buyers and government policies and regulations. These structures produce differing degrees of competition in markets and thus affect the product strategies of firms, pricing behaviour, the amount of research and innovation in the market, and the advertising and marketing efforts that companies must make. The structures and conduct choices subsequently affect financial performance of firms and the industry as a whole, as well as technical efficiency and the benefits of the market to society. One issue, therefore, has been the extent to which the Internet has altered the degree of competition in media markets.

Economies of scale and scope

For some types of industries - particularly those in which manufacturing and distribution are involved – the cost per unit produced are central to efficient operations and play an important role in determining company success and market structure. In such environments, economies of scale are beneficial to firms and to consumers because they lower the average costs as the quantity of output produced or plant size changes and as technological improvements create efficiencies. An extreme case of this is the 'natural monopoly' when there are ever increasing economies of scale so that average costs become ever lower; then marginal costs of supplying another unit of output are always below average costs and marginal cost pricing is not feasible. This is thought to apply with particular force in the media industries and has strong implications for regulation; whether the Internet stimulates competition or exacerbates the tendency to monopoly is a question of considerable importance to policy.

A similar type of cost efficiency is achieved through economies of scope, in which a firm's operations in different industries or activities provide shared elements that reduce overall costs. An example of economies of scope is merchandising offshoots from films or books; Disney has to a considerable extent exploited economies of scope for characters and images in children's films. From the mid-1980s onwards achieving such efficiencies became a key strategic goal for larger players in the media sector with activities stretching across a number of different sectors of the media industry, under the banner of achieving 'synergies'.

Network effects

Related to economies of scope is the idea of network effects where consumers benefit from the size of the network. The economics of networks dictate that when the value of a product to one user depends on how many other users there are, the product exhibits network consumption externalities or network effects. Communications technologies are a prime example: telephones, email, Internet access, fax machines all exhibit network externalities. The driving force here is positive feedback, which concerns the fact that the more people using a particular software, mobile phone network, etc., the more valuable it becomes, and the more new users it will attract, increasing both its utility and the speed of its adoption by new users. This creates a virtuous circle, whereby the increase in value attracts more members, and the addition of more members dramatically increases the value for all members, in turn attracting even more members and so on. This can be expressed in abstract terms in the form that for any communications network (not just computer networks) the number of nodes on a network yields that number squared in potential value. Therefore, the sum of a network increases as the square of the number of members, or as the number of nodes in a network increases arithmetically, the value of the network increases exponentially.

Lock in and switching costs

As technologies change, both producers and consumers face costs of adapting to them. If the costs of switching to new technologies are too high, a business might not be able to compete and is then said to be locked in to its existing technology or 'legacy systems'. Incumbent firms are obviously more vulnerable to this than new entrants. Such costs may prevent adaptation to a new environment and may be a reason why firms are 'destroyed' in the dynamic process of competition.

However, in an Internet environment it can make strategic sense for an organisation to seek to lock in customers and create high switching costs for them; indeed, the ideal strategic combination is to create a large network of users who are locked in, since once a consumer has chosen a technology, or a format for keeping information, switching can be very expensive, for example, changing email provider necessitates changing the email address, which brings switching costs in the form of informing all contacts, reprinting stationery, etc. Such costs lock in customers because they deter them from switching to a new provider.

Price discrimination

This economic concept involves the ability to charge different prices for the same product to different groups of customers based on their willingness and ability to pay, the amount they consume, their location and so on, which will increase revenues if conditions permit. In order to price discriminate, firms must have a degree of monopolistic power over the market and be able to exclude some customers from access to the product. The market also must be capable of being divided into segments with different willingness to pay for the product. The ability to price discriminate depends upon the nature of the product, the characteristics of the distribution system, the enabling technology and law and policy. Where these conditions are met, and it has been argued that by selling over the Internet, firms can customise or personalise and bundle goods to achieve the maximum sales revenue.

Business economics

As its title suggests, business economics concerns the application of economics to problems faced by businesses and deals with firm behaviour and the economic environment in which businesses operate.

Customisation and personalisation

Customisation refers to altering the presentation of content to suit the needs or interests of specific consumers or audiences. Thus a content packager or aggregator will use technology to create different presentations of materials of general audiences, businessmen and women, or persons with special interests in social policies or sports. Customisation uses data to identify users of content providers according to their general characteristics or interests and then automatically feeds a greater amount of preferential material.

Personalisation refers to altering content to suit the needs and interests of specific individuals using media. Media firms use information gathered on individual user preferences and interests, and patterns of content use, to create a personalised set of content for individual users. Both these business strategies are facilitated by the online environment and Internet-based commerce.

Bundling and unbundling

Bundling involves effort to sell multiple products in a group to reduce costs for the producer and to increase revenue by inducing consumers to buy more than they might otherwise choose. In media, this is evidenced by CDs that contain a dozen songs and by cable services tiers that bundle together different channels. In many cases the traditional structures of industries create cost and revenue challenges that are overcome through the benefits of bundling; however, bundling also means that consumers receive products – television channels or music tracks, for example – that they do not want. New distribution and sales mechanisms created by improvements in the information and communication technologies allow some unbundling (or debundling) to occur by overcoming the cost bases of the traditional structures. Track-by-track music licensing enables consumers to obtain a preferred personal selection of music and the Internet has proved to be very successful at supplying music.

Distribution economics

This area of theory involves the costs of getting products to customers and reveals that expenses are affected by distances, density of distribution and delivery time requirements (Picard, 2002). Distance affects distribution costs because it take more time, effort and expense to reach distant customers. Density affects costs because it is cheaper to physically distribute goods to many customers in a small area than to a few customers in a larger area. Time constraints affect physical distribution costs because if distribution time is short, there are few options for consolidating distribution with other products, producing a more logical distribution system, or benefiting from price competition among distribution firms. In some media industries, the need for large stocks of hard copies has been reduced by digital supply over the Internet and this has reduced storage and other such costs. In some cases, books can be printed up as required instead of being produced and stored to await sale.

Attention economy

Relating to consumer rather than producer behaviour, this approach argues that people's time and attention are scarce resources that can be seen as a market in which many products and services are rivals for that attention (Davenport & Beck, 2001). How well a firm serves needs, attracts attention and consumer time expenditures affect success in the market. The attention economy is affected by social and lifestyle changes that are increasing competitors for attention, changing the amount of time in which consumers' attention can be given (Gershun, 2000), and making it more difficult to gain regular attention and interaction between firms and customers. The vast quantity of information on the Internet as considerably exacerbated these problems.

Non-neoclassical economic approaches

The neoclassical and business economics approaches are not the only ones that have been applied to the economy in general and to analysing the impact of the Internet on the media industries in particular. Economics over the last few decades has espoused the transactions cost and property rights approaches to explaining firm size and consequently to the degree of integration, merger activity and so on.

Transaction cost economics

This theoretical approach is based on the idea that all exchange relationships involve costs. When firms acquire necessary supplies and services or when transactions take place between buyers and sellers, additional costs are incurred outside the basic expenses of producing the goods and services. This approach argues that firms seek to control the extent of transaction costs by structuring their relationships with their suppliers and customers (Williamson, 1985). Companies make efforts to control the costs through contracts, joint ventures, mergers and acquisitions, subscriptions and so forth. Transaction cost issues also arise within single firms with multiple business units and subsidiaries when they exchange resources and try to achieve synergies internally. Technological developments can alter costs of transacting and Internet sales of books and other media reflect this.

Property rights approach

Long before digitalisation highlighted the role of licensing rights to use in contrast to sales of hard copies of goods, economists realised that the exercise of property rights plays a significant role in economic dealings; one has to go no further than the stock market to see the truth of that. The growth of information goods have made this approach all the more appealing and the notion that rights such as copyright in print media, sound recording, film and suchlike are becoming ever more valuable now seems commonplace.

There is a link between transaction cost economics and property rights through the so-called Coase theorem (Blaug, 1997) which states that transaction costs are the cause of inefficient ownership of property rights; put the other way round, if transaction costs were zero, the initial distribution of ownership of property rights would not matter as they would be sold or licensed via the market to the party who could use them most efficiently. As long as economic agents are free to contract, the market mechanism will value the rights to use resources.

Contract theory

Some economists explain the structure of firms and industries in terms of contracting over property rights. Caves (2000) has applied this theory to the creative industries, both the non-profit arts and the for profit cultural industries including media. Starting from the problem facing any producer of a complex product – whether to make all component parts of the chain of production or to buy in some components from the open market, the so-called 'make or buy' decision – Caves analyses this in the context of industries in which content created by artists and other authors contract with commercial firms in order to reach their audience, the so-called 'creative industries' to which media belong.

Though in principle, the 'make or buy' problem is common to all producers, Caves argues that there are specific features of the creative industries that exacerbate the problem: a high degree of uncertainty about the quality of content produced by the creator and its reception by consumers; difficulties arising from dealing with many different types of creative people along the chain of production who typically have strong views about how their work is used; the longevity of some final products and the fact that they earn royalties and other income over a long time period; and the existence of deadlines that put pressure on all concerned with producing and marketing the product.

These features mean that contracts are incomplete in the sense that they fail to pin down all aspects of the contribution of each participant to the chain of production (such as quality or novelty or timeliness) and their value (because of teamwork, uncertain sales revenues) and so on. At each stage of the chain of motion picture production, new investments have to be made and much of the investment cannot be recouped in the event of the final product failing; this is called 'sunk' investment.

To overcome the problem of contract 'incompleteness', entrepreneurs in these industries opt for transferring property rights down the line of the chain of production in accordance with the outlay of sunk investment. Thus, to give some examples form the music industry: the composer or song writer is required to transfer some property rights (some of the bundle of rights we call copyright) to the music publisher and to the record label because these enterprises must invest in producing and marketing the products of the music. The contract is a royalty contract that shares revenues between the creator and the commercial enterprise (publisher or record label) and also shares the risk of the future success of the music on the market (Towse, 2001). Without the control of some rights, the commercial enterprise would not have an incentive to make the investment but the creator must rely on the commitment of funds as investment by the entrepreneur.

An ultimate solution to this problem is for the firm to control all aspects of the production process by full-scale integration. The much cited example of this is the Hollywood Studio system of the 1930s and 40s, in which every stage of the chain of motion picture production was controlled by the studio via the so-called Hollywood studio contract that appropriated property rights on the work of all those employed from script writer to film star.

Evolutionary economics and historical approaches

The term 'evolutionary' economics refers to a relatively new economic methodology modelled on biology that stresses complex interdependencies between competition, growth and resource constraints. As in the Darwinian scheme in the biological sphere, in the economic sphere, those firms survive that are able evolve through product and process innovation. The role of innovation in firms' ability to compete has been explored by Nelson and Winter (1982). This competition is referred to as 'dynamic' competition because it takes place over a period of time and is to be contrasted with 'static' competition as exemplified by the neoclassical model of perfect competition, in which firms are forced by the market to reduce prices to the lowest possible marginal cost of producing an item of the product.

Creative destruction

Although this concept was developed almost a century before digitalisation and the Internet, it has unique relevance in the contemporary business and media setting. The concept asserts the idea that innovations, especially technical innovations, can fundamentally alter the economic underpinnings of markets and industries and destroy existing market players and structures if adaptation and change do not occur (Schumpeter, 1983). This evolutionary process improves markets and benefits companies and consumers in the long run by reducing costs and improving products and services, the creative aspect. It is significant that it is assumed that monopolistic firms can achieve this effect of dynamic competition through technological innovation: without the element of monopoly, they would not be able to finance innovation. The implications are that competition law should not always seek to curb a monopoly firm if it is involved in innovation.

Economic historical approach

The evolutionary approach to business behaviour, emphasising as it does change over time and the development of new technologies, clearly lends itself to historical analysis; one topic of interest is the revolutionary nature of some inventions. Economic historians have asked themselves whether the Internet is the cause of a technological revolution comparable to the printing press or the steam engine. Carlaw et al. (2006: 660) argue that:

Innovative entrepreneurship operating in a world of uncertainty, where profit seeking innovation leads to new product creation with and from new technologies, where IP [intellectual property] has an important role to play, could equally describe the Industrial Revolution of the Information Revolution. The technologies differ and the relative mix of land, labour, capital and knowledge differs, but the general paradigm has explanatory power

And again:

In the old economy, reading, writing and the access to books was what divided the "haves" from the "have-nots" ... the modern analogy is access to the Internet and ICTs more generally. The "digital divide" is in part about access and acquisition of information, much as it always was.

They conclude that the debate over the role of the Internet and the wider question of a 'new' economy is an old one in a new guise.

One concept developed in the study of innovation by economic historians is the distinction between what Lipsey et al. (2005) call general purpose technology (GPT) and endogenous innovation that is specific to a firm or an industry. By contrast to GPT, endogenous technical change takes place within one firm that uses it to gain strategic advantage in the market over its rivals in the same industry. If successful, it can capture the full rewards to its investment in research and development, especially if there is an effective regulatory regime of intellectual property (IP) protection. Applying this perspective to digitalisation and the Internet, we can see that these are classic examples of GPT that has pervaded every industry, firm and household; that some firms have found it difficult to adopt and adapt – the 'majors' in the music industry are an obvious example; and that change has not been smooth, at least in some of the media industries. Not only have production processes changed but much wider unforeseen and unintended economic and social consequences have also come about, for example, the ability of people to download music. On the other hand, the return to the investment in the invention of the CD was capable of being appropriated by one innovating firm.

Regulation

Whether or not the Internet is viewed as an unprecedented technological change – one of the themes of this chapter – the task of analysing it and, therefore, understanding what policy measures are appropriate both within media firms and for government regulation has so far not necessitated any fundamental change in the disciplines adopted here. This may come about but has not done so yet.

Regulation is the use of laws and rules to alter economic and social behaviours and outcomes in accordance with some policy objective; regulation may be reactive or proactive, that is, it may seek to prevent something from happening or promote certain behaviour that would otherwise not come about. Examples of regulation are competition law that reacts to monopoly or other market dominance and copyright law, which protects creators and acts as a stimulus to creation.

Regulation is undertaken by a government in order to achieve its policies. Many policies are of a general nature, such as maintaining standards of social behaviour, for example, towards public decency and human rights, or economic goals, such as encouraging economic growth and the protection of consumers; others may be more specific, such as media ownership rules. Some regulation is self-regulation, whereby an industry imposes its own rules, such as film censorship or control of press content; the failure of self-regulation would lead to intervention by the state and that provides a stimulus to conform. Failure to comply with state regulations is punished by fines or even imprisonment.

One serious problem faced by the regulator is that the body responsible for it requires considerable knowledge of how the entity to be regulated operates so that appropriate regulations may be put in place. Where the impact of new technologies on an industry or on the whole economy is concerned, the regulator knows less than those in the industry who have invented or adopted the technologies. In such situations, the regulator must either wait until the full picture emerges before intervening or rely on the industry itself for the information it needs (Viscusi et al., 2005). The industry, therefore, holds the trump card and will use this superiority to its own advantage. Moreover, the representatives of an industry may well persuade a bureaucratic regulator to be sympathetic to its problems (real or not); this is known in the literature of regulation as 'regulatory capture' and is believed by political scientists and economists working in what is called 'public choice' theory (the economic analysis of political decision-making) to be a fundamental drawback of regulation. This analysis also demonstrates that producers combine to lobby governments in order to control regulation at the expense of citizens who lack the power to organise for such purposes. That has been a feature of recent deliberations over changes to copyright law.

Regulation affects the media industries at all levels, from individual authors creating content to huge media enterprises, and the main types of regulation are outlined below. In addition to regulation there has been a programme of deregulation and privatisation of many sectors of the economy, such as transport and telecommunications, and also including media, particularly television. These developments are not discussed here or in Chapter 6, but have been a factor in the changing business environment of media firms (see Chapter 7).

Competition law (antitrust)

Competition law seeks to control the effects of dominant firms on consumer welfare. Dominance is usually defined by rule of thumb as being in control of more than a certain percentage (often 25 per cent) of the market for a specific product. Thus oligopolies (several large firms) as well as monopolies are targeted by competition law. Moreover, competition law is concerned with all stages of the chain of production and distribution to the market. In the well known *Paramount* (1948) antitrust case in the USA that broke up the Hollywood studio system, the studios were forced to divest themselves of their distribution mechanism, the cinemas (movie theatres). Similarly, in the UK, an investigation in to the supply of recorded music by the Monopolies and Mergers Commission (1994) required some record labels to break their control over record shops. The motive for such interventions was both to enable greater diversity of supply for consumers and to prevent these enterprises from using their market dominance to raise prices and obtain monopoly profits.

The court or other statutory body enforcing competition law must conduct lengthy enquiries into the business it seeks to regulate and have judicial powers to obtain accurate knowledge. However, it cannot see into the future. Such courts have, therefore, tended to focus on the effect of dominance on prices and to espouse a view of static competition instead of adopting an evolutionary approach to dynamic competition. Excessive control of dominant firms introducing new technologies could inhibit their development and thereby reduce potential economic growth.

Copyright law

Copyright law in the Anglo Saxon tradition applies to both authors, performers and 'publishers' – the companies, such as producers of sound recordings and film. In the European civil law tradition, authors' rights pertain to human creators and neighbouring rights to the other groups. However, both bodies of law share the same essential features and here the term copyright is used loosely to refer to both traditions.

Copyright law protects authors and performers by establishing statutory property rights that enable them to control the exploitation of their works, granting them the exclusive right to authorise their use. It applies to works by an author or other 'creator'. A work may be a musical composition, a book, a poem, a painting, etc. and it may also be the creation of a sound recording or master copy of a film or broadcast. Copyright is in fact not just one thing but consists of an array of distinct rights and 'works'. In order to qualify for copyright protection, a work must be original, meaning that it was not copied from another work. In most Western countries, copyright lasts for 70 years after the author's death (50 years after the first fixation for a film or sound recording in Europe; in the USA, companies have been granted a 95-year term, the 'Sonny Bono' extension to copyright law that kept Mickey Mouse from going into the public domain). During that period, as long as the work continues to be sold (though the majority of copyright works are no longer in the catalogue), the author or her heirs receive royalty income.

Copyright law creates property rights that, when enforced, overcome what economists call the 'free-rider problem' associated with information goods that are non-rival and non-excludable, that is, ones that have the characteristics of public goods. The significance of these characteristics is that creators of such works cannot be fully (or even partly) compensated for their skill and the effort expended in producing them. Copyright law by giving authors exclusive rights to control the exploitation of their works on the market protects the so-called 'economic rights'; it also requires that authors be identified as the creator of a work and that their reputation and the integrity of their work is protected (the 'moral' rights). Besides protecting authors, some of the bundle of rights that constitute copyright law also protect publishers (through publication and distribution rights, and now the making available right for online distribution). 'Neighbouring rights' or 'rights related to copyright' (public performance rights are an example) apply to performers and firms or organisations in the cultural industries, for example, makers of sound recordings (phonogram producers) and broadcasters.

The simple economic rationale for copyright is that once a work has been set down in fixed form (printed, recorded, filmed), it can be copied and thus becomes a public good. Without 'privatisation' by statutorily created property rights, the creator could not cover the fixed cost of creation because a copier would only have to incur the marginal cost of making a copy, and with modern copying technologies, that is typically very low. An unauthorised copier can, therefore, supply the market at a price that does not cover the fixed cost, which decreases (or destroys) the incentive to create and distribute works. Copiers also avoid the risk of failure the first publisher takes as they only copy successful works (Towse, 2004).

In all copyright law, there are exceptions and limitations to the exclusive right of the author; these may loosely be called 'fair use' exceptions, utilising the term from US law that has become widely, if incorrectly, adopted. This means that copyrighted material may be used for certain non-commercial purpose by individuals without them needing to obtain permission from the copyright owner. It is this exception that has been disputed in relation to downloading copyright material from the Internet, particularly music. As copyright law is national law, different countries have different treatment of 'fair use', with downloading being legal in some but not in others.

Globalisation of trade in media and other copyright material has increasingly led to harmonisation of copyright law both internationally and regionally. On the world stage, the World Intellectual Property Organisation (WIPO) works to draw up treaties that are ratified by national governments thus achieving international alignment of copyright law; based in Geneva, it has taken over the role of the Berne Convention which since 1886 has sought to establish minimum reciprocal standards for the rights of authors in all signatory countries (and the 1961 Rome Convention has done the same thing for neighbouring rights). The EU is now the signatory body to international treaties on behalf of all member states and it mandates changes to national copyright law through Directives to the member states. The reason for this is to achieve harmonisation in both legal and economic terms for the pursuance of the internal market, a process which has had to overcome the difficulty of different legal traditions in the member states.

On the international level, WTO with its agreement on trade related aspects of intellectual property rights (IPRs) (TRIPS Treaty) sets down minimum standards for IP regulation. It was negotiated at the end of the Uruguay round of the general agreement on tariffs and trade (GATT) treaty in 1994. TRIPS requires that nations' laws must meet a wide range of IPRs including copyright. TRIPs also specifies enforcement and dispute resolution procedures and the use of trade sanctions against offending nations. The TRIPS agreement introduced IP law into the international trading system for the first time, and remains the most comprehensive international agreement on IPRs to date. It has important implications for media industries as well as for cultural and media policies.

Copyright law has been adapted over the years to accommodate new technologies. Digitalisation and Internet delivery of digital material has presented a particular challenge to copyright law as as the introduction of cheap and easy home copying devices. Copyright law has also become progressively stronger over the years as its scope and duration have been increased, as well as the penalties for non-compliance and this has happened again recently in response to the Internet. In 1996, WIPO negotiated the so-called 'Internet Treaties' specifically to deal with these problems. They are discussed in Chapter 6.

Media regulation

Broadcasting, film and the press are subject to a variety of rules and laws that deal with societal values such as standards of decency, protection of minors and minorities, privacy and so on, including censorship, libel and pornography laws. Economic regulation includes media and cross media ownership laws that restrict the same corporation from owning more than a certain percentage (typically 25 per cent) of one medium (Doyle, 2002). In the EU, audiovisual and media policy is concerned with encouraging the production and showing of European films on TV and recommends broadcasters to restrict the broadcast on TV and radio of non-European content in the attempt to ensure cultural diversity (Doyle, 2002).

Management theories

While the arrival of the Internet and the allied phenomenon of the emergence of global electronic networks gave rise to a substantial body of new management theory concerned primarily with networked environments (see below), it can also be viewed from the perspective of a substantial pre-existing area of theory that explores the complex inter-relationship between scientific advance and organisations. This focusses particularly on the implications of technological change for incumbent organisations, that is, those with an established track record and legacy architecture of systems, structures and strategies. For this reason this body of theory is particularly relevant to the question of how the Internet has affected the established mass media industries.

Theories of organisational technology

This stream of research is concerned the relationship between technology, organisations and innovation, and rests on two assumptions. The first is that technological change is a central engine of organisational adaptation, that is, of how an organisation changes in order to respond to or hopefully master its changing strategic environment. The second is that that the relationship between technological innovation and organisations flows in two ways: technological change affects organisations, altering core processes, rendering existing competencies obsolete, creating new markets and so on; but also that organisations' response to new technologies – for example, the way they commercialise them; the markets they address; the way products are priced – affect the path of technological change. A classic example of this is the way that Microsoft's corporate choices in terms of product/market strategies have determined the development of the personal computing industries. This body of theory, therefore, although it has technological advance as its focal point, cannot be classified as technologically determinist (Williams, 1974) in that it recognises that technological change arises from a complex interplay between scientific advance, social influences and institutional behaviour, and is a messy and unpredictable process.

Dominant design

A basic concept within this research stream is a Darwinian model of technology evolution known as the dominant design theory which proposes that in most industries innovation follows a cyclical pattern (Rosenkopf and Nerkar, 2001; Tushman and Anderson, 1986; Utterback, 1994; Tushman and Smith, 2002). The cycle begins with the emergence of a technological breakthrough or discontinuity. Such developments are stochastic events, and they trigger a period of ferment, where rival technologies compete intensively with each other and with the existing technological regime (Henderson and Clark, 1990). Examples from the media industry would include the invention of black and white photography in the 1820s, of the cinema and radio in the 1920s and the personal computer in the 1980s. These phases are confusing, rife with uncertainty, expensive and turbulent. They are also of tremendous strategic significance, since they only close when a so-called 'dominant design' has emerged which is now adopted as the standard – from the software field an example would be Microsoft's Windows operating system. Competitors must now adopt this design or risk market exclusion, and other paths of product innovation are in the main abandoned. After the 'technology transition' has occurred, technological advance will continue, but the developments will be more muted and less revolutionary in their impact.

Technology transitions

This so-called 'technology transition' ushers in a period of incremental as well as architectural innovation. From the perspective of firms, there are a number of important points to be made.First, a firm which pioneers a dominant design does not also automatically retain control of it. Indeed, studies by economic and business historians have shown that the initial inventor often does not perceive the full use to which the invention can be put and full exploitation is only achieved by newcomers. Second, technology transitions are always highly problematic for incumbent players. Third, the technology that becomes enthroned as the dominant design is not always the best on offer, but might have succeeded due to a range of other factors including time to market, the bundle of features on offer and socio-political dynamics in the strategic environment.

Thus not all technological change is the same. Despite the current fashion to label all dramatic technological developments as disruptive or radical, fine and critical distinctions can be drawn between technological advances, and in order to understand the impact of the Internet on the mass media this needs to be acknowledged. Abernathy and Clark (cited in Tushman and Smith, 2002) classify technological developments according to two dimensions; proximity to the current technological trajectory, and proximity to the existing customer/market segment. This classification allows a number of key terms from different bodies of management theory to be brought into a common typology.

'Incremental innovations' extend the existing technologies for existing subsystems and linking mechanisms. They push the existing technology trajectory by adding to established knowledge and current technological capabilities through steady improvements in either methods or materials to create better products and, therefore, higher customer satisfaction (Hill and Rothaermel, 2003).

'Architectural innovations' involve relatively simple technological or process innovations in subsystems and/or linking mechanisms and are often initially targeted at new markets that nonetheless have the potential to transform a product class or fundamentally change a key aspect of a business. The organisational challenge of architectural innovations lies in their apparently simple nature. This brings the risk that incumbents treat such 'seemingly minor' innovations as though these were merely incremental ones, and fail to perceive that they have undermined the firm's existing competence base, and the usefulness of deeply embedded firm knowledge (Henderson and Clark, 1990). Incumbents fail to see the need to restructure their organisations, seek new markets or alter their production processes. An example of an architectural innovation is the development of bubble jet desk top printers.

'Discontinuous innovations' bring 'discontinuous' change to a core subsystem causing cascading changes in other subsystems and linking mechanisms (Tushman and Murmann, 1998). They involve methods and materials that are novel to incumbents and are derived either from an entirely different knowledge base or from the recombination of parts of the incumbents' established knowledge base with a new stream of knowledge

(Hill and Rothaermel, 2003; Freeman and Soete, 1997). These developments are dangerous because they are 'competence destroying' (Tushman and Anderson, 1986), that is, they render existing competencies obsolete and make incremental improvement to existing products irrelevant. To respond, firms must develop new capabilities, which in turn demands absorbtive capacity (Cohen and Leventhal, 1990). Firms must also be able to 'de-commission' existing core competencies. Failure to do so might cause these to mutate into 'core rigidities' (Leonard-Barton, 1992).

'Market-based innovations' can be relatively simple technological developments that are targeted at new, less-demanding markets or customer segments. Their simplicity means they are often ignored by incumbents who fail to perceive their potential, which only becomes evident when the new players move upmarket and challenge the incumbent players. This is the scenario described in Christensen's *The Innovator's Dilemma* (1977), which became a seminal text for general managers during the Internet boom, where he describes how what he terms 'disruptive' innovations disrupt market structures and incumbents' organisational architectures (but are not technologically disruptive). It is suggested that this type of response underpinned the record industry's resistance to digital delivery of music via the Internet.

Implications for media organisations

This stream of research suggests that media firms need to distinguish carefully between types of technological change. All such change exerts pressure on existing firms, but the nature of that pressure, and the types of responses required, differ according to the nature of the change concerned.

Incremental changes require firms to extend existing core capabilities and a continuous improvement of production processes. Thus, electric typewriters required the print media to enhance current typing competencies. Architectural changes require alterations to basic production processes, and require organisations to address new markets, and usually restructure the organisation, thus desktop publishing systems allowed single-keystroking, which allowed journalists and advertising staff in the newspaper industry to set words in type without the help of printers. Discontinuous change requires firms to develop new competencies and perhaps abandon existing ones. The development of the CD-Rom was a discontinuous change for reference book publishers. For *Encyclopaedia Britannica* this development rendered existing competencies in book design, printing, binding and in door-to-door marketing irrelevant. Market-based innovations often require firms to create a 'new organisational space' where new company can develop strong market position in disruptive technology – an example is the new media divisions created by 'old' media firms to house their Internet activities (this is developed in detail in Chapter 7).

Further, technological transitions (the emergence of a new dominant design) tend to unseat dominant incumbents. This is due to a syndrome, which has been termed a 'pathology of sustained success' (Tushman and Smith, 2002:387) and has been observed in a wide range of different national and industry contexts by researchers from a wide variety of disciplines (Tushman and Nelson, 1990; Prahalad and Hamel, 1994; Utterback, 1994; Christensen, 1997; Tushman and Smith, 2002; Leonard-Barton, 1992). The reason is that that maturity, especially a successful maturity, creates inertia, and this reduces incumbents' ability to adjust to changes in the environment. The development route is as follows: companies with leading market positions and mastery of the dominant design strive to strengthen their leadership by extending their core competencies and engaging in continuous incremental innovation. When a technology transition occurs and a new dominant design emerges, the incumbent is trapped by its track record of success in existing markets, its focus on the competencies that were the basis of competition in the pre-transition days, and a cognitive set that deters it from searching outside its standard frame of reference (Levitt and March, 1988). The firm cannot reinvent itself and continue its market leadership, even though it is theoretically in a position to access the necessary competencies, resources and technologies.

Thus the current crop of leading firms is always likely to be superseded by a set of new players during technological transitions, which will themselves be superseded at the next transition. Current developments in the newspaper industry show signs of falling into this pattern. The newspaper industry has become accustomed to decades of reliable generation of high levels of cash. Years of profit have led to unwieldy and bureaucratic structures, high cost bases, slow decision making, complex reporting lines and moribund corporate cultures. Against the backdrop of aging populations, low growth and significantly the Internet, which is attracting high levels of classified advertising, they look set to be replaced eventually by a new news vehicle based around the Internet.

General management and business perspectives

Within general business and management literature over the past 15 years, especially publications designed for a 'general' rather than specialist audience, the notion of the Internet has been closely linked with a number of other concepts. Of these, the most 'contained', if not clearly defined, is convergence. The others are far more confused and, therefore, problematic to summarise and include: the 'new economy', 'network economy' or

'Internet economy', the 'knowledge economy/society' and the 'information economy/society'. All of these concepts were viewed as likely to transform industrial structures and society, and all were the subject of much analysis during the first Internet boom. While much of this concerns predictions about future developments, many of which have now been overtaken by the events and developments discussed later in this book, the terms nonetheless still exert influence over academics' and practitioners' understanding of the impact of the Internet, and for this reason are included in this chapter.

Convergence

There is a theory in high technology called the isoquantic shift which refers to a significant technological advancement that dramatically changes the way people do things and completely reorientates people's concepts of how things are done. We're seeing a new isoquantic shift taking place this decade that is replacing the old analogue communications we have known – digital compression communications. That's a very significant factor for all of us, because of the convergence of our respective industries, whether it's computers, communications, or content. They're all coming together. (John Scully speaking at National Association of Broadcasters Conference, 1993)

The concept of convergence was hard to escape in business literature during the first Internet wave. Its heavy usage derived from the magnitude of the changes it was expected to bring in its wake, for example, it was described as 'a second industrial revolution' (Henzler, 1998), 'comparable in scale to the biggest changes ever experienced by humans' (Barwise and Hammond, 1998). Like many terms of this era, despite frequent mention, it remained surprisingly vaguely defined. Overall, three broad types of definition can be identified:

1   Network-focussed definitions are favoured by the telecommunications sector – the sector responsible for supplying the 'conduit' for the new products and services arising from convergence. This usage of the term convergence can be traced back to an earlier idea, the 'information superhighway', which was prevalent in the 1980s. The shared concept in both definitions is that of a universal information pipeline. Thus network definitions of convergence foresee a world where all networks (broadcasting, satellite, cable, telephony) are each capable of providing all the different services (radio, television, voice telephony, data). The key technological driver of this form of convergence is advances in digital transmission technologies – once a variety of different messages are in a common digital format they can be transported and processed similarly, to create a: 'Swiss army network – a single integrated infrastructure capable of delivering voice, video, and data services', or a situation of 'all things over IP'. Baldwin, McVoy and Steinfeld describe this as: 'a broadband communications system that would integrate voice, video, and data with storage of huge libraries of material available on demand with the option of interaction as appropriate' (1996). This type of definition continues to be favoured by governments, and by the telecommunications sector.

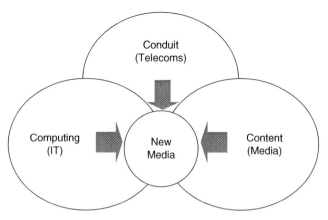

Figure 2.1 '3-C' model of convergence

2 Product-related definitions of convergence from the perspective of the end device upon which or with which content is consumed. Thus this group of definitions approaches convergence from the demand side, from the perspective of products and services, and tends, unsurprisingly, to be favoured by the consumer electronics industry. Initially the expectation was that convergence process would lead to the development of a universal convergence device, a multi-purpose 'information appliance' which combines the functions of converging sectors. Yoffie (1997:2) provides a product-centric definition of convergence when he defines it as 'the coming together of previously distinct products that employ digital technologies ... the uniting of the functions of the computer, the telephone and the television set', whereby, for example, 'a computer begins to incorporate the functionality of a communications device, and the telephone takes on the functionality of a computer'. While in practice devices appear to be diverging, rather than converging, with digital content being consumed on an increasing range of digital devices, the strategies of a number of big players, such as Microsoft or Nokia, are still optimistic that a single device might come to dominate the lion's share of some aspect of media consumption – at home consumption for example.

3 The third set of definitions is sector-focussed. These view convergence as the technologically driven fusing of the content (i.e. media), computing (i.e. information technology) and communications (i.e. telecoms and broadcast distribution) industries into a new 'media and communication' sector (Chakravarthy, 1997; Bradley and Nolan, 1998). This is the understanding of convergence most frequently espoused by the media industries, and it is commonly depicted in the so-called '3-C model of convergence'.

Convergence is the result of a combination of developments in the broader industrial environment. These include:

1 Improvements in computer performance, coupled with falling prices. This means that the cost of participation in the global networked electronic platforms (see below) is falling dramatically. It also means it is feasible to extend digitalisation of information beyond data to include voice, video and audio forms of content. The net result is that

the potential performance and benefits of computing power increase further, which in turn attracts ever more individuals to participate in the new information networks, enabling performance and benefits to be further improved (for further discussion, see Network Economics, below).

2   Increases in bandwidth capacity. The media industry developed in an environment where bandwidth was expensive and rationed. Now, however, developments in wireless technology, coaxial and fibre optic cable, routers and digital compression mean that telecommunications bandwidth, the speed at which data can be moved through the phone network, is increasing rapidly while its price is falling.

3   Standardisation of network architecture. Increasing agreement on standards for network architecture, indeed in more general terms the emergence of universal technical standards for communication allows information to be 'disconnected' from the proprietary channels upon which it has hitherto been carried (Evans and Wurster, 1999). Open standards ensure compatibility between devices, which in turn means the exchange of data between members of the network becomes easier. Combined with a rapid increase in the number of people and organisations connected by networks allows 'everybody to connect with everybody else at essentially zero cost' (Evans and Wurster, 1997:74), it also lowers communication and process costs, allowing the linkage of systems which were not compatible before.

4   Networked open electronic platforms. An important development arising from these various technological advances ranging from the standardisation of network architecture to advances in distribution technology is the development of new media platforms, namely high speed, open multimedia communications networks. Telephone communications, mass media transmissions and computer data exchanges are gradually combining to create an integrated, interconnected system of multiple digital broadband networks liked to video servers. This represents the tying together of all the recent advances in computing and telecommunication to link domestic and business computing power around the world. They combine both tangible (hardware such as computers, cables, modems and phones) and intangible elements (application software). The best known component is the Internet, but also included wired and wireless telephone networks and digital satellite networks. This represents a new infrastructure for global business and is both the prerequisite and a driver of convergence.

5   Network externalities. Networked electronic platforms, therefore, are developing into the backbone infrastructure for media and communication industries, and networked environments exhibit particular characteristics which are an important influence on strategy and structure in these industries, the network effects described earlier in this chapter.

6   Deregulation. Forces of industry deregulation have served both as a backdrop and a catalyst for the changes in the media and communications industries. Deregulation has affected a wide range of industries ranging from banking and aviation to public transportation and utilities over the last decade, but it is the deregulation of national telecommunications monopolies that has acted as an important catalyst for the digital revolution. The US Telecom Act of 1996 led to a restructuring of the telecoms sector and a flurry of consolidation activity in the broadcasting field. The World Trade Organisation's Telecommunications Accord (1998) triggered a wave of competition

in every world market by removing artificial barriers to entry and led to a wave of privatisations.

7 Globalisation. The globalisation of business is widely acknowledged as a defining feature of the closing decade of the twentieth century. Critically, markets are globalising too, as customers become increasingly accustomed on the one hand to sourcing goods from all over the world and on the other demanding access to the same brands and goods from any point on the globe. Organisations active in these markets must compete across geographic divides and meet the needs of customers, whereever they are, this in turn has created a highly competitive environment which has forced the pace for the development and adoption of digital technologies.

'Network economy', 'Internet economy', 'new economy'

Alternatively labelled the 'Network Era' (Bradley and Nolan, 1998), the 'Network Economy' (Kelly, 1997), the 'Networked Economy' (Schwartz and Leyden, 1997), the 'Era of Networked Intelligence' (Tapscott, 1996), the 'Internet Economy' (Evans and Wurster, 2000), this comprised the part of the economy that dealt with information goods and the supporting technology industries (Choi and Winston, 2000). Central concepts are the importance of digital technologies, the Internet, computers, information and the globalised networks they enable (Carlaw et al. 2006), and the assumption is that communication technologies allow firms to work together more effectively; to exchange goods/services and information easier; and to coordinate activities in ways that do not require single ownership of interacting firms (Tapscott, 1995; Evans & Wurster, 1997; Shapiro & Varian, 1999). These concepts received enormous amounts of attention in the business press, mainly due to a belief that they would create a fundamentally new business environment, one in which companies once celebrated as examples of best-practice would be disadvantaged, and where long-established management precepts would lose relevance. In practice, these assumptions proved erroneous, and these phenomena did not in reality alter basic economic and financial laws.

The basic concept was that electronic networks can transform how activities are performed and the linkages between them, reducing the time and costs of operations and allowing Internet-enabled networks of collaboration between distributors, customers and suppliers. These developments, coupled with a growth in alliance partnerships as a means of accessing resources and fostering growth, would lead to the emergence of new forms of fluid, flexible, network organisations, as well as clusters of organisations engaged in information goods and technology/communications-related activities, such as Silicon Valley in California. They would also bring about the 'death of distance' (Cairncross, 1997), whereby the Internet's ability to cross boundaries and link previously independent markets would give rise to 'virtual' marketplaces, shop windows in which companies can display goods to a world market.

Much research in this field focussed on supply chain management, which looked using the Internet and e-business applications as a means to better coordinate producers, suppliers and distributors. It was anticipated that production, marketing, distribution and transportations would blur into a single procedure, creating the need for fulfilment and re-engineering (Chandra and Kumar, 2000; Simchi-Levi et al., 2000). Such an environment also allows diverse and geographically dispersed companies to create alliances that represent advanced and dynamically changing networks that aim to become competitive by focussing their resources on bringing elements of e-business to specific market segments (Grieger, 2002; De Man et al., 2002).

Knowledge economy/society

While the network or Internet economy was a new phenomenon, the knowledge economy, and the information economy date are not. These terms are closely associated with the concept of 'new technology', and with innovations that allow knowledge to be applied to human work. A number of researchers, including Drucker (1969, 1984) and Toffler (1980) have drawn attention to the increasing importance of knowledge and knowledge creation in economic and social life and the implications this will have for institutions.

As with many terms discussed here, despite heavy use there is no commonly agreed definition of the knowledge economy/society. Describing the (joint) term as at best 'a widely-used metaphor, rather than a clear concept', Carlaw et al. (2006:650) provide a valuable analysis of the common characteristics that define its use. First, it describes an environment where knowledge has a central role in economic activity. By extension, there is a preoccupation with the role of innovation, as a product of human capital, in production and consumption (this, they argue, gives rise to the belief that intellectual capabilities are the fuel of the new economy), and particularly on the parts of governments on how this can be generated. Second, the term 'knowledge economy' is 'primarily concerned with knowledge as a commodity and the value of intellectual labour in the creation of wealth' and 'knowledge society' should 'concern the social climate in which the knowledge economy resides'.

Thus knowledge was highlighted as factor of production on a par with the classic trio land, labour and capital. Indeed, some economists emphasise 'human capital', meaning that people invest in knowledge and it is used to produce and increase productivity. In general, there is the notion that the present day economy needs workers with formal education and the ability to apply theoretical and analytical knowledge, rather than the less skilled employed in manufacturing or heavy industry of yesteryear. Indeed, one of the more descriptive terms is the 'weightless' economy, suggesting the antithesis of heavy industry. Underlying these various expressions is the idea that knowledge is a driving force of the new type of economy. The term 'knowledge society' also reflects this idea: science, innovation and expertise are held to be the moving forces of social change and development.

Information economy/society

The concept of the information economy or society focusses particularly on the importance of information and communication in modern economies (Harris, 2001: 23). The information economy or 'information age' is viewed as a progression from the machine age, where decisive assets are capital intensive, to one where competitive advantage lies mostly in the effective use of information. It is anticipated that this will be succeeded by the 'knowledge age', where competitive advantage involves the effective use of human resources (see, for example, Miles, Snow et al., 1997).

The structure of so-called 'industrial age' organisations reflected the coordination technologies available at that time: for example, the train, the car, the telephone and the mainframe computer. These technologies allow for slow and cumbersome communication (certainly in comparison with the networked digital environment), and it makes sense for transactions to be conducted internally, since they create the potential for economies of scale and scope. This gave rise to large, stable, hierarchical and often complex organisational structures characterised by centralised functions that are coordinated by an administrative bureaucracy. New information and co-ordination technologies, particularly the Internet, improve the efficiency of firms and markets, and, therefore, reduce transaction costs inside and outside firms (Bradley and Nolan, 1998). Thus large, complex, hierarchical organisation structures become less advantageous. Thus it was assumed by many theorists (see, for example, Evans and Wurster, 2000) that the Internet would cause organisations to reduce in size, with an accompanying shift from hierarchical governance structures to market exchange (the so-called 'law of diminishing firms').

A parallel concept that concerned the demise of the so-called 'industrial age organisations' was the emergence of the knowledge worker. This concept was developed by Drucker (1985). This new class of employee is involved with employing their minds, not their bodies, with producing intangible ideas, concepts and analysis, rather than tangible objects. These knowledge workers represent a large and growing part of employees in the developed world, and are the engine of value creation. They are, however, ill-suited to complex hierarchical organisational structures. This is partly because in order to create knowledge (especially in media firms with their emphasis on project-based work) they need to interact, collaborate and exchange specialist knowledge horizontally with their peers across the organisation, something that is hard to do in large complex hierarchical firms. It is also because knowledge workers tend to be self-directed individuals who do not thrive in hierarchical environments.

A further link between the information age and the media industry is the concept of 'information goods'. These are understood as intangible products that can be digitised (Shapiro and Varian, 1999). It was proposed that in the emerging information society information goods in digital form can be reproduced and distributed at near zero marginal cost independent of the medium by which it is delivered. This means that the Internet offers new opportunities to content owners that arise from the more flexible and cost-effective delivery of existing content, the development of new content and the possibility to enhance the value of content whose primary distribution takes place through traditional channels such as broadcast and cable TV. The Internet can be used to create services that broaden and deepen the audience's relationship with a film or TV show, thereby making the underlying media property more valuable through a larger audience. Media companies who wish to serve online markets must ensure online content offers new features and new value- added services. As a result these new forms of distribution require completely new business strategies, since online content products are frequently not an identical copy of the traditional products.

References

Baldwin, T. F., Stevens McVoy, D. and Steinfeld, C. (1996). *Convergence: Integrating Media, Information and Communication*. London: Sage Publications.

Barwise, P. and Hammond. K. (1998). *Media*. London: Phoenix.

Blaug, M. (1997). *Great Economists since Keynes*. Cheltenham: Edward Elgar.

Bradley, S. P. and Nolan, R.L. (Eds.) (1998). *Sense and Respond: Capturing Value in the Network Era*. Boston: Harvard Business School Press.

Busterna, J.C. (1988). 'Concentration and the Industrial Organization Model'. In Picard, R.G, Winter, M. McCombs, J. P. & Lacy, S. (Eds.). *Press Concentration and Monopoly: New Perspectives on Newspaper Ownership and Operation*. Norwood, N.J. Ablex Publishing: 35–53.

Cairncross, F. (1997). *The Death of Distance: How the Communications Revolution will Change Our Lives*. Boston: Harvard Business School Press.

Carlaw, K., Oxley, L., Walker. P., Thorns, D., and Nuth, M. (2006) 'Beyond the Hype:Intellectual Property and the Knowledge Society/Knowledge Economy', *Journal of Economic Surveys*, 20 (4): 633–90.

Chakravarthy, B., (1997) A New Strategy Framework for Coping with Turbulence, *Sloan Management Review*, Winter, 69–82.

Chandra, C. and Kumar, S. (2000). Supply Chain Management in Theory and Practice: A Passing Fad or a Fundamental Change? *Industrial Management & Data Systems*, 100(3), 100–13.

Choi, S. Y. and Winston, A. B. (2000). *The Internet Economy: Technology and Practice*. Austin TX: SmartEcon Publishing.

Cohen, W. M. & Levinthal, D. A. (1990). Absorbtive Capacity: A New Perspective on Learning and Innovation. *Administrative Science Quarterly*, 35:555.

Christensen, C. M. (1997). *The Innovator's Dilemma: When New Technologies Cause Great Firms to Fail*. Boston, MA: Harvard Business School Press.

Davenport, T. H. and Beck, J.C. (2001). *The Attention Economy: Understanding the New Currency of Business*. Boston: Harvard Business School Press.

Doyle, G. (2002) *Media Ownership: Concentration, Convergence and Public Policy*, London: Sage.

Drucker, P. (1969). *The Age of Discontinuity: Guidelines to our Changing Society*. London: Heineman.

Evans, P. and Wurster, T. S. (2000) *Blown to Bits: How the New Economics of Information Transform Strategy*. Boston: Harvard Business School Press.

Evans, P. and Wurster, T. S. (1997). *Blown to Bits: How the New Economics of Information Transforms Strategy*. Boston: Harvard Business School Press.

Freeman, C. and Soete, L. (1997) *The Economics of Industrial Innovation*. Cambridge, MA: MIT Press.

Harris. R. (2001). The Knowledge-Based Economy: Intellectual Origins and New Economic Perspectives. *International Journal of Management Reviews* (3) 1: 21–40.

Hill, C. W. and Rothaermel, (2003). The Performance of Incumbent Firms in the Face of Technological Innovation, *Academy of Management Review*, 28 (2): 257.

Gershun, J. (2000). *Changing Times: Work and Leisure in Post Industrial Society*. Oxford: Oxford University Press.

Henderson, R, M. and Clark, K. B. (1990). Architectural Innovation: The Reconfiguration of Existing Product Technologies and the Failure of Established Firms. *Administrative Science Quarterly*, (35): 9–30.

Henzler, H. A. (1998). *Communications and Media in the Digital Age.* Speech to mcm Forum, St. Gallen, Switzerland.

Kelly, K., (1997) 'New Rules for the New Economy. Twelve Dependable Principles for Thriving in a Turbulent World', *Wired*, Issue 5.09, September.

Leonard-Barton, D. (1992). 'Core Capabilities and Core Rigidities: A Paradox in Managing New Product Development'. *Strategic Management Journal*, Summer Special Issue, 13: 111–125.

Levitt, B. and March, J. G. 1988. 'Organizational Learning', *Annual Review of Sociology*, 14: 319–340.

Lipsey, Richard. G., Carlaw, K. I. and Bekar, C. (2005). *Economic Transformations: General Purpose Technologies and Long Term Economic Growth*. Oxford: Oxford University Press.

Monopolies and Mergers Commission (1994). *The Supply of Recorded Music*. HMSO Cm. 2599, London.

Nelson, Richard R. and Sidney G. Winter (1982). *An Evolutionary Theory of Economic Change.* Cambridge: Harvard University Press.

Picard, Robert G. (2002). *The Economics and Financing of Media Companies*. New York: Fordham University Press.

Prahalad, C. K. and Hamel, G., (Eds.) (1994). 'In Search of New Paradigms'. *Strategic Management Journal* 15, Special Issue. Chichester: Wiley.

Rosenkopf, L. and A. Nerkar (2001). 'Beyond Local Search: Boundary-spanning, Exploration, and Impact in the Optical Disc Industry', *Strategic Management Journal*, 22: 287–306.

Shapiro, C. and H.R. Varian (1999). *Information Rules: A Strategic Guide to the Network Economy*. Boston: Harvard Business School Press.

Schumpeter, J. (1983). *Theory of Economic Development: An Inquiry into Profits, Capital, Credit, Interest, and the Business Cycle*. Reprint Edition. Somerset, N. J. Transaction Publishers.

Scherer, F.M. & Ross, D. (1990). *Industrial Market Structure and Economic Performance* (3rd Ed). Boston: Houghton Mifflin.

Simchi-Levi, D., Kaminsky, P. and Simchi-Levi, E. (2000). *Designing and Managing the Supply Chain: Concepts, Strategies and Case Studies*. New York, NY: McGraw-Hill.

Schwartz, P. and Leyden, P. (1997). The Long Boom: A History of the Future, 1980–2020 in *Wired*, Issue 5.07 – July 1997

Tapscott, Don (1995). The Digital Economy: Promise and Peril in the Age of Networked Intelligence. New York: McGraw-Hill.

Toffler, A. (1980). *The Third Wave*. London: Collins.

Towse, R. (2001). *Creativity, Incentive and Reward*, Cheltenham: Edward Elgar.

Towse, R. (2004). 'Copyright and Economics' in Frith. S. and Marshall, L. (Eds) *Music and Copyright* (2nd Ed.), Edinburgh: University of Edinburgh Press; 54–69.

Tushman, M. L. & Anderson, P. (1986). 'Technological Discontinuities and Organizational Environments'. *Administrative Science Quarterly*, 31: 439.

Tushman, M. L. & Murmann, J.(1998).Dominant Designs, Technology Cycles, and Organizational Outcomes'. *Research in Organizational Behavior* 20: 213.

Tushman M. L., & Nelson, R. R. (1990). 'Introduction: Technology, Organizations, and Innovations.' *Administrative Science Quarterly*, 35: 1–8.

Tushman, M. L., & Smith, W.(2002). 'Organizational Technology'. In Baum, J. C. (Ed.) *The Blackwell Companion to Organizations*: 386–414. Oxford: Blackwell Publishers.

Utterback J. M. (1994). *Mastering the Dynamics of Innovation*. Boston: Harvard Business School Press.

Varian, H. (2005). 'Copying and copyright', *Journal of Economic Perspectives*, 19 (2), 121–138.

Viscusi, W. Kip, Harrington, J. and Vernon, J. (2005). Economics of Regulation and Antitrust, (4th Ed.), Cambridge, Mass: MIT press.

Williams, R. (1974). *Television: Technology and Cultural Form*. London: Fontana

Williamson, O. E. (1995). *The Economic Institutions of Capitalism: Firms, Markets, Relational Contracting*. New York: Free Press.

Wirth, M.O. & Bloch, H. (1995). Industrial Organization Theory and Media Industry Analysis, *Journal of Media Economics*, 8(2): 15–26.

Yoffie, D. B. (Ed.). (1997). *Competing in the Age of Digital Convergence*. Boston: Harvard Business School Press.

3

THE IMPACT OF THE INTERNET ON MEDIA TECHNOLOGY, PLATFORMS AND INNOVATION

Anders Henten and Reza Tadayoni

Introduction

The focus of this chapter is the technologies involved with the Internet. However, the Internet is just one branch of the development of digital technologies in the communication and media areas. Other kinds of digital technologies are used in, for instance, audio and video broadcasting and these technology solutions also have strong implications for the development of these media areas. Furthermore, digitalisation as such is the fundamental technological basis for the convergence between different media. The Internet, however, is one of the most important technological platforms within the broader digital development and it is unquestionably the most important common technological platform for the convergence between different kinds of communication and media industries. The reason is, first and foremost, that the Internet has proven to be a very efficient technology platform, e.g., in terms of reach, costs and quality. For media and content industries it, furthermore, provides a possibility for interactivity, which is a new development for the mass media that hitherto have been one-way media.

Figure 3.1 illustrates the development of the media with special emphasis on the Internet. In the upper part of the figure, the appearance of different media and communication technologies/applications in three different areas (text, audio and video) is shown. Emphasis is on one-way (distributive) technologies/applications, as media and content industries, formerly, have been one-way media. A limited number of two-way (communicative) technologies/applications, however, are also included, as they point to the convergence between one-way and two-way communications facilitated

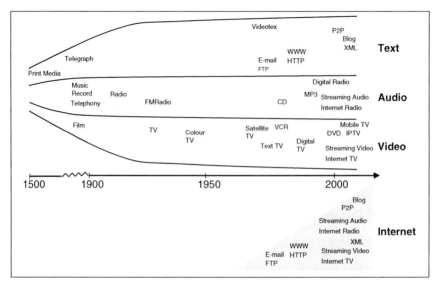

Figure 3.1   Media and communication technologies/applications: timeline

by the Internet. The lower part of the figure lists a number of the most important Internet-related technologies and applications. These technologies and applications are also included in the upper part of the figure but are in the lower part taken out separately to emphasise the increasing importance of the Internet for the media and content industries. The figure basically shows that new media and communication technologies and applications add to or substitute for the existing ones and that the Internet as a converged platform, including two-way as well as one-way communications, not only complements the existing forms of communication but also encroaches upon and substitutes for parts of existing one-way and two-way communications.

What is the Internet?

Placing the Internet at the centre of the developments of media and content industries means that what is meant by the term 'Internet' must be specified. In the present chapter, two specifications are emphasised. One is that the Internet is based on the Internet Protocol (IP) but that the IP also can be used in other technology contexts than the Internet proper, for instance, in managed IP-based networks. Not all IP-based communications use the Internet as technology platform.

The other specification is that the Internet is more than TCP/IP (Transmission Control Protocol/Internet Protocol). The basic definition of the Internet is communication using TCP/IP. However, what has come to be understood as the Internet encompasses a host of different technologies, e.g., the World Wide Web (the Web), compression technologies, streaming technologies, etc., where the different technological elements have different implications for the media. When talking about the Internet, all such technology solutions are mostly assumed to be included in the term. But it is important to understand that the Internet and IP-related technologies are not a finite thing but something that develops over time. Therefore, when examining media implications of the Internet, one should not only take a synchronic view on the Internet and IP implications but also include a historical and diachronic perspective (this is discussed later in this chapter).

Following the initial invention of packet-based technology in the 1960s, there has been a long row of complementary technology developments. According to some authors, this kind of development can be conceptualised as incremental innovations following an original radical invention and is often described as a cumulative process involving many different market players (Foster, 1986 and Christensen, 1997). Furthermore, when using the invention-innovation-diffusion terminology, first developed by Joseph Schumpeter (Freeman, 1994), the original invention is followed by subsequent innovations, and even in the diffusion phases, new developments will materialise. Even though the invention-innovation-diffusion framework can be interpreted in a unidirectional manner, it is important to acknowledge that technology developments also can take place late in the processes of innovation and diffusion. Technology providers will adapt their products to the manner in which they are taken up by the users. Furthermore, technology providers will learn from users. Moreover, the way users employ new technologies may change the way innovations were conceived by the technology providers. All such kinds of 'user-involvement' have been seen in the case of the Internet, which illustrates that a technology-determinist approach will not be able to understand the development of the Internet and how it has come to be what it is today.

The materialisation of the synergies between Internet technologies and the media is thus connected to a wide range of technological developments. It is, e.g., not economically feasible to transmit audio or video in raw digital form to end users in any network. Only professional internal broadcast networks are designed for this task. Therefore, coding and compression technologies are important. Furthermore, even in coded form it will take too a long time to download audio and especially video components within the current broadband networks. This has resulted in the development of streaming technologies which enable the users to start listening/viewing audio or video services without downloading.

The Internet itself has had huge impacts on the development of the media and content industries, but the real use of media services over the Internet or other IP networks is dependent on the development of broadband technologies and infrastructures. Broadband is increasingly becoming a driving force in the whole convergence process. Broadband establishes a platform for different services to be offered and for the development of interactivity. Broadband networks are competing technologies to other broadcast distribution networks. Broadband networks are also competitive in offering advanced services like video and audio on demand (VAoD) and giving access to online archival material. An important question is the extent to which broadband replaces the traditional distribution system and to what degree it will be more efficient to have specialised broadcast networks and what the parameters affecting this development are.

However, the Internet does not only allow for the kinds of interactivity connected with VAoD and searching for text material. The question of interactivity goes much further, with the Internet proving to be a technological platform for all kinds of point-to-point, point-to-multipoint and multipoint-to-multipoint communications, including blogs and peer-to-peer communications.

Looking at broadcasting once more, the development of the Internet and IP has, furthermore, had massive impacts on the production and contribution parts of the value chain. The widespread access to the Internet and advanced capturing devices establish a situation where every user of the Internet can be a contributor to programme production. The entry barriers to establish freelance journalism has decreased and there are many sources for news in competition with the traditional news agencies. The entry cost of establishing a Web radio and Web TV station is far below the traditional broadcast stations and they potentially have much wider consumer bases.

Moreover, mobile consumption has been one of the strength of broadcast services. The mobility has been a determining factor for the development of radio, long before residential communication became mobile. At present, we are witnessing that mobility comes to the media through mobile/wireless communicative networks. This is an important parameter in the future value creation and resource utilisation. Media products can be presented on different platforms, fixed and mobile, and this will not only lead to changes in the use of media products but also in their production.

Finally, it should be noted that the present chapter only deals with the technology aspects of the Internet and its implications on the media. In addition to the technology innovations related to the development of the Internet, there are many other and as important innovations regarding governance and organisation and also commercialisation of the Internet (Mowery & Simcoe, 2002). However, these innovations are, in the present chapter, taken for granted and only the technological potentials and limitations of the Internet and IP regarding media developments are taken into consideration.

The history of the Internet

In the paper, 'A Brief History of the Internet', a group of the 'founding fathers' of the Internet starts out with the following statement:

> The Internet has revolutionized the computer and communications world like nothing before …. The Internet is at once a worldwide broadcasting capacity, a mechanism for information dissemination, and a medium for collaboration and interaction between individuals and their computers without regard for geographic location (Leiner, Cerf et al., no year of publication).

This statement is absolutely true today – acknowledging, as the authors do, the previous developments of the telegraph, telephone, radio and computer, etc. – and is, indeed, the message of the present chapter. But it was not true from the beginning of the development of the Internet. The capacities mentioned came later, for instance, with respect to broadcasting. The purpose of this section is, therefore, to show: 1. that the Internet is not a fixed and finite thing – that the Internet has developed over time with different implications for the media; and 2. that it will keep on developing technologically with future consequences for media developments. First and foremost, the Internet is not just the TPC/IP protocol suite; it is much more. The aim of the chapter and this section is thus to go a couple of steps down in abstraction from 'the Internet' and look at the different technological elements and capabilities related to the Internet.

The Internet is based on packet switching technology, in contrast to the traditional telephone networks, for example, which are circuit switched. This means that, based on digital technology, communications are split up in packets and do not occupy whole circuits but share the capacity with packets from other communications. There are two basic kinds of packet switching technology, connection-oriented and connection-less. Connection-oriented means that specific paths are determined in advance, while connection-less means that packets from the same communication may follow different paths. Asynchronous transfer mode (ATM) is an example of a connection-oriented technology, and the Internet is an example of a connection-less network.

In their historical account, the 'founding fathers' explain that packet switching technology was developed at different places simultaneously. Work had been going on at Massachusetts Institute of Technology (MIT) and RAND in the US, and at national physical laboratories (NPLs) in the UK: 'in parallel without any of the researchers knowing about the other work' (Leiner et al., no year of publication). This happened in the beginning and middle of the 1960s, and in 1968 the overall structure and specifications of the advanced research projects agency network (ARPANET – the earliest precursor of the Internet) were finalised. In 1969, the first small network was built including four nodes and in 1970, the forerunner of TPC/IP, the network control protocol (NCP), was finished, which made it possible to develop applications for the network. Mowery & Simcoe (2002) explain that there was a parallel initiative in the UK at the NPLs – starting even before the development of ARPANET – and that there was also a French initiative a couple of years later, starting in 1972, called CYCLADES. But none of these networks became successful, partly because of lack of funding (Mowery & Simcoe, 2002).

Email was one such application. The first email programme for ARPANET was developed in 1972 and quickly became one of the most popular applications, and it still is. In 1973, work began on developing the protocol suite later to be called TCP/IP, but it was actually not until 1 January 1983 that TCP/IP was established as the standard for ARPANET. Furthermore, it was not until this time that the term Internet was used. In the 1970s and 1980s, many different technology developments, either closely or more remotely related to or totally in isolation from but with important implications for what came to be the Internet, took place. One such example is Ethernet local area network (LAN) technology, which has played a central role for the development of Internet. Another is, as mentioned, compression technology, without which the Internet would not be what it is today.

But from a media point of view, the most important thing is maybe that, in the 1970s and 1980s, what came to be the Internet did not have any implications for neither broadcasting nor the print media. It also did not have any immediate implications for the telecom sector – although this may seem strange today. But there were a number of other technology solutions being developed at the same time, some of them proprietary, for instance IBM's systems network architecture (SNA). Indeed, packet switching technology also entered the telecom world but was developed on a track separate from the Internet community, for instance, the X.25 standard for packet switching networks and the X.400 standard for message handling (email). But today, almost nobody remembers these standards. And in closer relation to the media world, the major part of the telecom sector was, until the mid-1990s, primarily preoccupied with videotex with the French Télétel/Minitel project as the pre-eminent example.

It was actually not until the development of the Web that the Internet began to have a serious impact on the media. Of course, the media industry also used email and file transfer, like any other industry sector for internal and external communications, and news group applications, bulletin boards and listservs were also developed earlier on. But for general media products the Internet did not play any significant role until the Web was launched. And even then, it took a while for the media as well as the telecom sector to realise that something had changed – which is, to some extent, still the case today. The media and the telecom sectors have still not fully adapted to the many uses of the Internet. But they have realised its importance – as new possibilities or threats.

In 1992, Conceil Européen pour la Recherche Nucléaire (CERN) released the first version of the Web. The central functionality of the Web is hyper-linking, which makes it possible for the users to browse around and find information on the net. In 1993, a graphical interface for the Web was developed resulting in the first popular browser, Mosaic. From then on, the implications of the Internet have grown for the media. In some instances, Internet technologies can substitute for technologies hitherto used and cause important upheavals in media industries. In other cases, the Internet supplements existing technical solutions and business models.

The Internet and IP

The impact of the Internet can be analysed in several ways. In this chapter, there is a distinction made between two ways: 1. the impact of the Internet as a global interconnected network; and 2. the impact of the IP as an efficient and widespread technology. These two aspects are closely interconnected. However, the distinction helps in understanding the development.

The first aspect, the impact of the Internet, can be analysed by studying the use of the Internet as a distribution channel for media services, e.g., the huge online activities of the traditional broadcasters. In this connection, the development of streaming technologies and peer-to-peer (P2P) applications has been decisive. Furthermore, the development in audio/video compression, which applies to the general development of digital media, has been an important factor.

The second aspect, the impact of the IP, can be analysed by studying the diffusion of IP as the technology for 'closed'/'private' infrastructures, which do not necessarily interconnect to the general Internet. These *managed IP* networks were initially developed within big companies as internal com-munication infrastructures, but presently the same types of infrastructures are developed in the residential markets, e.g., in broadband networks. The main difference between these infrastructures and the general Internet is that the general Internet is 'best effort', while in the managed IP networks it is easier to implement certain levels of quality of service (QoS). Another important difference is that the Internet is 'open' for service providers, where the 'openness' of managed IP networks depends on the applied business models of the owners of the infrastructures.

The underlying argument for the enormous success of the Internet and IP, and their influence on practically every media is connected to some of the design principles resulting in an efficient platform when it comes to resource utilisation as well as when it comes to the service creation environment.

One of the design principles of IP is scalability, i.e., the network can scale up and new users and components can be added to the network in a simple and efficient way, which, however, in the future development will suffer from shortage of IP addresses. But this problem is handled by the development of IP version 6, IPv6. Apart from solving the scalability problem, other issues like QoS and security are also addressed in the IPv6. The dominant Internet architecture, based on the client-server solution, is not necessarily the most efficient when it comes to organisation of content distribution, e.g., in video on demand (VoD) provision. In this case, P2P architectures, developed mainly for content sharing, can turn out to be more relevant.

The IP design

The emergence of the Internet is considered as one of the most radical innovations in the communication field in recent years. IP technology is designed in a way that enables a radically different environment for service development, innovation and competition when it comes to infrastructure platforms as well as service development platforms. In the following, some of the important characteristics of IP platforms are outlined:

- separation between network technology and services;
- end-to-end architecture, and the extension of intelligence from the core to the edge of a network;
- scalability; and
- distributed design and decentralised control.

The separation between the underlying network technology and the services, which are provided in the IP networks, removes entry barriers for the service providers in entering the network. The only precondition for service provision is access to the network. This has created huge dynamics in service development on the Internet. However, this also creates a problem of revenue sharing between the owners of the network infrastructures and the service/content provider. This is obvious in the broadband IP infrastructures that are mainly provided by the telecom operators. As flat-rate billing for connectivity has become a de facto paradigm, the development in value propositions is mainly concentrated in the service provision.

End-to-end architecture and the extension of intelligence from the core to the edge of a network is another factor that moves the development and innovation activities to the edge of network. The concept was first introduced in a paper named: 'end-to-end argument in system design' (Saltzer, Reed & Clark, 1984). Their main argument was that an efficient network design can be based on a 'dumb core network', where processing is moved to the edge of the network.

Scalability is yet another main feature of the IP design. One of the barriers for further scalability is the shortage of addressing space in the current IPv4 systems. As discussed in the sub-section on IPv6, the shortage of addressing space is a big problem especially for developing countries, mainly due to uneven allocation of the IPv4 addressing space.

Distributed design and decentralised control is a further characteristic feature that obviously has improved conditions for the development of services, innovations and the creation of new businesses. Different networks can easily connect to other IP networks, including the Internet, and obtain value-added from network effects, etc.

These characteristics of the technology create good conditions for the development of competition where several actors can be involved in service creation and provision. The general Internet is the major IP network in the world but it is far from the only IP network. In recent years, several private IP networks have been established and utilised for corporate as well as residential services, and the future of communication platforms, like the core of the next generation network (NGN) architecture, is based mainly on IP technology.

IP version 6

The current IP, which is primarily based on IPv4, has grown rapidly in terms of the number of IP enabled devices as well as of applications and services. IPv4, however, suffers from major weaknesses regarding the rapid growth in the number of devices connected to the Internet and the new applications and services. This has resulted in the standardisation of a new version of the IP, IPv6, to cope with the shortcomings of IPv4.

One of the main weaknesses of IPv4 is the amount of IP addresses available globally. The IPv4 address consists of 32 bits, meaning that there are about 4 billion addresses available. On the one hand, it is obvious that 4 billion addresses will not be adequate in a world where more and more devices and terminals become IP enabled. On the other hand, even those current addresses available are allocated so unevenly that many countries lack IP addresses to develop their ICT infrastructures. For example, according to a consultation paper on 'issues relating to transition from IPv4 to IPv6 in India' (Telecom Regulatory Authority of India – TRAI, 2005), 'India has merely 2.8 million IPv4 addresses compared to 40 million acquired by China'. Here it is important to note that any common US university has more IP addresses than India and that a US ISP, Level-3, alone has more IP addresses than China (TRAI, 2005). The distribution is much worse when it comes to less developed developing countries. Bangladesh, for example, has about 150,000 IP addresses.

IPv6 extends the address room to 128 bits, meaning that the number of IP addresses will cease to be a problem in the foreseeable future. This creates the possibility of allocating more addresses to different countries and regions. Furthermore, the allocation of IPv6 addresses does not suffer from the historical legacy that resulted in the uneven allocation of IPv4 addressing space.

The other issues dealt with in IPv6 are related to the applications. The main issues here are QoS and security. Quality of Service is important in relation to real time services like VoIP, IPTV, Interactive TV, etc., and security at IP level will be generally required by a number of services in the future.

Peer-to-peer technology

File sharing via peer-to-peer networking is one of the most debated implications of the Internet on the media. Especially the music industry, but also the film industry, is feeling threatened by unlicensed file sharing, infringing on copyrights. File sharing is thus clearly an example of implications of the Internet as a network.

Presently, the Internet is mainly based on a client-server approach. There are a number of servers in the networks doing specific tasks, like email servers, Web servers and so on. The end users install clients on their IP terminal (computers, mobile phones, personal digital assistants (PDAs), etc.) and connect to the servers for specific services. There is, however, another approach that is becoming more and more widespread whereby the end users' IP terminals act both as clients and servers. In this approach the IP terminals connect directly to each other and share information and files, etc. This approach is called P2P to indicate that the peers communicate directly with each other. P2P networking in its pure form means that all nodes of a network are equal peers. The combined resources of the network, including computing power and storage capacity, can be used by any of the nodes in the network and they are, furthermore, combined in an ad hoc fashion.

P2P technology was actually one of the basic technology concepts of the Internet. It was described in the very first request for comments (RFC) from 1969 documenting the interface message processor (IMP) for connecting computers on the ARPANET. However, the present Internet is dominated by client-server technology but allows for P2P networking solutions which are used in many applications. In the media context, the whole issue started with Napster. This was, however, not a pure P2P application but combined P2P elements (the sharing of files between users) with client-server elements (in the searching procedures).

P2P networking in its pure form means that all nodes of a network are equal peers. The combined resources of the network, including computing power and storage capacity, can be used by any of the nodes in the network and they are, furthermore, combined in an ad hoc fashion. The alternative network architecture is the client-server configuration where one or a number of the nodes function as servers for the other nodes (the clients). The two basic configurations can, as mentioned, be combined and are so in many of the applications based on the Internet.

One of the main challenges to make P2P networks operate efficiently is the location of information. This can be compared with the role of signalling in the telephony networks to locate the parties, which want to communicate with each other. Through the last five to six years, a number of P2P applications have been developed. Examples of applications are Napster, Gnutella, FreeNet and BitTorrent. The aim of these applications has been to facilitate document sharing and mainly sharing of music and movies. Furthermore, the voice over IP (VoIP) application Skype has based its signalling on the P2P approach.

Napster was the first large extensive P2P application for music sharing. This was developed in 1999 by a college student in order to share his music with his friends. Very soon after, Napster became popular among with users and very unpopular with the record industry and the content owners. Napster was closed down by a US court in mid-2000. Location of information in Napster was implemented by deploying a central index server, keeping track on available content on the net. So the approach was P2P but it still relied on a central server, which is why it was easy to bring a stop to the service by simply requiring that the index server should be closed down.

Gnutella and the other solutions mentioned here, on the other hand, have been designed with the requirement of not relying on a central server for indexing and locating of information. In Gnutella, every peer has connections to a few neighbour peers. For locating content, the peer will ask its neighbour peers, and if they don't have the content, they will ask their neighbour peers and in this way the content will finally be found and a connection to the content location will be established. This approach doesn't have the weakness of Napster with regard to centralism, but it consumes much more bandwidth because it sends requests in several directions.

Video, audio and text media

Video

Video technologies have been through a long history of development starting with the film industry and continuing with the broadcast television and consumer electronics industries. Today, video technologies are mainly based on digital technologies, which create a substantial synergy in the technological development within film, broadcast, home entertainment, Internet services and other video-based services.

In this section, four main technological developments that have important impacts on the development of video technologies are discussed: 1. Digital TV, which transforms the whole broadcast platforms; 2. IPTV, which combines the success of the Internet development with development in video/TV technologies; 3. Mobile TV, which utilises the development of video technologies in a mobile context; and 4. Digital rights management and CA, which enable the basis for the development of commercial business models.

Digital TV

Digital broadcasting denotes a broadcasting system, where the broadcasting signal is digital through the whole chain from content creation till the consumption of the service at the end users' sites. The digital signal at the end users' sites can directly be fed into the integrated digital television receivers or, in a transition period, through a set-top-box to a regular analogue TV receiver.

The simple digitalisation of an analogue signal was a revolution when it was invented but it is not a recent phenomenon. Digital technologies have been used in telecommunication networks since beginning of the 1960s. In broadcasting, the use of digital technology for transmission of signals has become relevant in the recent years due to the extensive development in audio/video coding and modulation of digital signals which make it possible to 'compress' the digital data and drastically reduce the required transmission capacity, and also by the deployment of more efficient modulation technologies. Consequently, the number of modulated bits per second per frequency unit has been increased and the frequency bandwidth needed to transmit a TV programme has been reduced substantially.

Presently, the frequency capacity needed for a transmitter to distribute an analogue TV-programme can be shared by several digital TV-programmes or TV/radio-services. (For digital broadcasting the concept service is used instead of channel. This is because there is no longer a unique relationship between the frequency and a television or radio channel.) Exactly how many services can share the capacity for one TV-channel depends very much on the quality requirements, deployed technology and the complexity of the video/audio sources. For example, high-definition TV (HDTV) requires much more capacity than standard definition TV (SDTV).

Digitalisation of TV started in the satellite networks, where the financial gains for the operators were obvious. Later, the cable and terrestrial networks were digitised. The modern cable networks are capable of offering huge amount of analogue TV channels, which has resulted in a hard time for the penetration of digital services to the households. Consequently, in many countries, cable operators have put their main focus on development of broadband. The level of development of digital terrestrial TV has been different in different countries and has been influenced by the political process aiming at defining introduction strategies. In Europe, the UK, Sweden and Spain were among the pioneers in introducing digital terrestrial TV. Presently, however, almost all European countries either have introduced digital terrestrial TV or have introduction strategies.

IPTV and IP-VoD

IPTV and IP-VoD started by offering different services using streaming TV over the Internet. In the last five to six years, we have witnessed the emergence of a huge amount of 'on demand' video services on the Internet, specific 'Internet TV' channels, and 'time-shifted' versions of parts of programming from traditional broadcasters. This development has been intensified in recent years, where the quality of streaming video signals is getting better and approaching the quality levels known from traditional TV services. Furthermore, broadband operators deliver IPTV services in their managed IP networks. In such a context, it is possible to deliver even better quality than traditional broadcast TV and many broadband operators have plans for the provision of HDTV based in IPTV technology. Also in the managed IP networks, a great deal of video content, mainly feature movies, is available in the VoD provisions. The IP-VoD is mainly based on client server architectures, but in the future development of P2P can be used as a more efficient content organisation architecture.

Three observations are important in relation to this development: 1. IP platforms, especially broadband platforms, are becoming a competing infrastructure for delivering television services. Until now, terrestrial, satellite and cable network have been the main delivery platforms and the main development has been towards digitalisation. 2. IP platforms, due to their inherent interactive component, are changing 'broadcast' in a fundamental way from a 'broadcast' service to an 'on demand' service. 3. The content providers can bypass service providers and directly offer services to the end consumers.

Regarding the first aspect, a number of broadband providers simply copy the business model from the multi-channel platforms like cable TV and satellite TV and offer services in different packages: a basic package, an optional package, a premium package and so on. They build up a head-end as with cable TV, take feeds from different TV stations, generate a live stream, form different packages and send them to the consumers.

The second aspect, the on demand transformation, is important because the characteristics of IP platforms are used to add value to broadcast services. If we look at the composition of TV programmes, we can see that the majority of programmes are not live and are distributed at certain times by the broadcasting station according to their schedules. In IPTV provision, this type of content can be put on a server so that users can use it when they want. A good case of this development is the Danish TV2 Sputnik, an on demand version of the Danish public service channel TV2, which can be accessed over the Internet.

The third aspect, bypassing the service provider, is not a new thing. In traditional analogue terrestrial broadcasting and free-to-air satellite broadcasting, there is no service provider. The programmes are sent to the transmitters (satellite or terrestrial) by the broadcasters and received by the users. The service or bouquet providers emerged in the era of multi-channel TV platforms like cable and satellite. To establish a business model, the service/bouquet providers form different packages of TV channels and sell them to the end users. On the IP platforms, it is possible to continue using this model, and as seen above this is done by several broadband providers. It is, however, also possible for the broadcaster to bypass this service provider function and sell the services directly to the users. This is, for example, done by the Danish TV2 Sputnik. It is interesting to follow this development and to see if this will become a successful model for the organisation of service provision. Definitely, this creates an incentive mismatch/conflict between broadband providers and content providers. A broadband operator does not get any revenue out of the huge traffic generated when the end users directly connect to a service like TV2 Sputnik. Another important question is if it is optimal for the broadcasters to maintain consumer subscription, etc.

Mobile TV, the case of DVB-H

Mobility has been propagated as one of the strengths of some of the digital terrestrial broadcast standards, including the digital video broadcast – terrestrial (DVB-T) standard. This has, not least, been an important argument which promoters of terrestrial digital television networks always have put forward to legitimise the use of this standard even in countries where other multi-channel infrastructures (cable and satellite) have been reasonably well developed – the argument being that terrestrial DVB, in contrast to satellite and cable, makes mobility and nomadic use (indoors as well as outdoors) possible. This is a valid argument as long as it concerns nomadic and mobile use of television as we know it, which is typically used in camping vans, cars, buses and trains. However, when we discuss mobile use of personal (hand-held) terminals, there are restrictions in DVB-T's possibilities for supporting mobility. One of the major problems is power consumption, which can be handled when watching TV on a train or a bus, but which will be a practical problem when using a mobile phone or PDA to watch TV. This problem has been taken care of in new mobile broadcast standards. The DVB group has standardised a new standard DVB-H, which is based on DVB-T but reduces the power consumption and other limitations of DVB-T when it concerns mobile use.

An important aspect of DVB-H, which is relevant for this chapter, is that it is based on IP data cast (IPDC). This is mainly done to get synergy from the developments in the IP world. The synergy is gained on the service and content side as well as at the hardware/terminal side. Even though one of the reasons for using IPDC is the potential it creates for accessing Internet content and services, the DVB-H IPDC network is a managed IP platform. The use of the IP platform in offering DVB-H services is a good example of IP's impact on broadcast TV as IP technology as well as access path to content on the general Internet.

DRM and conditional access

Digital rights management systems cover a number of technologies, which are used to protect the copyright on digital content. The open mobile alliance (OMA), for example, defines the scope of their implementation of DRM: 'to enable the controlled consumption of digital media objects by allowing content providers to express usage rights, e.g., the ability to preview DRM content, to prevent downloaded DRM content from being illegally forwarded (copied) to other users, and to enable new business models with super distribution of DRM content' (OMA).

In the broadcast world the protection of content rights has been implemented using CA systems, with the aim of controlling the provision and consumption of TV/radio channels. The CA systems were first implemented in the analogue satellite and cable networks. The aim was to establish a business model for the provision of direct to home (DTH) satellite services and to be able to offer premium pay the TV the cable networks by simply excluding the non-payers. CA systems are further developed in digital broadcasting and are also deployed in digital terrestrial broadcast provisions.

The scope of CA systems is, however, more than excluding the non-payers. The CA systems consist mainly of two functions:

- Encryption/decryption of signals. The signals are encrypted in a way that only authorised users are able to decrypt and use. The information necessary for decryption of the signal is transmitted alongside with the signal.
- The CA management: The management function has the task of network management and subscriber management. The CA management system consists of two parts: subscriber management system (SMS) and subscriber authorisation system (SAS). The SMS is the administrative system dealing with the consumer bases and storing data on the consumers, the services they subscribe to, and facilitating financial transactions. The SAS is a technical system that implements processing of the data from SMS

into commands that can be used by the receiver equipments. These commands are transmitted alongside the data to the decoders and facilitate the decryption of the signals the users are authorised to use.

Audio

Developments in the audio technologies are driven by the developments within radio and music industries as well as the developments within the telephony industry. In this sub-section, the focus is primarily on the media industry and hence the technologies relevant to the radio and music industry. Two main sets of technologies are discussed: 1. Digital radio, which is the main innovation in radio history since FM; and 2. Internet audio, which establishes new applications and platforms for radio and music delivery.

Digital radio

Digital radio is the main innovation within the radio industry since the introduction of frequency modulation (FM). Digital radio is not one single global standard and in different continents different technologies are dominant. However, the heart of many of these standards, i.e., that coding is based on the moving picture experts group (MPEG) solutions, which creates a mass market for vital components in the digital radio industry.

Digital audio broadcast (DAB) is the European standard for digital radio. Digital audio broadcast needs new frequency allocations and operates in the very high frequency (VHF) band as well as in the L-band. In many European countries DAB is introduced either as regular radio provision or extended trial projects. The pioneer market for DAB has been the UK and later on Denmark, where several new DAB channels are available. Digital multimedia broadcast (DMB), which is a mobile TV standard promoted by South Korea, is also based on DAB technology.

In band on channel (IBOC) is the standard used in the US. It was introduced in 2002 and the technology gives the FM and AM stations the possibility to send one or two digital radio channels within the same frequency bands as their analogue radio channels. Hence, IBOC does not require new frequency allocations, which is one of the main advantages of the technology.

Digital radio mondiale (DRM) is a digital radio system for short-wave, AM (Amplitude Modulation)/medium-wave and long-wave. Digital radio mondiale is standardised by the International Telecommunication Union (ITU), International Electrotechnical Commission (IEC) and European Telecommunications Standards Institute (ETSI). Initially, DRM was designed to cover the broadcasting bands below 30 MHz. Recently, major efforts have been put on extending the system to the broadcasting bands up to 120 MHz.

Internet Audio

The development of Internet audio is directly connected to development of Streaming technologies and P2P technologies. Streaming technologies are the basis for the huge development of Internet radio we are witnessing.

A recent phenomenon of combining MP3 players with Internet-based content provision is becoming relatively important for the future of music industry. An example is the introduction of iTunes, which in combination with iPods, impacts dramatically the music industry. iPods have primarily been used for listening to music, but recently it has evolved to include Podcasting services and audio books. Furthermore, video services are also becoming an integrated part of the iPod world. iTunes offers an Internet-based system for the delivery of audio content to the consumers. Podcasting services are delivered mainly by radio stations around the globe.

Text

As for all other information and communication-based activities, email and the Web have had a huge impact on text media with respect to information and news gathering. In the present sub-section, however, there is emphasis on the use of the Internet for the presentation of the products using text-based media. The Web application in particular has tremendous potential in terms of new presentation platforms, hyper-linking, faster updating, user-access to archive material and interactivity with users. Furthermore, eXtensible markup language (XML)-based technologies are increasingly central in building up search facilities, which are becoming more and more important on the Internet.

For text media, it is the Web platform in itself with its hyper-linking facilities which is the primary new asset that the Internet offers. The Web constitutes a whole new possibility for offering text-based material to the users. However, the way these new possibilities fit into the business models of text media is not a discussion which is covered in this chapter (but is discussed in Chapters 4 and 7). But there is no doubt that the Web is one of the major new challenges that text media is facing and will continue to face in the coming years.

In comparison with the two other major traditional media forms, audio and video, text-based media place smaller demands on the Internet and related technologies. The hyper-linked Web was originally designed for text purposes, and the transmission of text requires much less capacity than the transmission of audio, let alone video. However, the audio and video transmission possibilities offered by the Internet are also increasingly used by media with a text-based point of departure when different media converge.

In addition to the presentation of the existing media products on the new platforms – which does not only include PC-based Internet access but also Internet access via, for example, mobile terminals – the Internet provides the possibility for continuous updating, for the presentation of additional background material including linking to sources, for giving users access to archival material and for improving the interactivity with and among readers which hitherto relied on letters from the readers. Text-based media, present on the Internet, often encourage readers to react electronically via emails or by uploading their reactions on the website of the newspaper, magazine, etc.

This creates a blogging possibility for the media which can add to the value of the products offered. Often, however, the most important effect is the strengthening of the community of users around the media. It thus constitutes a possibility for trying to tie-in users closer to the media product. An example of the use of blogging by a newspaper is *USA Today*, which has a blogging part of its website with the following headings: news, travel, life, tech and weather.

Specifically with respect to newspapers, blogging has been discussed as an alternative to the existing news media – as has the Web as such with its possibility of finding information and news without reading a newspaper or watching or listening to TV or radio news. Indeed, there is no discussion that the new electronic possibilities for accessing news not only complements the traditional print media but constitutes a huge challenge. The Internet has lowered the entry barriers into the news market and has created alternative sources of access to news and information.

Conclusions and discussions

The aim of the chapter is to emphasise the important implications that the Internet and the IP already have and will, even more so, have in the coming years. As examples, the paper touches upon the implications of peer-to-peer technology for the music industry and the increasing importance it also has in the video area on the film industry. The implications of the Internet are felt in almost all areas of the media in the production phases (for instance, information gathering by journalists) as well as the distribution phases (for instance, online radio). But it is not only the Internet as such but also the IP, which deeply affects the media area. Significant implications may actually not be related to the Internet as a network but to the use of IP as a common technology platform for the development of media industries. This applies, for instance, to the upcoming mobile broadcast area. Such developments are, of course, closely related to the development of the Internet as a world-wide network, as the basic protocol used is the IP. However, they are not strictly

Internet developments and do not necessarily use the Internet as transmission network.

This is important to remember in order not to limit the implications of Internet and IP to the Internet as such. IP will increasingly function as a common technology platform for convergence developments among the different media branches. Digital technology is the basic technological precursor for the convergence developments between broadcasting and other media industries and the IT, and telecom areas. However, IP is the most likely candidate for the actual materialisation of such convergence possibilities.

In this context, it is furthermore important to consider that the Internet is not a fixed and finite thing. Basically, the Internet is defined as a network of networks using TCP/IP. TPC/IP is thus the basic defining criterion of the Internet. But the Internet is much more than this. A host of different technologies are part of what we understand to be the Internet. This is also part of the explanation why a historical approach is helpful in understanding the implications of the Internet and IP. The first 'generations' of the Internet did not have any implications for the media. It was only when the Web was developed that the Internet began to impact on the media. Many other technology solutions such as compression and streaming technologies are equally important for the Internet to have impacts on the media.

In connection with this historical approach, the discussion could be raised whether the media industries have underestimated the importance of the Internet and IP for the development of their business areas. This certainly seems to be the case. The question can be divided into two aspects. One aspect, the fundamental one, deals with the question whether the media industries have not sufficiently realised the implications for their business areas of the convergence tendencies technologically enabled by digital technology and more specifically packet switching technology. The other aspect concerns the more specific development of the Internet and IP as the dominant technology trajectory of digital and packet switching technology. With respect to both aspects, the answer is yes, however, with the modification that industries often quite reasonable will seek to exploit their existing technological bases as much as possible before venturing into new technology solutions and the more specific modification that the Internet and IP were not the only technological options available until a few years ago. At present, the Internet and IP certainly is the dominant avenue, but this was not the case a few years ago.

The final issue to approach here is whether the media, conversely, have affected the development of the Internet and IP. The paper describes the influence of the Internet and IP on the media, but does the influence also go the other way round? The answer is affirmative, and it applies with respect to the Internet as such as well as the use of IP in non-Internet contexts. The potentials in using the Internet as a network platform for media industries contributes to the development of the Internet and Internet-related technologies, and the same applies to the use of IP as a common technological platform for convergence developments in the media.

The important thing in the context of the present chapter is to step down from the highest levels of abstraction dealing with the Internet as such and to look at the many diverse technological elements that go into what the Internet is today and what it will develop into in the coming years. Among these technological elements should be mentioned, first and foremost, streaming media, multicast, peer-to-peer, broadband and mobility. And, there are many others. With respect to the Internet itself – understood as a network of networks based on the TCP/IP protocol suite – the diffusion of IPv6 instead of the presently dominating IPv4 protocol will also have great implications. Among other things and in addition to an immensely expanded addressing scheme, IPv6 includes improved security, QoS and enhanced mobility.

References

Christensen, C. (1997). *The Innovator's Dilemma*. Boston: Harvard Business School Press.

Foster, R. (1986). *Innovation: the Attacker's Advantage*. Orangeville, Canada: Summit Books.

Freeman, C. (1994). Innovation. In *The New Palgrave: A Dictionary of Economics*. 2: 858–860. London: Macmillan Press.

Leiner, B., Vinton, C., Clark, D., Kahn, R., Kleinrock, L., Lynch, D., Postel, J., Roberts, L., & Wolff, S. (no year of publication). *A Brief History of the Internet* http://www.isoc.org/internet/history/brief.shtml.

Mowery, D. & Simcoe, T. (2002). 'Is the Internet a U.S. Invention? – An Economic and Technological History of Computer Networking'. *Research Policy, 31*, 1369–1387.

Saltzer J.H., Reed D.P. & Clark D.D. (1984). *End-to-end arguments in system design*. Boston: M.I.T. Press.

TRAI. (2005). 'Issues relating to transition from IPv4 to IPv6 in India'. TRAI Consultation Paper No. 8.

4

THE IMPACT OF THE INTERNET ON MEDIA CONTENT

Richard van der Wurff

Introduction

In this chapter, we first consider the economic reasons why the Internet increases the availability of existing content rather than adding new content and new content formats. We then discuss the role of the Internet as platform for social communications and user generated content. Next, we look more specifically at content that is offered on the Internet. We try to estimate how much content is available, discuss the different types of content offered and highlight the role of search engines to make all this content accessible. Special attention is paid to the availability of news on the Net. The chapter ends with conclusions and a brief outlook into the future.

More content rather than new content

The emergence of the Internet has contributed to a tremendous increase in the accessibility of content. As students and scholars, we now have easy Internet access to scientific journals, governmental statistics and a whole range of other sources – whereas 15 years ago accessing those sources might have required extensive travelling and consultation of information specialists. In a similar way, interested citizens from all over the world can read thousands of daily and non-daily newspapers (see www.onlinenewspapers.com); music enthusiasts in Belgium and Senegal alike can tune in to more than 2,500 online radio stations (see www.radio-locator.com); and family and friends can read our travel diaries and admire our holiday pictures at websites such as www.whereareyou.net.

The emergence of the Internet has also changed the way in which we access content. Whereas traditional media offer bundled content packages (magazines, CDs, evening television programme schedules), the Internet primarily offers unbundled content items (articles, songs, video files). Hyperlinks enable us to combine these elements as we see fit into our own individual content experiences. From these hyperlinks the activity of Web surfing originated – now the normal way to navigate the Web, but not so long ago a new and exiting activity, enjoyed by novices and experienced users that shared interesting uniform resource locators (URLs).

Hardly any new content or new formats

In contrast to these implications for the accessibility of content, the Internet so far has had remarkably little impact on the types and formats of content that is presented to audiences (for that reason, the subtitle for this book could have been 'old wine in smaller and more accessible bottles'). By far the largest share of Internet content – most text, audio and video files that we can access – is content that could, actually is, or previously was presented in similar ways in old media. Online newspapers, for example, may provide individual articles rather than news pages, but these articles tend to be identical to the ones published in the print paper. New content, specifically made for the Internet – such as real-time stories that are updated during the day – is scarce, and new content formats – such as interactive reporting – are even scarcer. The same holds for non-media websites, such as corporate websites that offer product information, vacancies, financial statements, annual reports and press releases (Esrock & Leichty, 1999). The ease with which we can access this content is a remarkable and new phenomenon – the implications of which should not be underestimated. Yet, the content and in particular the content format are not 'new' or innovative.

There are, of course, exceptions. Many websites offer some new content or make some use of Internet-specific features like chat rooms and discussion forums. Moreover, several new and innovative types of content and online communication have been introduced. Examples include personalised Web pages, weblogs, interactive advertising, online forums and social networking sites – new formats where the hyperlinking and interactive opportunities of the Internet are deliberately put to use. New content and new formats can in particular be found in areas where users are willing to pay for content (for example, retail financial services), or in areas where enthusiastic 'amateur' content producers set the trend. These examples give us a rough idea of what the ultimate impact of the Internet on content might be. Yet, for the time being and for the average user, these examples are easily lost in the flood of traditional content that dominates the Web.

The impact of the Internet on content costs and availability

To understand why the Internet has developed as distribution channel for traditional content – content that is or in principle could be distributed via other media – rather than as a medium with its own new dedicated content and content formats, we must look at the cost structure and resulting economics of the Internet (Van der Wurff, 2005a). By and large, Internet technology reduces the costs of content reproduction and distribution, but not the costs of content production. This basically means that organisations and individuals can easily use the Internet to distribute existing content at trivial or no additional costs to large or small audiences – including audiences that could not be served cost-effectively before. The production of new content itself, however, is not made significantly easier by the Internet. Costs of original content production (a newspaper article, a television programme, a sound recording or a scientific paper) remain high, regardless of whether content is made for the Web or other media. If there has been any impact of the Internet on content production, it is that it has become more difficult to recover production costs by selling content to audiences.

More efficient distribution

Accordingly, we see that media organisations use the Internet as a cost-effective, additional promotion and distribution channel, to serve existing and some new audiences. Likewise, non-media organisations increasingly use the Internet to communicate directly with (prospective) customers. Examples of this development have already been mentioned above. They include local newspapers, radio stations and TV programming that now can be accessed by expatriates around the globe; stock market quotations and other types of professional content that nowadays are available to the professional and residential consumer alike; and product and governmental information that is distributed on the Web.

Besides distributing already published content, media and non-media organisations as well as individuals use the Internet to distribute content that was not made public before – primarily because audiences were too small or dispersed and distribution costs consequently were too high. Examples include pop groups, scholars and authors who were not able to publish a CD, book or article with an established record company or publisher, but nowadays can distribute their content via the Web. Other examples include the websites of small and dispersed communities such as emigrants or refugees which allow them to present their causes to the general audience and provide information to group members (Bakker, 2001; Siapera, 2004). In all those cases, the diminishing effect of Internet technology on reproduction and distribution costs results in increased publication (rather than production) of content.

Obviously, once organisations start to distribute content via the Internet, users' experience and expectations increase, and competition for audiences stimulates or forces organisations to improve their content offerings and add additional features and content. The distinction between content originally produced for old media and new content produced for the Internet moreover loses its significance in areas where the Internet has become an established distribution channel (for example, in scientific publishing where it makes little sense to distinguish between print and online content, or even print and online revenues). Nevertheless, the Internet results primarily in wider distribution of existing content and in additional publication of content that previously would not be made public.

Limited new production

The production of new content – i.e., content specifically developed and designed for the Internet – remains limited. One important reason is that would-be providers foresee hard times to recover the relatively high costs of producing new content on the Internet alone. This is mainly due to the fact that many non-media organisations and individuals use the Internet to distribute their content for free to their audiences. The main objective of these organisations and individuals, in terms of their Internet activities, is to inform (potential) customers, to advocate their causes, to persuade anyone interested or just to draw the audience's attention – but not to make money by selling content or advertisements. The presence of such non-media organisations on the Web creates substantial challenges for media organisations that want to recoup the costs of content production and, if possible, make a profit in the process, too. Consequently, new and Internet-specific types of content are primarily found in three areas: content niches where audiences are willing to make substantial payments (such as retail financial and investment services, professional and scholarly information or porn); areas where 'amateur' content providers are very active and do not put a price on all costs (for example, weblogs and social networking sites); and on websites of organisations where the profit motive is not dominant or even absent (for example, websites of European public broadcasters).

User-generated content

One area of Internet use that so far has only be hinted at, but that is growing rapidly in popularity, is the use of the Internet as platform for social communication. Recently, social networking sites such as *MySpace* have attracted a lot of attention, both online and in the popular press. Social networking sites integrate personal networks of members in an online environment, allowing registered users to contact 'friends of friends'. They offer not only features such as address books and profiles, but also enable members to post and share different kinds of content, including photos, music, diaries, messages and videos. Starting musicians and bands have jumped upon this new opportunity to publicise and promote their music (Hansell, 2006).

The number and size of social networking sites is growing rapidly. In October 2006, there were 89 'notable' social networking sites ('List,' 2006). The smallest open network, ActiveRain for real estate professionals, counted approximately 5,500 members in September 2006; whereas the largest network, MySpace, at that time could boast 113 million users. National networking sites count between 39,000 in Estonia, 2.3 million in the Netherlands and 5 million in Japan ('List,' 2006). Social networking sites are especially popular among young users. With such audiences, the largest networking sites are considered attractive advertising vehicles and major Internet and media companies have bought or developed their own networking sites. So far, however, only MySpace, owned by Rupert Murdoch, seems to be an advertising success (Wood, 2005).

Virtual communities

Smaller and dedicated social network sites, like *ActiveRain*, may also be considered examples of online or virtual communities. Online communities enable their members to interact and communicate with like-minded members. The emphasis in virtual communities is more on information sharing than on networking. The traditional example of virtual communities is USENET, set up in 1979 to enable users to exchange information on the UNIX operating system. Starting with three newsgroups and two posts per day, new topics and members were added rapidly, and in 1994 USENET counted 73,000 postings per day to almost 11,000 moderated and unmoderated groups. These groups are subdivided in nine major 'hierarchies' – Computer discussions, Usenet news, Recreation and Entertainment, Science, Social discussions, Controversial topics, Humanities, Miscellaneous topics and Alt.* for topics that are too controversial for the other eight hierarchies – which give a rough idea of the breadth of topics covered ('Usenet', 2006).

Other examples and usages of virtual communities include bulletin-boards, multi-user dungeons, electronic mailing lists, chat rooms, massively multiplayer online games (MMOGs), education-based communities (Haythornthwaite, 2000; Rosen, et al., 2003), religious networks (Campbell, 2004) and health-related communities (Josefsson, 2005; Rodgers &

Chen, 2005). A final example is the Wikipedia online encyclopaedia. Formally established in January 2001 as a free online encyclopaedia that is written and edited by more than 2 million 'Wikipedians', the Wikipedia has been doubling in size (as counted in numbers of articles) every year since October 2002 ('Wikipedia:Modelling', 2006; 'Wikipedia:Wikipedians', 2006).

The success of Wikipedia underlines that the contribution of interested Internet users to online content should not be neglected. The willingness of Internet users to supply content in their own areas of expertise and interest has not escaped the attention of media managers, who increasingly predict that user-generated content will be a major (and free) building block of their online content offerings (Fagerjord, Maasø, Storsul & Syvertsen, 2006). It should, however, be kept in mind that most content contributions are made by a small minority of users (Gapper, 2006; 'Wikipedia:List,' 2006).

How much content?

This chapter discusses the impact of the Internet on content. The primary impact that floats up from the discussion so far is the tremendous increase in the amount of content that is made available via the Internet. The amount of online information is so enormous, and its growth so rapid, that it is virtually impossible to estimate how much information is actually available. Besides, most available data on the size of the Internet have been collected for other purposes than a scholarly assessment of the information content of the Web. To my knowledge, only two research projects have attempted to measure and assess the Internet on the basis of a sample of websites. One is the five-year 'Web Characterization Project' by the office of research of the US-based Online Computer Library Center (OCLC), which analysed an annual sample of between 2,800 and 9,000 sites (Web characterization, 2003). The other is the 'How Much Information?' project by Lyman and Varian at the School of Information Management and Systems at the University of California at Berkeley, which analysed 9,800 sites (Lyman and Varian, 2003).

The size of the World Wide Web

One indication for the size of the Internet can be derived from the number of hosts, that is, the number of computers or computer systems that are connected to the Internet and have a registered IP address. The number of hosts can be counted relatively reliable. It increased from four in December 1969 (when the Internet was created) to 313,000 at the end of 1990 (just before the Web was invented and the first Web server was created), to 353 million in July 2005 (Zakon, 2005). Hosts include both servers – computers that offer services – and clients – computers used to access those services. To get an idea of how much content is available on the Internet, the number of Web servers is relevant. Web servers are computers that offer one or more websites. Their number increased from the original first one in 1990 to 68 million in July 2005 (Zakon, 2005).

A third estimate is provided by the number of registered domain names – addresses that we can visit on the Web. This number increased from 18,000 at the end of 1991 to approximately 18 million in July 2000, and further growing to more than 63 million in 2005 (*Internet growth data*, n.d.; *Quick stats*, 2005; Zakon, 2005). The number of domain names, however, is less informative than we may think at first sight. Many domain names are only registered, but not active; and different domain names may refer to the same website (Tehan, 2003). The most informative, but unfortunately also the least reliable numbers are counts of websites and Web pages. Estimates of websites start at 130 in June 1993 (when the Web was not even two-years-old) (Zakon, 2005), reach about 4.4 million active websites in 2000 (*Web characterization*, 2003) and approximately 35 million active websites in 2005 (Livraghi, 2005). The total number of Web pages at that time (2005) was estimated at around 8 billion pages (*Quick stats*, 2005), growing from 80 million pages in early 1997 and 2 billion pages in 2000. The average lifespan of these Web pages (in 2000) was 44 days (*Internet growth data*, n.d.). Among these Web pages, we could find, in 2003, more than 3 million registered and at least 1.6 million active weblogs (Greenspan, 2003). The growth of the Web is shown in Table 4.1.

Surprisingly, HTML pages make up only 18 per cent of the total size of websites. The largest share is taken up by images (23 per cent of the total file size). Other major file types are dynamic PHP files (13 per cent) and PDF files (9 per cent). Audio and movie files take up relatively little space (2.6 per cent and 4.3 per cent respectively) (Lyman & Varian, 2003).

Table 4.1 Selected Web size indicators

	hosts [a]	domain names	Web servers [a]	active websites	Web pages
1969	4				
1989	130 thousand	4 thousand [a]	- -	- -	- -
1993	1,776 thousand	26 thousand [a]	130	130 [a]	
2000	93 million	18 million [b]	18 million	4.4 million[c]	2 billion [b]
2005	353 million	63 million [d]	68 million	35 million[e]	8 billion [d]

Sources:
a. Zakon, 2005
b. *Internet growth data*, n.d.
c. *Web characterization*, 2003
d. *Quick stats*, 2005
e. Livraghi, 2005

Dynamic, closed and non-www sites

One problem encountered in measuring websites and Web pages is that more and more Web pages are created dynamically by users when they access online databases. In 2000, BrightPlanet estimated that 400 to 550 times more information was available via these dynamic Web pages than was offered on static Web pages (depending on whether you count the Web in bytes or documents). They refer to these dynamic pages as the 'deep web' and contrast it with the 'surface web' consisting of static pages (Lyman & Varian, 2003; Tehan, 2003). Another problem, already hinted at above, is that not all websites offer content to the general public. According to data collected by the OCLC, a substantial and increasing proportion of websites is 'private' rather than 'public' – 12 per cent in 1998; 29 per cent in 2002 – meaning that access to content is restricted to a particular audience (for example, a paying audience) rather than provided for free to all. Another third of the websites at any time is 'under construction' or otherwise does not provide meaningful content (*Web characterization*, 2003). A third issue to take into account is that WWW-sites represent only part of the content available on the Internet. Another important source of content is peer-to-peer file sharing. The 3 million active users on Kazaa, for example – which was one of the most popular peer-to-peer networks in the early 2000s – shared 600 million files or 5,000 terabytes of data. As can be guessed from discussions on music file sharing, audio files constitute the most frequently shared type of files (62 per cent of all shared files). Video files (for example, movies) are less frequently shared (8 per cent of all shared files). However, since video files tend to be large, video files account for 59 per cent of all bytes shared on peer-to-peer networks, and audio files for another 33 per cent (Lyman & Varian, 2003). Usenet groups added one MB worth of postings per day in 1985, increasing to a data feed of one GB in 1995 and two TBs at the end of 2005 ('Usenet', 2006; Zakon, 2005). The growth in recent years reflects the growing use of Usenet as distribution channel for pornography and music files ('Usenet', 2006).

Internet content in bytes and books

The amount of information available on the Internet has been compared by O'Neil and colleagues (2003) to the amount of information available in libraries. Although these estimates must be taken with several grains of salt, they are nevertheless illuminative. According to Lyman and Varian (2003), an average Web page sizes 18.7 KB, while an average 300-page book would take up 1 MB of space. The 8 billion Web pages that make up the Web in 2005, therefore, present 150 terabytes of data, which is equivalent to 150 million books; 10 times as many books as are available in the library of

Harvard University (O'Neill et al., 2003). The 'deep web', estimated at more than 90,000 terabytes would add another 90 billion books. In comparison, weblogs are relatively small: Lyman and Varian (2003) estimate that in 2003 all weblogs together amounted to 81 GB of data, or 81,000 books.

Obviously, not all of these terabytes represent observable and meaningful information. An unknown percentage of data includes formatting instructions and metadata, and an unknown number of Web pages provides duplicate or 'useless' information – or, at any rate, information that is no match for the content provided in published books (O'Neill et al., 2003). Nevertheless, if only 0.1 per cent of all data on the Internet is equivalent to the content of published books, the Internet would still present six times more information as Harvard University Library.

What types of content?

Given the size of the Web, and the problems involved in measuring it, only a rough indication can be given of the types of content that are available on the Internet. One distinction that can be made, is in terms of the language and country origin of Internet content; another is in terms of content topic.

Country and language

A large majority of websites (72 per cent) is in the English language, and about half of all websites is made by US organisations or citizens. The second and third largest countries on the Web are Germany and Japan. Approximately 6 per cent of all websites are in German and another 6 per cent are in Japanese; likewise, content providers in Germany and Japan make 6 per cent and 5 per cent, respectively, of all websites. Other important languages, accounting for 1 per cent to 4 per cent of all Web pages, are Chinese, French, Spanish, Italian, Dutch, Korean, Portuguese and Russian (*Nombre total*, 2000; *Web characterization*, 2003). Taking the number of native speakers into account, there are not only relatively many Web pages in English, but also in Scandinavian languages (including Islandic) (*Nombre total*, 2000). Librarians suggest that the language distribution of Internet content is not so different from what is found in the worlds' libraries (O'Neill et al., 2003).

The Yahoo! Directory offers some insight in the breadth of topics covered on the Internet. This directory presents an overview of websites that are considered worthwhile by the directory's editors, subdivided by topic. Commercial sites are indicated separately, and specialised sites are placed in more specific categories, so the directory gives a rough idea whether a site offers commercial or non-commercial, and general or specific information. The largest major category consists of regional sites (59 per cent; as of

10 January 2006). These regional sites are subdivided into area and category. An example of how specific this classification system gets, is provided in Table 4.2. Excluding regional sites, the second largest category is Business & Economy (17 per cent of all entries; 41 per cent of all entries except those classified as regional). Other categories are relatively small.

Internet resource surveys

Internet resource surveys sketch a more detailed picture of the types of content that are available on the Internet. These surveys are produced by librarians and information specialists. These specialists select and describe websites that they consider useful for other professionals or consumers, in journals such as *College and Research Libraries News* (also available on <www.ala.org>), *Health Care on the Internet, Internet Reference Services Quarterly* and *Journal of Library Administration*.

What kind of topics are covered by surveys in these journals and consequently on the Web? For residential consumers, available resources present information, *inter alia*, on diseases (endometriosis, HIV/AIDS), politics (the Kosovo crisis, liberalism, bioterrorism), health and lifestyle (alcohol abuse, genetically modified food, vegetarianism, alternative medicine, dying well), entertainment (music, film and television) and practical issues (home schooling, taxation). For students and professionals, we can find additional resources providing content that is relevant for many (specialist) studies and sciences (chemistry, English, but also piano pedagogy), health issues (including statistics, biomedicine and diseases) and business (general business information, but also Internet sources for interactive marketing, online advertising and agriculture).

A case study: Endometriosis

To get a better understanding of the types and quality of content that can be found on the Web, we look more closely at an Internet resource survey produced by a nurse researcher and resource librarian. In May 2004, Deevey (2005) found that Google produced 794,000 hits when she searched for information on endometriosis; a female health condition where uterus lining tissue is found elsewhere in the body. When we repeated this search in January 2006, the number of hits tripled to 2.55 million. But what do these websites and documents contribute to someone looking for information on this unfamiliar disease? Deevey studied the top five websites or documents retrieved by the top ten search engines in May 2004. She found that 62 per cent (31 of 50 hits) lead to commercial sites that concern women's health and health products but provide little information on endometriosis. Another five bring the interested reader to an infertility medical practice.

Table 4.2 Websites and documents accessible via Yahoo! Directory (on 10/01/06)

Main category	Count	%	Example path
Arts & Humanities	152,643	3.7%	Arts > Humanities > History > U.S. History > By Time Period > 20th Century > People > Presidents
Business & Economy	695,231	16.8%	Business and Economy > Shopping and Services > Travel and Transportation > Lodging > Bed and Breakfasts > Directories
Computers & Internet	20,592	0.5%	Computers and Internet > Internet > World Wide Web > Weblogs > Entertainment > Comics
Education	80,405	1.9%	Education > K-12 > Schools > High Schools
Entertainment	164,960	4.0%	Entertainment > Music > Artists > By Genre > Rock and Pop > Punk and Hardcore > Oi!
Government	30,127	0.7%	Government > U.S. Government > Politics > Elections > Past Elections > 2000 Elections
Health	27,264	0.7%	Health > Diseases and Conditions > Cancers > Organisations > Children > Camps
News & Media	56,294	1.4%	News and Media > Radio > Amateur and Ham Radio > Personal Pages
Recreation & Sports	264,421	6.4%	Recreation > Travel > Destination Guides > Convention and Visitors Bureaus > Organisations
Reference	9,900	0.2%	Reference > Libraries > Public Libraries
Regional	2,452,894	59.3%	Regional > U.S. States > California > Metropolitan Areas > San Francisco Bay Area > Counties and Regions > Silicon Valley > Business and Shopping > Business to Business > Computers > Software > Consulting > Custom Programming
Science	50,447	1.2%	Science > Biology > Zoology > Animals, Insects and Pets > Mammals > Dogs > Breeds > Basset Hound > Organisations > Rescue Organisations
Social Science	12,569	0.3%	Social Science > Linguistics and Human Languages > Languages > Specific Languages > English > English as a Second Language > College and University Departments and Programs
Society & Culture	118,252	2.9%	Society and Culture > Religion and Spirituality > Faiths and Practices > Christianity > Denominations and Sects > Catholic > People > Popes > Pope John Paul II (1920–2005) > 1981 Assassination Attempt
Total	4,135,999	100.0%	

Note: The 'example path' gives some indication of the levels of subcategories available. The example path is found by selecting, at every level, the largest topical subcategory. Regional subdivisions are excluded, except in the example path for regional websites.

Only five hits would bring users to more substantial information. Three point to the advocacy organisation International Endometriosis Association, and two would bring users to US government sites with relevant health information.

Of course, there are more relevant sites. Deevey mentions the website of the National Library (that gives access to scholarly and consumer information), websites of individual or groups of physicians and personal websites (of those suffering from the disease), in addition to the websites of the US government and advocacy organisations already mentioned. But these are not easily found via search engines. Deevey (2005:70), therefore, concludes: 'in general, search engines retrieve a large number of hits for the term endometriosis, but do not consistently lead the researcher to quality information and are not recommended as a starting point for medical librarians.' An exception is the Yahoo! directory that does point the user to useful resources.

Abundance of information from many non-media sources

Other surveys of Internet sources paint a similar picture. Like in the endometriosis example, they show that there are many sources available to the general public; including sources that previously were only available to paying professionals. According to a former research librarian at the Federal Reserve Bank, Chicago:

Banking data and research, once available only through specialized government publications or by request from many sources, are now increasingly available through the Internet. Students, scholars, banking professionals, and public patrons can now more easily find many different levels of financial information, especially within the United States' (Humphrey, 1999: 1).

The Internet resource surveys also show that many relevant sources are offered by non-media organisations, in particular governmental organisations, NGOs, student organisations, universities, research organisations, consul-tancies, commercial companies and personally interested amateurs. For information on alcohol abuse, we can visit advocacy organisations (mothers against drunk driving), governmental organisations (US bureau of alcohol, tobacco and firearms), AA websites, educational and research institutes (higher education center for alcohol and other drug prevention; alcoholic beverage medical research foundation), as well as some databases that index online and print sources (Schmitz, 1997). Likewise, in 2001 a major online directory in the Netherlands listed 2005 websites with agricultural information. These websites were published by farmers, their suppliers, advisors and customers and by other relevant organisations (such as the farmer associations). Publishers offered not more than 1 per cent of these websites (Van der Wurff, 2005a).

Finding Internet content

The overall impression that emerges from the Internet resource surveys is that there are countless websites that provide information on almost any topic. At the same time, the authors of these surveys argue that it can be very difficult to find valuable content within this plethora of information. Moreover, the credibility of sources and the reliability of the information are difficult to establish, and many websites copy and paste the same information. In 'Touring the scientific web', Ivar Peterson, an editor at *Science News*, found that 'despite the abundance of websites that feature science and medical news, there appears to be no corresponding diversity of news items. Most news organisations derive their headlines and articles from the same small group of primary sources' (Peterson, 2001: 252). Research into news sites in the Netherlands shows a similar picture. They obtain their news from a few sources, including a major newspaper and the national press agency.

This lack of diversity, not so much in the supply but in the actual reception of content, turns out to be a common feature of the Internet. Researchers from Altavista, Compaq and IBM found in 2000 that only 30 per cent of all websites constitute a strongly connected core where users can easily hyperlink from site to site. Incidentally, this core includes many corporate websites. In addition, two times 24 per cent of websites either refers to this core, or can be reached from this core, but none of these websites is reciprocally related to the core. The remaining 22 per cent of websites is not related to the core at all (*Altavista, Compaq*, 2000; *IBM research*, 2000; Tehan, 2003). Taking into account that search engines rank results in terms of the number of pages that refer to a particular page (Sullivan, 2003), these results mean that ordinary users that rely on search engines might never access a large part of the Web. Supporting this argument, Alexa Internet reported in 1998 that 50 per cent of all Web traffic goes to not more than 900 best-visited websites (*1.5 million*, 1998). A similar fate awaits users that start searching the Internet from library home pages. Prabha and Irwin (2005), investigating librarians tend to make those Web resources available that are referred to by many other websites.

Finding controversial content

A consequence of the way in which the Internet is organised, and content is made available, is that controversial information remains frequently hidden from the general public. Gerhart (2004) studied what information one would find if one would use search engines to find information on five different topics – distance learning, Albert Einstein, female astronauts, Belize and St John's Wort (a popular herbal remedy). Assuming that average Internet users would limit their searches to the 50 or 100 first mentioned hits, Gerhart discovered that these users would incidentally learn that the effectiveness of St John's Wort is disputed and that the US space programme discriminated against female astronauts. Yet, they would miss controversial information on the commercialisation of distance learning, the contribution of Einstein's first wife to his discoveries and the border dispute between Guatemala and Belize – unless they specifically knew to look for this information. She concludes: 'Each controversy was well represented on the Web in search results posed with the right query. However, we do not believe many searchers would be exposed to the controversies by search or surfing alone, without off-Web experience [of the dispute]' (Gerhart, 2004).

These glimpses of Internet content suggest that specialists and knowledgeable amateurs can find high-quality information on almost any topic on the Web. This includes new content (for example, technical information on Internet standards) and new types of content (for example, source codes) that could not be distributed efficiently via other means. Yet, for the interested but not very knowledgeable Internet user, much of this information may remain hidden behind a general cloud of company and public relations (PR) information.

Media and the Internet

The organisation and selection of information is a key activity of media organisations, and one that adds considerable value to content. So far, however, research indicates that media organisations are reluctant to take up this organising and selecting role on the Internet. One reason is that media organisations have difficulties finding a business model that enables them to continue making a profit by selling information and advertisements. Another reason is that media organisations find it difficult to leave the conventions and traditions of their old media behind when they start to operate on the Internet. Radio stations in particular find it difficult to translate their aural tradition to the text and image-based Internet – apart from streaming radio programming to end users. Radio websites are relatively limited, with less news and weather information than websites of other media. They primarily promote the station itself. Public TV broadcasters, on the other hand, face fewer obstacles. With an increasing number of broadband Internet connections, TV content can be relatively easily transferred to the Web. Besides, public and advertising-based broadcasters do not run the risk that their online ventures cannibalise their offline revenues (Lin & Jeffres, 2001; Randle & Mordock, 2002; Van der Wurff & Lauf, 2004).

For newspapers, cannibalisation is a more serious issue. Newspaper content can be easily transferred to the Web, and most newspapers nowadays have a website where part of the newspaper can be read for free. The major question that most newspapers nevertheless face is how to earn money with their websites. Several newspapers have experimented with selling content, but only a very few have been successful (Mings & White, 2000). The general trend, therefore, seems to be that newspaper publishers use their websites as tool to attract and maintain good relationships with print subscribers, and sell additional services such as access to archives.

Newspaper content

In 2003, researchers from 16 countries compared the front pages of major national print and online newspapers. Their analysis confirms what has been found in previous studies within individual countries (Van der Wurff & Lauf, 2005). First of all, print and online newspapers turn out to be very similar as far as the news offering is concerned. Basically, online newspapers repurpose print news. On average, 70 per cent of the most important online news stories are identical to news stories published in a print newspaper.

The repurposing of content does not rule out that different types of news are emphasised in print and online. Researchers in Italy found that front pages of print newspapers emphasise more serious news whereas front pages of online newspapers pay more attention to peripheral issues (Fortunati & Sarrica, 2005). In a different way, researchers in the UK found that the classic news agenda as presented by the serious press dominates online, whereas this agenda is downplayed in the print world by the emphasis of tabloids on entertainment, sports and personalities (Sparks & Yilmaz, 2005). Nevertheless, in spite of these differences in emphasis, the general conclusion still must be that print and online news are to a large extent identical.

The significant degree of overlap of print and online news indicates that there is little, if any, new online reporting to be found in the main quality online newspapers in Europe – at least not on the front pages. There are, for example, very few hyperlinks inserted in news items – which would have been an obvious way to improve traditional ways of reporting in an Internet fashion. Also other types of Internet-specific features – multimedia, interactivity, real-time news – are sparsely found in the online newspapers. The exception – in line with the general trend on the Internet – is user-generated content. One-third of the investigated major national quality newspapers offered their readers the opportunity to submit comments, one-sixth offered the opportunity to participate in chat rooms or discussion forums and another third offered both options. In merely one-fifth of the newspapers, no user generated content is solicited or displayed.

Online presentation

Even though online newspapers present primarily the same content as print newspapers, and do so under the same masthead, they organise the content in a different way. Front pages of print newspapers primarily provide news, including full news items, and add some other types of content. Front pages of online newspapers, instead, provide an overview of a larger number of news items that are to be found on other pages, and add a large number of pointers (hyperlinks) to other types of information. This makes print front pages rich in content and simple in structure, whereas online front pages have a more complex structure but are less rich in content (Finnemann & Thomasen, 2005).

The differences in presentation partly reflect technological differences and partly express choices of online editors and publishers. They imply that online front pages offer different functionalities than print front pages. Online front pages offer a starting point for navigation, in which users have more opportunities to define themselves what is important and what not. This contrasts with the print front page where the editors define what is important.

The average European online newspaper

These similarities and differences between print and online newspapers can be found across Europe. Hence, online newspapers in Europe are to some extent homogenous. The 'average' European online newspaper uses half of its front page for news, a quarter for pointers (hyperlinks) to other pages and the remaining part for other services, including interaction, service information, display advertising and self-promotion. The majority of textual pointers (like plain hyperlinks) refer to news; graphic pointers (images) first of all refer to self-promotion. About half of the most important (that is the largest and the most prominently positioned) news items are teasers (short introductions with a 'read more' hyperlink) and a quarter consists of single headlines. Only 5 per cent are full stories, and breaking news is almost absent. One-fifth of the most important news items has no by-line, whereas two-thirds is attributed to a journalist (anonymous or by name). As already indicated above, 70 per cent of these news items is identical to a print newspaper story. In addition, the average online newspaper in Europe provides some tools for user feedback (several e-mail addresses and letters to the editor), some opportunities for content interaction (a search engine and a news archive) and increasingly also a PDF edition, but no multimedia. Arguably, this online newspaper is more suitable for checking headlines than for reading in-depth background information (Van der Wurff, 2005b).

Innovative news practices

In the European study we also looked at other Internet news resources offered by Internet service providers and press agencies. Another study in the Netherlands compared news services from different media (Van der Wurff & Lauf, 2004). Both studies suggest that online newspapers and other online news services are very similar in content and structure. For innovate news, we, therefore, have to look elsewhere.

One obvious place to look for innovative reporting is in blogs. Matheson (2004) discusses the weblog produced by British *The Guardian* as a new experiment in online journalism, where traditional conventions of news reporting are renegotiated. He presents *The Guardian* blog as a product of journalistic research skills, where journalists set readers 'along paths of exploration' (p. 456) by providing references to 'noteworthy reads online' (p. 455). Here, knowledge about events is replaced by the knowledge how to find information and how to judge its quality and relevance. In this way, blogs may make Internet content available in a qualitatively different way than search engines (that refer to the most popular rather than most interesting sources) and online versions of traditional newspaper articles (that refer to other articles in the same newspaper rather than external sources; cf. Dimitrova, Connolly-Ahern, Williams, Kaid & Reid, 2003).

Another place to look for innovative reporting is online traditional news media at times of crisis. Salaverría (2005) studied how online newspapers responded to the airplane attack on the Twin Towers in September 2001. Although he is critical of the quality of online reporting, and in particular of the way mistakes are rectified, he nevertheless shows that online newspapers do play an important if not innovative role, by keeping the audience up-to-date and managing to provide analysis and background in real-time.

Conclusions

This chapter discussed the impact of the Internet on content. Several implications are highlighted. One is that the Internet is used by media and non-media organisations alike to distribute existing content on a much wider scale than ever before. Another is that the Internet makes it feasible to publish content that hitherto could not be made public at affordable costs. Both of these developments lead to the conclusion that the Internet increases the availability and accessibility of traditional content, content that is, or could be, distributed via old media.

One major break with the past is that content is distributed via the Internet in an unbundled way. Instead of acquiring newspapers, magazines and long-play records – combinations of content that are compiled by professionals – Internet users access individual newspaper and magazine articles and songs. This reduces the impact of editors and other professionals on user selection (see Tewksbury & Althaus, 2000). Combined, improved accessibility and unbundling increase user choice, but at the same time make users more dependent on their own information skills. The end result is that the Internet offers almost everything, but only to those who know where to look.

New Internet techniques to facilitate user searches do exist: search engines are among the most profitable Internet businesses and hyperlinks are a defining characteristic of the Internet. Yet, these new navigational techniques need to be developed much further to enable average users to profit substantially from the increase in content accessibility. At present, hyperlinks and search engines tend to bring Internet users to a subset of most frequently visited and linked websites. These encompass a substantial number of commercial websites – that provide product and PR information – and relatively few websites that provide high quality and controversial information. This reduces substantially the impact of the Internet on content for average users.

If new types and formats of Internet-specific content are to be developed in the future, these types and formats will resemble combinations of navigational items and content items. Examples are weblogs, interactive advertising and social networking sites. Further development of new content and in particular new Internet formats, however, has been hampered by the costs of Internet content production and the lack of Internet content revenues. Consequently, new content is primarily produced in specialist areas, by amateurs, and by not-for profit content providers.

These trends were illustrated for the news sector. Overall, online newspapers add little to the news that is already provided in print newspapers, apart from making news from all over the world accessible to users. The major difference between print and online newspapers is the way in which the same news items are presented. Online newspapers allow users to choose more directly and exclusively for the news that they are interested in. Thus, the Internet makes the same news better available, but it depends on the knowledge, experience and desires of each individual user whether and how the plethora of available news items is accessed and used. Weblogs are one example of how new navigational techniques can be integrated with content into new Internet-specific news services that complement traditional news services.

The developments in the news sector underline the general conclusion of this chapter that, so far, the Internet has primarily changed the distribution of content rather than the content itself. The Internet has not yet become a new medium with its own characteristic way of presenting types of content that are typical for the Internet. Whether this will change in the future, depends first of all on whether ways can be found to earn money with content on the Web. If this is the case, new Internet formats will look like weblogs, online newspaper front pages and other hybrid formats that combine content and navigational services.

References

1.5 Million Web Pages Born Daily, according to Alexa Internet (August 31, 1998). Retrieved January 5, 2006, from http://www.clickz.com/showPage.html?page=10381

Altavista, Compaq and IBM Researchers Create World's Largest, Most Accurate Picture of the Web (2000). May 11). Retrieved January 11, 2006, from IBM Research website: http://www.almaden.ibm.com/almaden/webmap_release.html

Bakker, P. (2001, February). *New Nationalism: The Internet Crusade* (revised version). Paper presented at the International Studies Association Annual Convention on 'International relations and the new inequality', Chicago, IL. Retrieved January 8, 2006, from http://users.fmg.uva.nl/pbakker/VN/InternetCrusade.pdf

Campbell, H. (2004). Challenges Created by Online Religious Networks. *Journal of Media and Religion*, 3(2), 81–99.

Deevey, S. (2005). Endometriosis: Internet Resources. *Medical Reference Services Quarterly*, 24(1), 67–76.

Dimitrova, D.V., Connolly-Ahern, C., Williams, A.P., Kaid, L.L., & Reid, A. (2003). Hyperlinking as Gatekeeping: Online Newspaper Coverage of the Execution of an American Terrorist. *Journalism Studies*, 4(3), 401–414.

Esrock, S.L., & Leichty, G.B. (1999). Corporate World Wide Web Pages: Serving the News Media and Other Publics. *Journalism and Mass Communication Quarterly*, 76(3), 456–467.

Fagerjord, A., Maasø, A., Storsul, T., & Syvertsen, T. (2006, April). *Personalised and Participatory Media: Studying Fortune-Telling in the Media Industry*. Paper presented at the COST A20 Conference on The Impact of the Internet on the Mass Media in Europe, Delphi, Greece.

Finnemann, N.O., & Thomasen, B.H. (2005). Denmark: Multiplying news. In R. van der Wurff & E. Lauf (Eds.), *Print and Online Newspapers in Europe: A comparative analysis in 16 countries* (pp. 91–103). Amsterdam: Het Spinhuis.

Fortunati, L., & Sarrica, M. (2005). Italy: Going Online Without Exploiting It. In R. van der Wurff & E. Lauf (Eds.), *Print and Online Newspapers in Europe: A comparative analysis in 16 countries* (pp. 172–185). Amsterdam: Het Spinhuis.

Gapper, J. (2006, September 25). The Digital Democracy's Emerging Elites. *Financial Times*. Retrieved October 4, 2006, from: LexisNexis Academic.

Gerhart, S.L. (2004). Do Web Search Engines Suppress Controversy? *First Monday*, 9(1). Retrieved January 11, 2006, from http://firstmonday.org/issues/issue9_1/gerhart/index.html

Greenspan, R. (2003, July 23). *Blogging by the Numbers*. Retrieved January 5, 2006, from http://www.Internetnews.com/stats/print.php/2238831

Hansell, S. (2006, April 23, 2006). Making Friends Was Easy; Big Profit Is Tougher. *New York Times*. Retrieved October 4, 2006, from: LexisNexis Academic.

Haythornthwaite, C. (2000). Online Personal Networks: Size, Composition and Media Use among Distance Learners. *New Media & Society, 2*(2), 195–226.

Humphrey, R.K. (1999, November). Banking Data and Research: Free Information is now Available to You. *C&RL News, 60* (10). Retrieved January 11, 2006 from http://www.ala.org/ala/acrl/acrlpubs/crlnews/backissues1999/november5/bankingdataresearch.html

IBM Research Maps the Web (2000, May 11). Retrieved January 11, 2006, from IBM Research website: http://domino.research.ibm.com/comm/pr.nsf/pages/news.20000511_bowtie. html

Internet Growth Data (n.d.). Retrieved January 9, 2006, from University of California, Berkeley, School of Information Management & Systems website: http://www.sims.berkeley.edu/research/projects/how-much-info/Internet/rawdata.html

Josefsson, U. (2005). Coping with Illness online: The Case of Patients' Online Communities. *Information Society, 21*(2), 143–153.

Lin, C.A., & Jeffres, L.W. (2001). Comparing Distinctions and Similarities across Websites of Newspapers, Radio Stations, and Television Stations. *Journalism & Mass Communication Quarterly, 78*(3), 555–573.

List of social networking websites (2006, October 4). In *Wikipedia*. Retrieved October 4, 2006, from http://en.wikipedia.org/wiki/List_of_social_networking_websites

Livraghi, G. (2005, July 7). *NetMarketing*(75). Retrieved October 4, 2006, from http://www.gandalf.it/netmark/netmar75.htm

Lyman, P., & Varian, H.R. (2003, October 27). *How Much Information*. Retrieved January 5, 2006, from University of California, Berkeley, School of Information Management & Systems Website: http://www.sims.berkeley.edu/how-much-info-2003

Matheson, D. (2004). Weblogs and the Epistemology of the News: Some Trends in Online Journalism. *New Media & Society, 6*(4), 443–468.

Mings, S.M., & White, P.B. (2000). Profiting from Online News: The Search for Viable Business Models. In B. Kahin & H. R. Varian (Eds.), *Internet publishing and beyond* (pp. 62–96). Cambridge, MA: The MIT Press.

Nombre total de pàgines web, dividides per idiomes (2000). Retrieved January 9, 2006, from Vilawebsite: http://www.vilaweb.com/media/imatges/especials/5anys/enquesta.html

O'Neill, E.T., Lavoie, B.F., & Bennett, R. (2003, April). Trends in the Evolution of the Public Web: 1998–2002. *D-Lib Magazine, 9*(4). Retrieved January 9, 2006 from http://www.dlib.org/dlib/april03/lavoie/04lavoie.html

Peterson, I. (2001). Touring the Scientific Web. *Science Communication, 22*(3), 246–255.

Prabha, C., & Irwin, R.D. (2005). Characteristics, Uniqueness and Overlap of Information Sources Linked from North American Public Library Websites. *First Monday, 10*(8). Retrieved January 8, 2006, from http://firstmonday.org/issues/issue10_8/prabha/index.html

Quick stats (2005). Retrieved January 5, 2006, from http://www.cyveillance.com/web/newsroom/stats.htm

Randle, Q., & Mordock, J. (2002). How Radio Is Adapting Weather to the Web: A Study of Weather Strategies on Local News/Talk Radio, Television, and Newspaper Home Pages. *Journal of Radio Studies, 9*(2), 247–258.

Rodgers, S., & Chen, Q. (2005). Internet Community Group Participation: Psychosocial Benefits for Women with Breast Cancer. *Journal of Computer-Mediated Communication, 10*(4), 00–00. http://www.blackwell-synergy.com/doi/abs/10.1111/j.1083-6101.2005.tb00268.x

Rosen, D., Woelfel, J., & Krikorian, D. (2003). Procedures for Analyzes of Online Communities. *Journal of Computer Mediated Communication, 8*(4), 0–0. Retrieved October 4, 2006, from http://www.blackwell-synergy.com/doi/full/10.1111/ j.1083-6101.2003.tb00219.x

Salaverría, R. (2005). An Immature Medium: Strengths and Weaknesses of Online Newspapers on September 11. *Gazette, 67*(1), 69–86.

Schmitz, C.M. (1997). Alcohol Abuse and Alcoholism: Internet Resources. *Reference Services Review, 25*(3–4), 51–78.

Siapera, E. (2004). Asylum Politics, the Internet and the Public Sphere: The Case of UK Refugee Support Groups Online. *Javnost: The Public, 11*(1), 79–100.

Sparks, C., & Yilmaz, A. (2005). United Kingdom: The Triumph of Quality? In R. van der Wurff & E. Lauf (Eds.), *Print and Online Newspapers in Europe: A Comparative Analysis in 16 Countries* (pp. ©259–273). Amsterdam: Het Spinhuis.

Sullivan, D. (2003, 31 July). *How Search Engines Rank Web Pages*. Retrieved January 11, 2006, from http://searchenginewatch.com/webmasters/article. php/34751_2167961

Tehan, R. (2003). *Internet Statistics: Explanation and Sources* (Report for Congress). Washington DC: Congressional Research Service. Retrieved January 5, 2006, from http://www.thememoryhole.org/crs/RL31270.pdf

Tewksbury, D., & Althaus, S.L. (2000). Differences in Knowledge Acquisition among Readers of the Paper and Online Versions of a National Newspaper. *Journalism & Mass Communication Quarterly, 77*(3), 457–479.

Usenet (2006, October 2). In *Wikipedia*. Retrieved October 4, 2006, from http://en.wikipedia.org/wiki/Usenet

Van der Wurff, R. (2005a). Online competition and Performance of News and Information Markets in The Netherlands. *Gazette, 67*(1), 9–26.

Van der Wurff, R. (2005b). A profile of print and online newspapers in Europe. In R. van der Wurff & E. Lauf (Eds.), *Print and Online Newspapers in Europe: A Comparative Analysis in 16 countries* (pp. 27–51). Amsterdam: Het Spinhuis.

Van der Wurff, R., & Lauf, E. (2004). *Online dagbladen en pluriformiteit: Een onderzoek naar de bijdrage van print en online dagbladen aan de pluriformiteit van de nieuwsvoorziening in Nederland* [Online newspapers and pluriformity]. Amsterdam: University of Amsterdam, ASCoR.

Van der Wurff, R., & Lauf, E. (Eds.) (2005). *Print and Online Newspapers in Europe: A Comparative Analysis in 16 countries*. Amsterdam: Het Spinhuis.

Web Characterization (2003, April). Retrieved January 5, 2006, from Online Computer Library Center website: http://www.oclc.org/research/projects/archive/ wcp/default.htm

Wikipedia: List of Wikipedians by number of edits (2006, October 7). In *Wikipedia*. Retrieved October 7, 2006, from http://en.wikipedia.org/wiki/Wikipedia:List_of_ Wikipedians_by_number_of_edits

Wikipedia: Modelling Wikipedia's growth (2006, October 2). In *Wikipedia*. Retrieved October 7, 2006, from http://en.wikipedia.org/wiki/Wikipedia: Modelling_Wikipedia's_growth

Wikipedia: Wikipedians (2006, October 6). In *Wikipedia*. Retrieved October 7, 2006, from http://en.wikipedia.org/wiki/Wikipedia:Wikipedians

Wood, M. (2005, June 2). *Five Reasons Social Networking Doesn't Work*. Retrieved October 4, 2006, from www.cnet.com/4520-6033_1-6240550-1.html

Zakon, R.H. (2005, August 28). *Hobbes' Internet Timeline v8.1*. Retrieved April 4, 2006, from http://www.zakon.org/robert/Internet/timeline/

5

THE IMPACT OF THE INTERNET ON USERS

Piet Bakker and Charo Sádaba

Introduction: users, technology and technological determinism

In 1999, readers of the free Dutch newspaper news.nl were offered an InfoPen they could connect to their computer. With the pen they could scan barcodes under articles in the newspaper, the Internet browser would then automatically connect to a website with more detailed information. Needless to say, it was a complete failure. Many boxes with unused pens still rest in forgotten corners of the publisher's headquarters to remind too eager executives that it is not easy to force new technologies on the audience.

Such an example is a warning for any researcher who tries to map and explain the impact of new technologies on users. Many technologies were short-lived or complete failures (quadraphonic music, 3D-movies, pagers all come to mind) while other technologies are adopted enthusiastically but used in ways not intended by the inventors. SMS was invented for telephone mechanics to leave messages; the first Walkman was a personal gadget for a Sony CEO, while the developers of the Internet never foresaw downloading music and films.

The fact that technologies are used in a social context and have to fulfil existing needs cannot be emphasised enough (Castells, 2001). The use of a technology is better explained by looking at the user than at the possibilities and potentials of the technology. Choosing a 'Uses and Gratifications' approach (Katz, Blumler & Gurevitz, 1974; McQuail, 2005) instead of a technological-deterministic perspective, however, does not mean that technologies have no impact on users. It would be very hard to argue that the Internet has not affected the way in which people work, study and look for information or communicate with others. In a classic McLuhan-like sense, the Internet has been an extension of man (McLuhan, 1964). In this chapter we address the question of how these changes have impacted the use of other media, but from the perspective of the user. Below, we will cover possible uses briefly, mainly by exploring the 'interactivity' concept. Thereafter, we will focus on actual use.

Users who have been empowered by information and communication technologies do not only substantially modify their work or information-getting routines, but they also affect the way people around the world interact with media, content and other users. These changes have taken place in a very short time span: the Internet only took seven years to reach 50 million users, against, for example, the almost 50 years needed for the telephone or the 20 years for television. In 2006, the number of Internet users worldwide reached one billion (Internet World Stats, 2006).

An important question concerning the impact of new media on users is why these technological devices, adopted at an unprecedented pace, were able to affect how people communicate and live. Users' acceptance, their willingness to deal with the new media despite of the difficulties of their complex structure, is, of course, a reason for their success. Reaching a critical mass is an accepted measure of success for a new product or service. As was said above, there have been many InfoPens examples in the last years. So why has the audience adopted the Internet with so much enthusiasm?

The concept of users

In contrast to the classic understanding of an audience, that is, a more or less passive group expecting information or entertainment, Internet users are in many cases active, looking for those pieces of content to satisfy their particular and concrete needs.

The concept of the 'user' can perhaps explain the attractiveness of the medium: the Internet must be used, played, searched, surfed, navigated. Engagement is almost an obligation. No two Internet experiences are the same as the user decides what to see, when and where. That free-dom, far away from the limited choice available with a remote control, allows the building of a personal medium. Of course, this freedom can sometimes end in frustration when the user cannot find what he or she needs or is confused by redundant information. But no other medium has offered the user so much power and so many opportunities. In fact, the Internet exceeds the idea of a medium as an information or entertainment container. It is a strong personal communication vehicle, and a social platform as well.

Connected to the user perspective is the interactive nature of the medium. Interactivity has been analysed from various perspectives. In this chapter, on the impact of the Internet on users, we focus on interactivity as an activity that recognises the central role of the user. Sheizaf Rafaeli (1988: 111) elaborated the first definition of the concept from the Communication Studies field:

Interactivity is a variable characteristic of communication settings. Formally stated, interactivity is an expression of the extent that in a given series of communication exchanges, any third (or later) transmission (or message) is related to the degree to which previous exchanges referred to even earlier transmissions.

What is relevant in Rafaeli's contribution is the idea of a variable interactivity (it admits degrees), and its relationship with the influence on messages. Steuer (1994) defined interactivity as 'the extent to which users can participate in modifying the form and the content of a mediated environment in real time'. More recently, Jensen (2001: 38), stated that interactivity is the 'measure of a medium's potential ability to let the user exert an influence on the content/or form of the mediated communication.' The Internet user is part of its evolution. Users are involved because the medium requires from users that they are not mere viewers, but that their active role is essential.

The time hypothesis

Although we do not consider it very likely that basic social practices have changed because of the Internet, we expect people who have access to the Internet on a regular basis, and most of all those groups who have broadband access to this medium and have grown up with it, will differ from comparable groups without this relation with the Internet. First of all, they will spend more time with this medium and time spent with one medium cannot be spent on other media and other entertainment sources. We would, therefore, expect effects on the use of media that are also primarily consumed at home (radio, television, newspapers, recorded music) in countries and among groups with high Internet access.

It is not expected that a functional replacement will take place. The hypothesis is, therefore, in line with Riepls law, formulated by the German researcher Riepl in 1913 and confirmed even in respect to the Internet in 1999 (Hagen, 1999). The central thesis is that established media are not replaced by technically more advanced media, although it is possible that they will have to change their content and could be used in different ways (see also Waldvogel, 2002).

The media-use hypothesis

A second development is harder to pin down, but if people do use the Internet for a considerable amount of time, it could very well be that they will incorporate this medium in their social practices, making use of the specific features of this medium. Looking more closely at these possibilities, it is clear that a computer connected to the Internet is a very versatile medium; it is, among other things, a typewriter, a calculator, a jukebox, a telephone, a movie theatre, a photographic studio, a newspaper, magazine, a TV and a radio. There is a sheer endless amount of information and entertainment available. But the Internet is different not only because of what can be found on it, but also because of what can be done with it. It is much more a 'communication' medium with possibilities of email, feedback, chats, blogging, MSN, etc., as has been stated above. And it has many possibilities of being active (interactivity), ranging from determining your own path by clicking on links to making your own blog or webpage. We expect, therefore, also that the way in which people relate to this new medium but also to existing media, might change because of their experiences with the Internet (Dimmick, Chen and Li, 2004).

Related technologies

The focus here is on the use of the Internet and the impact this technology has had on users and media use in general. Mapping penetration and use, focusses on ownership and use of computers with Internet connections. The use of mobile phones, game computers, satellite TV, mobile music players, digital cameras and other gadgets is sometimes also related to Internet use. A clear case is the advance of the digital music player, often referred to as the MP3 player, with the iPod as the most visible example. Although these players can be used without connecting to the Internet, filling it with downloaded music is the most common use. Without the Internet, iPods and other digital music players probably would not be around. Worldwide more than 42 million iPods were sold until 2005 (Van Veelen et al. 2005). In 2004, for instance, one in every 20 people in the Netherlands bought a digital music player, far exceeding expectations (Fair, 2005). Moreover, the booming sales of digital cameras can only be explained because of the introduction of multimedia PCs. A third example is the market for computer games that in the past developed independently from the Internet but in the last years has increasingly relied on online business models.

It could be said that network benefits apply here to these technological appliances: as the new gadgets improve the optimisation of the previous ones (the Internet, the PC), they are really welcomed by users.

There have been several attempts to create a one-stop device, grounded on the possible benefits of simplification. But users' behaviour confirms that there are needs that must be addressed in different ways depending on the situation: in a work environment, mobility is a requirement and small screens and high-speed connection devices are needed in order to be more efficient. At home, entertainment requires a bigger screen, a high sound quality and a comfortable usage situation. So, technological convergence has to deal with needs that must be satisfied in different ways.

But younger users show more interest in media convergence. According to research by the European interactive advertising association (EIAA), the 'digital generation' could be in a few years using a single platform to access several media content: in 2005, 93 per cent of 16–24 year olds own a mobile phone, and 38 per cent of them currently use it to receive and send emails and surf the Internet. And forecasts are more interesting, as could be seen in Table 5.1. Watching television, through 3G terminals, and listening to radio are activities that will take place on their mobile phones.

This research, alongside other studies showing how young people are adopting digital media faster than the rest of population, indicates that the age factor is important in understanding how the Internet and other ICTs will affect users, and technological advances (as 3G on mobile phones) have also a strong impact once those have been adopted by the audience.

Adoption, penetration and consumption

A central question is to what extent people in different countries are connected to the Internet; below we see that there still is a steady rising penetration level of this technology. In countries with an already high level of Internet penetration, however, growth seems to be flattening out. Broadband connections (cable, DSL) are still rising while dial-up is losing ground. We also cover the question of what people do online; what applications, functions, content or kind of use is preferred and what is the time spent online. Gender, educational, income, age and country differences are also addressed.

Penetration

In 2003, Luxemburg, UK, the Netherlands and the Nordic countries had a Internet penetration of 50 per cent of more, with Germany, Belgium, Italy and Austria having a penetration level of more than 40 per cent — the majority of the users could access the Internet at home (eInclusion revisited, 2005). In 2005, 70 per cent of European homes were already connected to the Internet (Home Broadband…, 2005); in the Netherlands, almost 80 per cent of households were connected (De Digitale Economie, 2005).

In the US, a PEW study revealed that in 2004, 63 per cent of the population was using the Internet, while 81 per cent of the teenagers (12–17 olds) go online. Growth, however, seems to be flattening out (Pew Internet Project, 2005: 58–59). In 2005, 71 per cent of American teenagers

Table 5.1 Percentage of European 16–24 year olds intending to use their mobile/PDA/Blackberry to ...

	Europeans	UK	France	Germany	Spain	Italy	Belgium	the Netherlands	Denmark	Norway	Sweden
Surf the Net	22	19	29	16	23	25	26	20	10	38	40
Watch TV	25	29	28	17	32	19	23	28	22	40	41
Email	33	24	37	27	40	40	36	30	43	52	45
Radio	39	31	44	33	51	32	37	46	59	53	64

Source: EIAA, Mediascope Europe, 2005

(aged between 12–17) had access to the Internet from home according to another more recent study (Teens Read Newspapers, 2005).

There are still notable differences when Internet penetration and use are standardised according to the percentage of people living in different continents. In North America, Oceania/Australia and Europe; Internet penetration is much higher than in other areas whereas the usage is concentrated in Asia, North America and Europe (Table 5.2).

In the second half of 2004, the worldwide total of broadband lines grew by 21 per cent to 150 million. Leaders in broadband in Europe are, not surprisingly, Germany, France, the UK, Italy and Spain. Growth was greater than average in Turkey, Poland, Hungary and the UK. Broadband penetration in 2005 and 2006 is particularly high in the Netherlands, Denmark, Switzerland, Belgium, Sweden and Norway. Outside Europe Taiwan and Canada are in the same range while penetration is only higher in South Korea and Hong Kong (World Broadband Statistics, 2005; 2006).

European household broadband penetration according to strategy analytics in *eMarketeer* (July 2005) is highest in the Netherlands (56 per cent). Switzerland (51 per cent). Denmark (49 per cent) and Norway (48 per cent). The fact that ADSL (broadband through regular phone lines) is available in almost every home in many countries has driven this growth.

Growth in broadband, however, also seems to be flattening out; in Germany, it is expected to grow more slowly (although still with a yearly 20 per cent rate). The same pattern is expected for Internet use in general, with growth slowing down and use growing to ± 60 per cent in 2006 (Harms, 2004). In the UK, where home broadband is also growing at a fast speed, it is also expected that a saturation level is reached when 60 per cent of the households are connected via broadband.

The growth in broadband is also explained by the competitive market. Many ISPs invest in technologies more advanced than cable or

Table 5.2 World Internet usage and population

	Per cent of world population	Per cent of population (penetration)	Per cent of usage
Africa	14	4	3
Asia	56	11	36
Europe	12	38	28
Middle East	3	10	2
North America	5	70	21
Lation America/Carribean	9	15	8
Oceania/Australia	1	54	2
Total	100	17	100

Source: Internet World Stats, 2006

(A)DSL connections. Most ISPs are active in (wireless) *WiFi* and experiment with *wimax* (long-distance wireless) technologies, offer Internet through satellite and explore the new 3G mobile phone generation. Mobile Internet services were in 2004 and 2005 already responsible for a substantial part of the growth of mobile services in general (Commission of the European Communities, 2004). Also triple play (television, phone and Internet) is offered in some markets while in Germany the old plan of offering Internet through the electric grid is being revived. Important investments are also in fibre-to-the home connections. Apart from that, there is still strong competition by prices for broadband connections, speed and service, which makes switching from dial-up to broadband attractive. All these developments will drive more consumers to the Internet or to faster and 'always-on' Internet connections. An introduction of Web 2.0 technology, where desktop computing is being replaced by central (social) software technologies, will probably again drive the demand for broadband.

Penetration and age/gender divides

In *UK Children Go Online* (Livingstone & Bober, 2005), is it reported that in the UK 75 per cent of children between 9 and 19-years-old have access to the Internet at home, a third of whom has a broadband connection, while access at school is almost universal. There is, however, a distinctive class effect: 88 per cent of the middle class children have Internet access but only 61 per cent of working class children do. A majority of the children interviewed spend less than an hour per day on the Internet. A small group (16 per cent) does not use the Internet or only does so occasionally. The mobile phone, not the Internet is used for communication. There is a clear generation effect: children use the Internet more than their parents. Gender differences are modest, although boys use the Internet more than girls. Data from Portugal also support a strong relation between age and Internet use, the vast majority Internet users being 34 years or younger; for non-users this was the other way around (Centre for Research and Studies in Sociology, 2006). According to a research being conducted in Spain (Civertice, 2006), boys and girls between the ages of 10 and 18 prefer the most interactive medium: if they have to choose among television and the Internet, 38 per cent of them would prefer Internet over the 30 per cent that would chose television.

The digital gender divide, however, seems to be narrowing since the 2000s as women speed up their Internet take-up. Also, the 55-year-old plus group is increasingly using the Internet. Education and wealth, however, are still strong predictors for Internet use: 'higher Internet use seems to be remain clearly and consistently related to higher educational and occupational status', according to a European Commission report, *eInclusion revisited* (2005: 9). The cost of computers is one of the main obstacles for getting online; also Internet penetration is lower in rural and remote areas, as the example from Portugal makes clear (Centre for Research and Studies in Sociology, 2006). According to *eInclusion revisited* (2005), 43.5 per cent of the EU15 population was using the Internet, when the EU enlarged to 25, this dropped to 41.4 per cent. In all the new member states, however, more than 25 per cent of the population is using the Internet. The EU is actively stimulating investment, innovation and competition in these areas by requiring the opening up of the markets for electronic communications (formerly telecom markets) in all member states (European Commission, 2004).

Internet use

Research from European Interactive Advertising Association (EIAA) revealed a 17 per cent growth in time spend on the Internet from 2004 to 2005, a quarter of the users are 16 hours or more online with France leading the way with 13 hours average, the UK and Spain following with 11 hours and after that the Nordic countries and the Benelux, with 10 hours. The Internet is Europe's preferred medium (EIAA, 2005). Using email, getting news, checking the weather and doing job-related researches are the activities most mentioned in a US-study (Pew Internet Project, 2005). Portuguese data also reveal that communication (email) is the most popular activity, followed by net-surfing, consulting libraries atlases, etc., participation in chats and newsgroups and finding online news (Centre for Research and Studies in Sociology, 2006). Data from Spain are similar: 51 per cent of 10–18-year-olds use the Internet to communicate (chat or messenger); 49 per cent of them to download material and 33 per cent to play online (Civertice, 2006).

However, political and social participation, the development of new online communities and new forms of online activism that was expected by some scholars (see Rheingold, 1998) does not seem to be flourishing in the way it was expected. In *UK Children Go Online* (Livingstone & Bober, 2005) 25 per cent of the children interviewed had sent a message to website, and more than half of the sample (N=1511) visited websites concerned with civic or political issues. Also, there is no overwhelming proof that globalisation or cultural change is taking place because of people getting online and using the Internet for communication and as an information source. In the Netherlands for the last five years, the 20 most popular websites have been domestic ones, with buying, banking, information seeking, communication and news as the most popular categories (Multiscope, 2000–2005).

Consequences for other media

What are the results of these changes for the use of other media? In this section, we distinguish between two sorts of possible or probable effects, corresponding with the two hypotheses formulated above. First order effects concern time spent on the Internet that is not spent on other media – or to be more precise: time that would probably have been spent on other media if the Internet were not around. Second order effects have to do with use of other media: do people expect other things from traditional media because of their online experiences?

First order effects

Probably, the most visible effect of Internet use on other media is the use of traditional media by the so-called Net-generation. In general, the younger generation's use of traditional media, particularly of newspapers, but also of radio, television and recorded music has dropped. There also might be other reasons for not using these media for the younger generations but the Internet probably has had a profound effect in these cases.

Kaye and Johnson (2003: 271) concluded that already by 1996, television news in the US suffered from the Internet, while in 2000 news magazines and radio news also lost readers and listeners to the new medium and, although a majority of the users claim that their media use has not changed, the authors state that: 'the trend indicates that those Internet users whose media pattern have changed are abandoning traditional media at a much greater rate than they are increasing their use'. For 1998/1999, Hagen (1999) found that in Germany time spent on the Internet only diminished time spent on traditional mass media to a small extent. But that was when the Internet was still developing; Hagen added that: 'as long as the average online-time per user will not drastically increase, the effects of the Internet on the use of traditional mass media will continue to be moderate at most'.

Waldvogel (2002) examined shifts in media use in the US and concluded that there is clear evidence of substitution between the Internet and broadcast TV and between the Internet and daily newspapers. At the beginning of October 2006, research carried out among 5000 people by Jupiter Research in the five biggest European markets (UK, France, Germany, Spain and Italy) revealed that time spent online (four hours a week) had overtaken time spent on newspapers (stable at three hours a week for the last two years) for the first time. Television had not suffered; the average amount of time spent on TV rose to 12 hours a week. It was also mentioned that the rapid introduction of broadband was expected to accelerate this trend (Edgecliffe-Johnson, 2006).

Reading in general seems to be affected by the use of other media in the Netherlands; in 1975, 59 per cent of the youngest generation and 82 per cent of the oldest generation read newspapers – in 2000 these percentages dropped to 21 and 76 per cent respectively. The pattern for reading magazines and books is the same: everybody reads less but younger generations show a sharper decline (Tijdsbestedingsonderzoek, 2005). Over a 30-year period (1975–2005), the amount of time devoted to reading dropped sharply in the Netherlands, from 6.1 hours to 3.8 hours; Internet/computer time rose from 0.5 hours in 1990 to 3.8 hours in 2005. TV-viewing time showed a steady increase until 2000 but dropped in 2005, a change attributed to the time spent online (Tijdsbestedingsonderzoek, 2006). Data on this issue, however, is somewhat inconclusive. Day-to-day audience research by Stichting Kijkonderzoek (2006) reveals that the Dutch watch more television every year. The cause for the difference, can be partly attributed to different methods used, but the main reason probably has to to with what is measured. Stichting Kijkonderzoek (2006) simply measures whether the TV is on, while Tijdsbesteding (2006) asked what participants did and measured mainly primary use so every TV-use in the background was not measured.

Cole (2006) comes to similar conclusions based on research carried out within the World Internet Project (WIP). Media users in 12 countries were studied over a five-year period (from 2000 to 2005). In every country Internet users watch less TV than non-users and while 5 per cent of users interviewed stated that they watch more TV, 31 per cent report that they watch less. At the same time Internet users are increasingly multi-tasking, and watch TV when they are also online. A small majority of American users is even occupied with three of more tasks at a time.

Newspapers have seen their circulation drop in almost every part of the world for the last decade – which in fact points also to other causes than the Internet. But an accelerating drop in the last years and the rising age of the average reader (*World Press Trends*, 1996–2006) points also to the Internet as possible cause. Lauf (2001) already pointed out that every European generation reads less than the preceding one. Dimmick, Chen and Li (2004: 19) concluded that news in newspapers and on TV is probably less important for many people because of high Internet use: 'the Internet has a competitive displacement effect on traditional media in the daily news domain with the largest displacements occurring for television and newspapers'.

In *World Press Trends* (2006), media consumption in general is covered. Unfortunately, only six out of 216 countries report changes in use in different media over the last five years. In those countries, only one trend is clear: the total amount of time devoted to the Internet is rising; television time is dropping in four cases, and rising slightly in Canada and Taiwan. Time spent on newspapers is more or less stable in four of the countries, but drops in

Table 5.3 Time spent (in minutes) on different media in six countries, 2001–2006

	2001	2005	2001	2005	2001	2005	2001	2005	2001	2005
	newspapers		magazines		radio		TV		Internet	
Canada	48	49	17	17	121	114	114	115	45	65
China	54	38					184	150	75	164
Spain	15	13	4	4	94	110	226	222	9	27
Sweden	29	29	17	14	127	105	102	96	23	32
Switzerland	51	37	31	21	85	94	90	88	25	43
Taiwan	22	22			62	51	182	188	38	73

Source: *World Press Trends*, 2006

China and Switzerland (Table 5.3). On the whole, the time spent on media seems to go up. The general conclusion from these examples could be that time spent online only partly comes from other media, but in all countries some media seem to suffer from the new competition.

Television use by younger people also seems to be affected by the Internet. In the Netherlands in 2000 for the first time, the only age group that did not watch more than in the preceding period was the youngest (Tijdsbestedingsonderzoek, 2005).

A medium that claims to be affected is recorded music. Since the end of the 20th century, CD sales indeed have been dropping sharply, while the popularity of file-sharing P2P-services like Napster, Kazaa and Limewire rose. Although other causes cannot be ignored, a relation between these two developments is more than possible (Bakker, 2005a). The example of the music industry, however, also points to the fact that media use is not equal to content use. Listening to music probably has not suffered because people buy fewer CDs. On the contrary, the amount of downloaded music far exceeds the drop in music sales.

Second order effects

Although the most prominent feature of the Internet is the interactive nature of the medium, this feature hardly has contaminated other media – apart from the fact that these media can be better reached by readers, viewers or listeners (the number of 'letters to the editor' has sharply gone up because of email). There is in fact very little proof that other media have become more interactive or open to discussion because of people's expectations formed by Internet use.

Where the use of news is concerned, there is, however, another possible effect. News on the Internet is, almost by definition, free. Although many newspapers have experimented with a paid model, the free model is almost universal (van der Wurff and Lauf, 2006). Also, the new free daily newspaper model is becoming more and more important in many countries, for instance, in almost every European country, North America and in many Asian countries. In Europe, 24 million copies of free dailies are distributed every day, reaching an average market share of 20 per cent in the countries were they are available (newspaperinnovation.com). These newspapers are particularly popular with younger users (Bakker, 2005b). The notion that news should be 'free' is becoming a reality. This, in turn, could have effects on paid newspapers and other news media that charge readers or viewers. But not only news is being affected by the 'free' issue: in 2006, most of the US television series could be downloaded by the US users for free, directly from networks websites.

Conclusions

Data on Internet penetration, Internet use and the availability of broadband tend to differ, depending on the sources used. Nevertheless, the trend is quite clear. Many developed countries are already in a situation where the majority of the population uses the Internet on a daily basis. Broadband is gaining fast on dial-up connections. Younger people use the Internet more, and there is also a distinct income gap. The gender gap seems to be closing, and urban areas are better equipped than rural areas. Growth, however, seems to be flattening out, meaning that there will be a saturation level much lower than 100 per cent – 70 or maybe 80 per cent will be more realistic. There is, in other words, quite a substantial group of people who does not use or does not want to use the Internet.

Other media seem to suffer from the quite impressive use of the Internet. Particularly (paid) newspaper reading seems to be affected – with the younger generation changing most rapidly. Also, there are some signs that TV could lose viewers because of the Internet. It is, however, in no way a zero-sum game – much of the time spent online seems to come from former non-media time: people seem to spend more time with media and communication in general than they did before. The time-shift hypothesis is, therefore, only partly supported. When we look at what people do online, communication, shopping and looking for information seems to be very important, meaning that there is a time-shift but not so much a functional shift.

Some questions still need to be addressed. If people change their media-use pattern, and thereby, the type and amount of information they consume, possible effects on the general knowledge level could be expected. A recent study by British research company Telecom Express among 1000 respondents, however, revealed that although a lot of people use the Web, trust in this medium is quite low. Television was trusted by 66 per cent, newspapers by 63 per cent and radio by 59 per cent – websites and blogs on the Web scored only 36 per cent and 24 per cent (*Study: Newspapers, TV far more trusted...*, 2006, August 21). Moreover, participation could be different in the digital age. It is, however, not yet clear that people use less serious news or participate less. But they certainly use media in other forms and for other purposes.

References

Bakker, P. (2005a). 'File-sharing – fight, ignore or compete; paid download services vs. P2P-networks'. *Telematics and Informatics* 22: 41–55.

Bakker, P. (2005b). 'Growth in a Shrinking Market'. *Ideas; the Magazine of Newspaper Marketing*, July/August, 8–13.

Castells, M. (2001). *The Internet Galaxy – Reflections on the Internet, Business, and Society*. New York: Oxford University Press.

Centre for Research and Studies in Sociology (2006). *The Network Society in Portugal*. Available online at: http://www.cies.iscte.pt/en/linhas/linha2/. Accessed: 18/07/06.

Civertice (2006). *From Television to Internet: a study about the use of new media technologies*. Downloaded from www.civertice.org. Accessed 6 December 2006.

Cole, J. (2006). Internet and society in a global perspective: Lessons from five years in the field. In Castells, M. & Cardoso, G. (Eds.). *The Network society: from knowledge to policy*. Washington: Johns Hopkins Center for Transatlantic Relations: 305–13.

European Commission (2004). *European Electronic Communications Regulation and Markets*, 2004. Brussels.

De Digitale Economie (2005). Centraal Bureau voor de Statistiek, 19 January 2006.

Dimmick, J., Chen, Y., & Li, Z. (2004). Competition between the Internet and traditional news media; The Gratification-Opportunities Niche Dimension. *Journal of Media Economics*, 17(1), 19–33.

Edgecliffe-Johnson, A. (2006, October 8). Web overtakes newspapers. *The Financial Times*. Retrieved on October 9, 2006 from www.ft.com *eInclusion revisited: The Local Dimension of the Information Society*. (2005). Commission Staff Working Document. Brussels: Commission of the European Communities.

EIAA (European Interactive Advertising Association) (2005). *Press Release, 29 November 2005*.

Hagen, L. M. (1999). Riepls Gesetz im Online-Zeitalter. Eine sekundär Analyse über die Grenzen der Substitution von Massenmedien durch das Internet. In U.-D. Reips, B. Batinic, W. Bandilla, M. Bosnjak, L. Gräf, K. Moser, & A. Werner (Hrsg). *Aktuelle Online Forschung - Trends, Techniken, Ergebnisse*. Zürich: Online Press. Available: http://dgof.de/tband99/

Harms, M. (2004). *Stand und Ausblick der digitalen Wirtschaft*. Hewlett-Packard Development GmbH.

Home broadband sign-ups 'soaring'. (2005, November 28). *BBC News*. Downloaded from news.bbc.co.uk/go/pr/fr/-/hi/technology/4477492.stm. Accessed 20 December 2005.

Internet World Stats (2006, September 18). downloaded from www.internetworldstats.com. Accessed 18 September 2006.

Jensen, J. F. (2001). 'Virtual Inhabited 3D Worlds: Interactivity and Interaction Between Avatars, Autonomous Agents and Users'. In: Qvortrup, Lars (Ed.): *Virtual Interaction: Interaction in Virtual Inhabited 3D Worlds*. London, Springer: 23–47.

Katz, E., Blumler, J. G., & Gurevitz, M. (1974). 'Uses of Communication by the Individual', in W. P. Davison and F. T. C. Yu (eds.) *Mass Communication Research: Major Issues and Future Directions*. New York: Praeger: 11–35.

Kaye, B.K. & Johnson, T.J. (2003). 'From here to obscurity?: Media substitution theory and traditional media in an online World'. *Journal of the American Society for Information Science and Technology* 54(3), 260–273.

Stichting Kijkonderzoek (2006). Jaarrapport 2005. Retrieved on December 15, 2006 from from www.kijkonderzoek.nl.

Lauf, E. (2001). 'The vanishing young reader, sociodemographic determinants of newspapers use as a source of political information in Europe 1980–98'. *European Journal of Communication* 16(2), 233–243.

Livingstone, S. & Bober, M. (2005). *UK Children Go Online: Final Report of the Key Project Findings*. London: Economic & Social Research Council.

McLuhan, H. (1964). *Understanding Media: The Extensions of Men*. New York: Signet.

McQuail, D. (2005). *McQuail's Mass Communication Theory* (5th Edn.). London: Sage.

Multiscope (2000–2005). *Yearly top 20's*. (http://www.multiscope.nl)

Rafaeli, S. (1988). Interactivity: From new media to communication. *Sage Annual Review of Communication Research: Advancing Communication Science* 16: 110–134, Beverly Hills, CA.: Sage.

Rheingold, H. (1998). *The Virtual Community*. Downloaded October 21, 2005 from www.rheingold.com/vc/book/

Sector Report 1: The European Newspaper Market. (2004) Publishing market watch. Turku: Turku School of Economics and Business Administration; London: Rightscom Ltd; European Commission.

Steuer, J. (1994). Defining virtual reality: Dimensions determining telepresence. In F. Biocca & M. Levy (Eds.), *Communication in the age of virtual reality*. Hillsdale, NJ: Lawrence Erlbaum Associates. Available online at: http://cyborganic.com/People/jonathan/Academia/Papers/Web/defining-vr1.html. Last accessed: 18/01/03.

Strategy Analytics in eMarketeeer (July 2005), *Alain Neuville Newsletter October 2005*.

Study: Newspapers, TV far more trusted than Web Sites, Blogs (2006, August 21). Editor & Publisher. Downloaded from www.editorandpublisher.com August 22, 2006.

Teens Read Newspapers. (2005, 23 November). Center for Media Research. Downloaded from www.centerformediaresearch.com/cfmr_brief_cfm?/fnl=051123

Tijdsbestedingsonderzoek, het (2005). Retrieved on August 28, 2005 from www.tijdsbesteding.nl

Tijdsbestedingsonderzoek, het (2006). Retrieved on October 20, 2006 from www.tijdsbesteding.nl

Pew Internet Project (2005). *Internet: The Mainstreaming of Online Life*. Downloaded from: www.pewInternet.org/pdfs/Internet_Status_2005.pdf

Van der Wurff, R. & Lauf, E. (Eds.) (2006). *Print and Online: Newspapers in Europe, A Comparative Analysis in 16 Countries*. Amsterdam: Het Spinhuis.

Van Veelen, T., De Kloet, J., Bakker, P. & Ter Bogt, T. (2005). *Portable Sounds in the Age of Digital Reproduction. How iPod affects sonic experience*. Paper presented at the First European Communication Conference. Amsterdam, 24–26 November 2005.

Waldvogel, J. (2002). *Consumer Substitution among Media*. Federal Communications Commision.

World Broadband Statistics: Q4 2004 (2005). London: Point Topic Ltd.

World Broadband Statistics: Q1 2006 (2006). London: Point Topic Ltd.

World Press Trends (1996–2006) Sector Report 1: The European Newspaper Market (2004). Paris: World Association of Newspapers.

6

THE IMPACT OF THE INTERNET ON MEDIA POLICY, REGULATION AND COPYRIGHT LAW

Des Freedman, Anders Henten, Ruth Towse and Roger Wallis

Introduction

This chapter focusses on public policies concerning the regulation of mass media industries in the context of the emergence of the Internet as a significant challenge to the existing communications environment. It tackles, in particular, the issues of content regulation, competition law and copyright policies and examines the impact of the Internet on both the development and efficacy of current approaches to media regulation, largely in Europe but also drawing on experiences in the US.

There are three key reasons for devising policies that are specific to the media:

- Economic: the scarcity or natural monopoly characteristics of the media often require intervention to open up audiovisual markets given that the lack of competition in a monopoly situation may lead to higher prices and lack of innovation.
- Political: given the democratic importance of media in facilitating free speech and producing informed citizens, special attention is required for the media industries.
- Socio-cultural: the acceptability (or not) of particular forms of media expression and the media's role in facilitating specific cultural (national, ethnic, religious) values requires special mechanisms of support and control (Garnham, 1998: 211–12).

The main objectives of public policy in relation to the media concern aspirations like freedom, independence, localism, order, efficiency, competition, consumer protection as well as pluralism and diversity (see Hutchison, 1999: 69–122; McQuail, 1992: 32; Napoli, 2001). The latter two objectives are often confused with each other but actually refer to different phenomena; while pluralism is related to the variety of media sources – broadcast channels, websites, newspaper titles, radio stations – diversity is connected to expressions of difference in media content. All of these aspirations, however, are seen as key to the pursuit of a democratic and competitive media system in which intellectual property is protected, profitability maximised, innovation encouraged and the needs of distinct audiences addressed.

Media and communication policies always reflect a mixture of economic, technological and cultural impulses and visions, and are frequently coloured by the lobbying activities of parties with resources and clear impressions of their vested interests. The same can be said of policies that have emerged from the notion of the 'Information Society'. The vision is of a society where digital technologies are seen as the key to new and more effective ways for citizens, businesses and governments to share and store services and products and partake actively in everyday social life. The implementation involves a patchwork quilt of different types of legislation and initiatives; often these take the form of policies that seem to move in mutually incompatible directions.

The different economic, technological and cultural factors rarely result in a homogenous view of progress, but in opposing forces which need to be carefully balanced. Regulation versus the free market, and cultural diversity versus cultural uniformity are two such opposites.

Development of information society policy

These issues are not a new phenomenon resulting solely from the specifics of the Information Society, however. In the 1970s, UNESCO eagerly promoted the concept of a 'free flow of information'. A critic of this stance maintained that: 'there are no real policy recommendations, just a belief that more and more media are a good thing' (Tunstall, 1977: 211). We can see similar elements in current information society policies involving slogans such as 'broadband for all' and 'affordable access'. Domestic satellite technology made its entrance in the 1980s and once again a new technology became the focus of both visions and concerns. The Council of Europe (CoE) began to address the notion of European identity (the term 'cultural diversity' had not yet entered the debating arena) and set up the Council for Cultural Cooperation in 1987 to study the: 'trend towards uniformity and the blurring of European identities' (CoE, 1990).

The European Commission (EC) began to take a greater interest in media and communication policies in the 1980s. It had previously tended to view media and cultural products as 'ordinary' goods in that they should be traded in a market with a minimum of regulatory restraints. A result of this was that the concept of 'public service' media became heavily criticised, even if a goal shared by all was to increase the quality and availability of European audio-visual products across the Union. Soon, quantitative studies of the effects of satellite transmissions across borders showed that public service broadcasters provided a far greater access to European programmes than their new commercial competitors and this is still the case (CoE, 1990; Blomkvist et al., 2005). For the Commission, providing a free flow of media and information products across European borders using satellites was nevertheless the best guarantee for achieving its goal of stimulating broadcast material of European origin.

The Internet first entered the media policy arena during the 1992 US presidential election where Al Gore, the vice-presidential candidate, made a great play of the importance of building an 'information superhighway', a digital infrastructure that would transform the economy, labour, education and health as well as the media. In a famous speech to the International Telecommunications Union (ITU) in March 1994 (Gore, 1994), he outlined the five principles on which his plan for a 'global information infrastructure' (GII) would be built: the need for private investment, the promotion of competition, the creation of flexible regulation, the provision of open access and the guarantee of universal service (see Freedman, 1996). In order to build this digital 'network of networks' that, according to Gore, would facilitate: 'robust and sustainable economic progress, strong democracies, better solutions to global and local environmental challenges, improved health care and – ultimately – a greater sense of shared stewardship of our small planet' (Gore, 1994), policies were required that emphasised, above all, private sector participation and the entry of new private players into existing markets.

The EU Bangemann Report

The above approach was reflected within European media policy-making with the publication of the 1994 *Bangemann Report, Europe and the Global Information Society* (EC, 1994), undoubtedly inspired by the US debate on the information superhighway and all that it offered in terms of stimulating the competitiveness and efficiency of a modern 'service economy'. This European analysis of the digital world took as a starting assumption the view that there is an inexorable increase in the scope of digitalisation. One of the prophetic texts of the era was *Being Digital* (Negroponte, 1995), together with a wide variety of terms emphasising intangibility, for example, *Living on Thin Air* (Leadbeater, 1999) and the *Weightless Economy* (Quah, 1996). If any product or service could be digitalised, then this would happen and the physical equivalents would disappear. A plethora of e-prefixes emerged to cover all these opportunities: e-commerce, e-work, e-democracy, e-health and so on.

Bangemann and his colleagues expressed much concern over the observation that there were 34 PCs for every 100 US citizens, but only 10 on average in the EU. The answer was to stimulate major investments in digital networks, driven primarily by attractive content which consumers would purchase, thus making the networks 'tick' and generate traffic revenues. Video-on-demand was regarded as a likely driver. But this proved to be an incorrect conclusion. Content owners were loath to release their copyrighted materials into a new environment where perfect copies could be made at the click of a mouse and the legal protection of their copyright revenues was unclear. With a minimum of regulation there were no mechanisms such as compulsory licences or 'must-carry' conditions which could ensure attractive content being made available in the new networks of the information society (Wallis, 1998: 52). Historically, services such as gambling and pornography have often played an important role in driving the uptake of new media technology. A decade prior to the Bangemann Report, producers of 'adult movies' had been credited with contributing heavily to the success of the VHS Cassette, rather than its BETAMAX rival. Currently, the success or failure of the new blu-ray video discs in the market is being discussed in similar terms (Anonymous 2007). That other services such as pornography and gambling could play an important role as a driver, as such things have done historically, was not mentioned in any official documents referred to above.

Convergence

'Convergence' in the media was a major buzzword during the latter half of the 1990s, although as one speaker at a conference in 1999 put it, convergence is rather like the term culture: we all know what we are talking about but no-one can define it. As discussed in chapter 2, convergence referred loosely to the integration of the information technology (IT), telecommunications and entertainment industries. The Internet, however, is the quintessential example of convergence in the information and communication technology (ICT) area as it can be seen as a combination of IT and telecommunications and can be used for broadcasting purposes and by other media, including text media. The Internet is thus the most important platform for convergence developments and a key driver of many of the important changes taking place in the communications and media industries.

Convergence implies that similar services can be conveyed on different platforms and, conversely, that individual platforms can carry different services. It is, therefore, increasingly difficult to differentiate between different platforms with the implication that policies and regulations have to be changed. It should be acknowledged, however, that pressures for ownership convergence had existed for decades before technology convergence and the

Internet and have been legally constrained in a number of countries in order to limit media power. But there is no question that technology convergence has significantly changed the conditions for the convergence of previously distinct markets in the communications and media industries.

As argued in Chapter 3, technology convergence has been evolving for many years – as has the Internet – and has played an important role in the ongoing changes in communication policies for a good number of years. However, at the EU level, it was not until the 1997 *Green Paper on Convergence* (EC, 1997) that it was placed on the political agenda for European communication policies. This process resulted in the eventual adoption of the New Regulatory Framework for communication infrastructures and related services implemented in EU member states in 2003 (EC, 2003a). Convergence and its most important expression, the Internet, is thus the technological basis for many of the changes in the communication policies and regulations from the early liberalisation to the more developed regulatory framework of 2003. The same applies to other regions and countries, for instance, the Telecommunications Act of 1996 in the US and similar changes all over the world.

The basic tenet of these policy changes is that it becomes increasingly meaningless to differentiate in terms of regulations between different technological platforms installed originally for different purposes, for example, telecommunication or broadcasting. It would even be counterproductive to do so, as this could be a barrier to the development of inter-platform competition and the marketing of services across platforms, including all the new multimedia services based on technology convergence. In terms of regulations in the EU, this has led to the promotion of the concept of technology neutrality, which means that all different infrastructures carrying essentially similar services should be regulated in the same manner.

Impact of the Internet on policy

In summary, we can identify five ways in which the Internet has affected the mechanisms of and possibilities for public policy concerning the media:

1   The Internet is the emblematic technology of a period in which we are seeing a broad shift in public policy where the traditional social contracts underlying policy in Western Europe have been torn apart by a new political and economic consensus about the centrality of the private sector, together with the experience of economic recession and technological innovation.

The questioning of the rebalancing mechanism that was called the social contract goes together with the fact that for the first time since World War II, the best regulating mechanism is considered to be a minimally regulated market, in particular with regard to the information society (Burgelman, 2000: 59).

2   Convergence threatens traditional distinctions between and separate forms of regula-
    tion of different media and, in particular, muddies the difference between traditional
    'broadcast' (interventionist) and 'telecoms' (less interventionist focussing on network
    but not content) modes of regulation. It also necessitates a technology-neutral policy
    and what Collins and Murroni (1996: 175) call 'fuzzy law' that 'increases regulatory
    discretion' and, in particular, calls for more self-regulation and co-regulation.
3   Broadband Internet threatens to abolish the phenomenon of spectrum scarcity undermin-
    ing the traditional justification for applying special measures to broadcast industries.
    According to the economist Tim Congdon (1995: 11–12):

> As spectrum scarcity is overcome and more suppliers are involved, and as the scope
> for pricing individual programmes to individual customers evolves, the structure of the
> media market begins to resemble that in competitive industries. The argument for special
> treatment is therefore increasingly obsolete.

4   Multiple sources and outlets facilitate competitive flows, constitute a barrier to
    regulation and undermine the efficacy of antitrust and ownership regulations. Helen
    Coonan, the Australian communications minister, put it very clearly:

> Media policy has traditionally achieved its objectives by closely controlling who may
> enter the market and what services they may offer .... In a converged environment it
> will become almost impossible, and certainly counterproductive, to stop new players and
> new services from emerging. In my view, regulatory strategies need to move away from
> relying on controlling market structures in the way they have to date, to a new framework
> that allows some efficiencies of scale and scope while encouraging new players, new
> investment and new services (Coonan, 2005).

5   There is a diminished role for the state in the 'push' environment of the Internet where
    users are able to actively seek out their tastes and not be subject to the tastes of others.
    'Soft' regulation is, therefore, deemed to be more appropriate than 'hard' regulation
    in this new environment.

We now turn to examining the impact of the Internet on three specific areas
of media policy and regulation: content, competition and copyright law.

Content policy

Pluralistic and diverse media systems have been promoted through a variety
of statutory obligations, institutional forces and legal barriers. Rules on
advertising time and content, images of sex and violence in pursuit of the
'protection of minors' and the origin of material have coincided with support
for public service broadcasting structures and other forms of public subsidy to
create a complex array of national regulatory structures that deal with media
content. The key European-wide piece of legislation on media content is the
Television without Frontiers Directive (TVF), originally passed in 1989 with

a commitment to transmit at least 50 per cent of EU originated material 'where practicable' and with a host of other rules designed to stimulate a competitive, democratic, diverse and relevant European audiovisual space. TVF lays down basic rules concerning obligations aimed at, for example:

- protecting consumers from unfair commercial practices;
- protecting minors from inappropriate material;
- protecting the right to reply;
- promoting the production and distribution of *European* audiovisual material; and
- guaranteeing European audiences free access to events of major importance (see EC, 2003b: 13).

The *Directive* was being revised at the time of writing (2006) to meet the challenges of digital technologies, including the Internet, which are seen to be unsettling and rendering inappropriate existing forms of content regulation. The increase in broadband penetration and general expansion of Internet communication is stimulating a discussion about which delivery platforms should be exempt from traditional rules as material is 'sought out' by audiences rather than generally disseminated to them. The UK white paper on communications notes that audiences have different expectations of different media and an approach to regulation: 'which sought to impose the same rules on all media despite these differences might have to adopt the standards of the medium where regulation was hardest to enforce and least justified, which, today, is the Internet' (DCMS/DTI, 2000: 61).

While this is neither desirable nor likely, a clear distinction has now been drawn between linear and non-linear 'push' and 'pull' technologies and a consensus formed around the need for a 'two-tier' approach to regulation. Representatives of the non-linear industries (ISPs, online content producers, advertisers, etc.) are calling for minimal regulation in order to stimulate innovation, creativity and diversity. According to the UK broadband stakeholder group: 'New audio-visual content services, made possible through innovation in digital technology and the Internet, should be given time to evolve and develop rather than being shackled by premature and unnecessary regulation [sic] intervention by the EU' (quoted in Williams, 2005: 4). The perception of regulation as 'stifling' and the equation of innovation with the freedom to manoeuvre in the market is becoming increasingly powerful in policy debates and is shaping regulatory approaches not just to non-linear but also to traditional linear services. This perspective was popular in the 2005 TVF negotiations where online content producers and intermediaries sought to fend off statutory obligations in favour of self- and co-regulatory approaches. 'Commercial broadcasters', however, also 'indicated that they could support a Content Directive if the level of regulation was lower than the present *Directive*, especially in relation to advertising rules' (EC, 2005: 3). The Internet, in other words, is being used as a precedent to minimise regulation not just in emerging sectors but also in traditional broadcast sectors where battles over the relaxation of rules concerning advertising time, excluded sectors and product placement are at the heart of the revision of TVF.

For some, any proposed distinction between 'strong' regulation of linear services and 'light touch' regulation of non-linear services is increasingly untenable because of the challenge posed by the Internet. James Murdoch, CEO of BSkyB, asked this question at the Liverpool Broadcasting Conference: 'Should Internet audio visual content be regulated in the same way as television currently is, or should TV increasingly be deregulated towards the way that the Internet is currently?' (Murdoch, 2005). Given that 'the first option is for the birds', he insisted that '[o]ver time, lessening of [broadcast] TV content regulation is inevitable (ibid).

Competition (antitrust) policy in Europe

It is, however, increasingly competition policy and not content policy that is shaping contemporary European communications. The starting point, once again is the 1994 *Bangemann Report* and its vision of a European information society where the Internet is seen as a key basic prerequisite for a competitive service economy. The route to critical mass goes via deregulation (above all of the telecommunications industry) and attractive services which will draw investment capital. The report notes that no one owns the Internet, and that serious security flaws can arise without any actors having to take overall responsibility. The role of competition policy should be dynamic: 'not to freeze any sets of regulations, but rather to establish procedure and policies through which the exploding dynamism of the sector can be translated into wealth and job creation' (EC, 1994: 20).

More than ten years later, it can be seen that applications such as file-sharing have produced the critical mass but have also created, as predicted, opportunities for the rapid spread of malicious software (viruses, worms). Competition policy has had to move forward from simple analysis based on market-share in a specific industrial sector to looking at combinations of effects as convergence has brought the IT, telecommunications and content industries closer together, in a number of strange relationships, often coloured by a desire to tame the un-regulated Internet.

Horizontal and vertical integration and competition

Telecommunications deregulation followed the pattern of other former monopoly utility industries such as radio/TV, electricity and water. Deregulation produced numerous new suppliers offering competitive prices for consumers. By and by, what was presented as an inevitable process of concentration of ownership produced an inevitable oligopoly. Competition law could handle a simple case of members of an oligopoly providing the same services/products seeking further internal mergers (horizontal integration), by measuring the resulting market share in a specific sector of any proposed new amalgamations. But vertical integration, where different mixes of products and services are integrated within the same conglomerate, provides a much tougher analytical challenge. The music industry is a typical case. Publishing (controlling copyrights to musical works), production and production rights, distribution channels (physical and virtual), broadcasting, etc., can all be integrated within the same conglomerate. This gives rise to a number of synergy opportunities with the result that actual market power in any particular sector (e.g., record production) can be greater than apparent market share. The following examples illustrate the difficulties experienced in using competition law to analyse possible resulting threats to competition and a well-functioning market.

Time-Warner/AOL and EMI (2000)

Internet-facilitated convergence led to a new and more complex form of vertical integration which, in the case of the music industry that we shall now focus on, initially involved record companies buying music publishers. By the mid-1990s, five record companies controlled almost 75 per cent of global phonogram sales, and their sister publishing divisions controlled almost the same percentage of all music copyrights. These two groupings formed de facto oligopoly cartels, which were to have considerable implications for competition in the area of music, for example, as the Internet's potential for music distribution exploded.

Competition law seemed to fail to apply to and confront the very intricate form of collective dominance in the music market that was to have considerable significance, both via actions and lobbying, as the Internet developed. However, it became impossible for European competition authorities to ignore the issue of collective dominance when, in 2000, the world's largest ISP AOL/Time Warner, with its wide interests in music, publishing, film and broadcasting/narrowcasting, announced its plans to join up with EMI, (with its major interests in sound recordings, and owner of the largest music publishing company). At this time, music delivery via the Internet had exploded, thanks to Napster. Most of it involved the illegal swapping of music files and virtually no legal alternatives were available that offered online materials from the major record companies/publishers. The EC, charged with examining the implications of the proposed merger, found that a new Warner-EMI might be able to bypass the traditional copyright collection societies, thus raising entry barriers and costs for smaller players, and concluded that the merger would create a: 'dominant position on the markets for online music and music software' (EC 2000 Paragraph 130: 33). In terms of collective dominance, the conclusion was that the merger would provide: 'the first vertically integrated broadband content provider ... which would have a considerable advantage over non-integrated content providers or firms able to supply a more limited range of content' (EC, 2000 paragraph 149:41). EMI and AOL/Time Warner then decided to shelve plans for the merger.

Sony and Bertelsmann's record companies (2004)

Sony and Bertelsmann announced a planned merger of their record companies in early 2004. In many ways it resembled the EMI-Time Warner proposal, but with one difference, the media conglomerate's two music publishing divisions would be retained as separate entities within the two owner-corporations. Otherwise there were many similarities. Sony had its own Internet distribution network (Sony Connect). Bertelsmann, as well, had extensive interests in broadcasting, the Internet, etc. In May 2004 the Commission published a Statement of Objections (case COMP/M.3333 Sony/BMG 24.05.2004 D/202145) (EC, 2004a). The Commission had concluded that the merger: 'would enhance a situation of collective dominance' (Paragraph 142, page 45). The result would be less competition in the online market and reduced consumer choice.

These statements were followed by a public hearing and a final ruling less than two months later involving a 180-degree turnaround. The merger was compatible with the common market: 'It is not likely that the merger would lead to the creation of a collective dominance of the remaining four majors on the market for online music' (Commission Decision COMP/M.3333 Sony/BMG C (2004) 2815: 48).

An initial statement that the merger would most likely lead to the coordination of publishing activities became a conclusion that: 'there is no evidence that the joint venture would have as its object the co-ordination of the Parties' competitive behaviour in music publishing'. It also noted that, even if this were to occur, the effects would be limited since it is the collective rights management (CRMs) organisations (otherwise known as copyright collecting societies') in the music industry and not the major publishers who decide tariffs. Once again the music industry's dual oligopoly (publishers/record companies) had convinced the EC that vertical integration was not a problem, but that the problem lay with the monopoly intermediaries, the CRMs.

A few weeks prior to the final ruling, on 8 July 2004, the then European Commissioner for competition policy, Mario Monti, gave a keynote speech on the development of competition in the new media market. Monti noted that the distinction between infrastructure services and content services was becoming increasingly blurred, at the same time that: 'their interaction is becoming increasingly vital to the success of both' (Monti, 2004: 2).

The importance of access to attractive content for the success of all media is generally recognised by most operators ... since the Commission's general objective is to keep media markets open and to stimulate growth as much as possible, the Commission needs to ensure that access to key inputs in the markets for delivery of content is not unjustifiably restricted. ... We certainly do not have the illusion of having removed once and for all the obstacles that, as far as content is concerned, might hamper the development and opening to competition of new media markets ... in many cases, innovation builds up as a challenge to existing technologies and/or processes. As such, it pits new players against established firms. Such configurations obviously create incentives for the incumbents to try to block or curtail the new dynamics in the market place, to try to maintain their position at the expense of the innovations (Monti, 2004: 8).

The Sony-BMG record company merger was one of the last cases to be decided during the reign of outgoing Commissioner, Mario Monti. One wonders how he would have reacted if he had known then that Sony-Ericsson – a 50/50 joint venture between the Ericsson telephone company and Sony of Japan – manufacturer of mobile phones, would soon launch a service to provide embedded recordings in each new phone – these recordings would only be provided by the new Sony-BMG record company (a corporate decision). Other content providers would be excluded from this new type of music delivery channel. Or that this decision was followed by a demand by Sony publishing to do internal deals regarding any embedded songs in Sony-Ericsson mobiles where the publishing division had a contractual interest (thus bypassing the CRMs, something DG Competition had warned against in the EMI-Time Warner case).

Not everyone accepted the final ruling. In Europe, the independent record companies association IMPALA, representing smaller record companies in Europe, filed a complaint with the Court of First Instance in Luxembourg, maintaining that issues of collective dominance had been ignored when allowing Sony and Bertelsmann to merge their record company divisions.

IMPALA's arguments were the following:

- A state of collective dominance existed already in the recorded music industry, and the merger would strengthen dominant positions.
- A state of collective dominance would be created for the resulting four major record companies in the market for online music.
- That Sony would achieve an individual dominant position in the market for online distribution of music.

- The merger would have the effect of coordinating music publishing activities of the parties, even if the divisions were formally excluded from the merger.

The findings of the court were announced in July 2006. (Court of 1st Instance, Luxembourg, Case T-464/04.) The Commission's decision to allow the merger was rejected, mainly on the grounds of pricing issues, where a smaller number of majors could be expected to integrate their pricing strategies. DG Competition had failed to prove that this would not be the case. The sudden change of view between the initial statement of objections (SO) and the approval a few weeks later was, in the court's words, 'not sufficiently reasoned and is vitiated by manifest errors of judgement' (paragraph 531).

Further merger attempts

While the EU competition authorities, in accordance with this ruling, were reviewing the situation regarding the BMG and the Sony *record* production divisions, another merger proposal emerged, namely that between the *music* publishing divisions of the Bertelsmann empire (BMG Publishing) and Universal-Vivendi (Universal Publishing). Universal's parent had offered 1.6 billion Euros for BMG publishing. This amounts to almost 11 times the annual net publisher share (what publishers retain after paying what they owe to composers), and is a good indication of the lucrative nature of a music publishing business which controls large swathes of music copyrights, many of which are governed by agreements which extend for 70 years after the death of the composer.

Several individual music composers and composers' organisations in Europe registered objections in late 2006 to the proposed Universal-BMG publishing merger. They argued that a larger publishing house with less staff would mean less resources for actively promoting works in the market (the essence of a publishing contract), less competition between publishers and could be a threat to creativity and cultural diversity. Even IMPALA, opposed the merger, arguing that it would facilitate coordination of activities between different divisions of large media conglomerates (e.g., between record production, publishing, broadcasting, etc.) and thus create barriers for smaller players unable to engage in such synergy activities.

Warner Music Group (WMG) had failed to arrange a marriage with EMI in 2000, but attempts to seal the wedding have continued over the past half-decade. Many observers got a major surprise in February, 2007, when WMG announced a renewed plan to amalgamate with EMI. This time they would do it with the support of the very groups that had so successfully opposed the Sony-BMG record company merger, namely, the independent record companies organised in IMPALA.

A WMG press release announced a number of concessions to IMPALA in return for their support in selling the planned merger to the regulatory authorities in Brussels (Warner music group 2007). The WMG-IMPALA deal involved WMG promising:

- support via funding for a new digital rights licensing platform established by the independent music labels to represent the world's independent sector;
- to ensure the divestiture of certain recorded music assets to reinforce the market power of the independent record sector; and
- to pursue various other behavioural commitments which have the aim of benefiting the recorded music market as a whole, and, in particular the independent sector.

The full details of this letter of intent are not clear at the time of writing (February 2007). But it indicates, once again, the difficulties facing the competition regime in an environment characterised by vertical integration. With the EU approval of the Sony-BMG record company merger being turned down by the Court of First Instance, at the initiative of IMPALA, WMG have chosen a route via an IMPALA deal to clear the hurdles. What effect this may have on the EC's view of IMPALA's credibility as a champion of the small to medium-sized (SME) business sector is another matter. Significantly, neither the WMG press release, nor the equivalent release from IMPALA, make any reference to possible plans to merge the music publishing interests of EMI (the world's largest music publisher) and those of WMG (Warner Chappell publishing).

The growth of oligopolies in the music industry, with fewer players controlling more rights (both on the publishing and the recording side), has also provided opportunities for new types of business deals, not least in the Internet environment. Here new business models and actors have appeared and sometimes disappeared. Often copyrighted materials appear on Internet sites where individual consumers have become producers or adapters of content, posting their own 'versions' on sites for others to view. Examples from 2006 are MySpace and YouTube. In the case of YouTube, the major record companies were rattling sabers throughout the early autumn of 2006, threatening to sue the company. The search engine Google, however, was also interested in getting access to YouTube's huge consumer base and planned a takeover. Shortly before this took place, three of the major record companies agreed to a settlement with YouTube involving small equity stakes in return for cancelled litigation. The Google deal meant that these stakes provided each of the three with an estimated 150 million dollars in equity profit, according to reports in trade magazines. The interesting point about this is not the exact size of the windfall, but that the ownership of repositories of rights could allow major record companies to generate profits (by referring to the rights controlled) without having to share any of the spoils with the artists who had created the same rights. This provides an interesting aspect of how legislation on IPRs can be used for other purposes than rewarding those who originally created them (Anonymous 2006).

Arguments about ownership restrictions

Many justifications for proposals to loosen ownership rules in the US can be found in US literature. For example, in 1996, the technology guru Nicholas Negroponte had argued that the centrifugal logic of digital 'bits' was overwhelming analogue 'atoms' and making it increasingly difficult to justify traditional media ownership rules. 'Guaranteed plurality', he wrote in *Being Digital*, 'might require less legislation that one would expect, because the monolithic empires of mass media are dissolving into an array of cottage industries' (1995: 57).

> Media barons of today will be grasping to hold on to their centralized empires tomorrow .... The combined forces of technology and human nature will ultimately take a stronger hand in plurality than any laws Congress can invent. But in case I'm wrong in the long term and for the transition period in the short term, the FCC had better find some imaginative scheme to replace industrial-age cross-ownership laws with incentives and guidelines for being digital (ibid: 58).

That is precisely what former FCC chairman Michael Powell attempted to do eight years later in his proposed (and ultimately unsuccessful) loosening of media ownership rules in 2003. Drawing on the communication 'abundance' facilitated by the Internet, he argued that:

> the most striking difference between the world today and the world pre-remote [control] is that Americans now have access to a bottomless well of information called the Internet. ... The time has come to honestly and fairly examine the facts of the modern marketplace and build rules that reflect the digital world we live in today, not the bygone era of black-and-white television (Powell, 2003).

This is also the approach of the British government in its commitment to relax ownership rules. In the section on 'A Changing Market and a Changing World' in its *Consultation on Media Ownership Rules* (DTI/DCMS, 2001), it argued that Internet-led convergence is delivering greater convenience and choice while spectrum abundance is also stimulating competition and pluralism. 'Against this background', it argued, 'we will be as deregulatory as possible, in the knowledge that new competition legislation should be more effective in preventing companies from abusing a dominant market position' (ibid: 11).

The argument that the dynamism of an Internet-nourished 'new economy' undermines the need for competition rules is an argument that perished with the collapse of the (first) dotcom bubble and has had little serious impact on media policy today. Far from technologies like the Internet undermining the power of competition authorities, it is the latter which are increasingly influential in structuring existing and future digital and online communications markets. Indeed, as more and more traditional media policy objectives (concerning diversity and pluralism in particular) are to be pursued using economic rather than political or cultural mechanisms, the Internet has contributed to a strengthening, rather than a weakening, of competition authorities.

Copyright and IPR policies

Copyright, author's rights and neighbouring rights

One of the most influential forms of media regulation is copyright law, a precept that has existed in the UK and the US since the 18th century and in most European countries since the 19th as an author's right, therefore, predating the development of all media industries with the exception of literary and music publishing. There are differences between the legal tradition of authors' rights on the one hand (found in much of continental Europe and in many other countries, including Russia, Japan and most of South America) and copyright law (originally in England, then the US and many Commonwealth countries) on the other. One way of characterising this difference lies in the emphasis placed in the law on economic effects, with copyright law emphasising economic rights and the civil law tradition emphasising the natural rights of the author. This difference has implications for the impact of the Internet on copyright law and also makes for some difficulties in the harmonisation of authors' rights and copyright law internationally (Koelman, 2004), that is increasingly regarded as necessary to deal with globalisation of trade in media products and their delivery by Internet.

Besides the author's right, neighbouring rights (rights related to copyright) offer protection to works created by performers, sound recording makers, broadcasters and film producers and others. The duration of copyright protection in countries of the EU and in the US (as well as in most other developed countries) is now 70 years after death for authors. However, the duration of neighbouring rights differs quite a bit: in the EU, it is 50 years from the date of fixation, while in the US since the Sonny Bono Copyright Term Extension Act (1998), the term has been 95 years for company copyrights, such as those in the film and sound recording industries. By contrast, the US did not recognise for a long time performers' rights in their sound recordings, though most European countries eventually became signatories to the Rome Convention (1961). Such differences can make for friction in international trade and for the reciprocal 'national' treatment of copyright owners.

Copyright law has always had to adapt to technological progress. It has coped successfully with the introduction of sound recording, moving pictures, television (wireless, cable and satellite), photocopying, fax machines and audio and video cassette recorders – the last four being copying devices that enable individuals to make their own copies of the works of others. Throughout its adaptation to these developments, the basic principles of copyright have been maintained: that the author has the exclusive right to control the exploitation of her work until such time as the copyright expires and her works then enters the public domain; and that there are certain exceptions and limitations to this rule (called 'fair use' in US law – a term that has erroneously come to be widely used elsewhere) to facilitate private study and research and what might be called 'free speech' – the use of copyright material for quotation, criticism, parody, etc., – without the author's permission. Copyright and authors' rights are in fact a bundle of rights covering many different ways of reproducing and distributing works of literature, art, music, dramatic works and performances and so on, and copyright owners and their representatives, such as the CRMs or copyright collecting societies, license use of all these rights in all possible media, including the Internet. By and large, the main reward to the copyright holder is obtained through royalty payments for licences to use works in specified ways.

Copyright and downloading

Despite being considerably influenced by international treaties, and in the case of the EU, subject to harmonisation under Common Market rules, copyright law is nevertheless national law and there is some variation as to the treatment of certain items in different countries, as noted above. One notable difference is the treatment of exceptions and limitations to copyright with respect to the legality of private use by individuals of material downloaded from the Internet, especially in the case of music and increasingly also with film. While it is illegal to upload copyright works without authorisation, in many countries it is not illegal to download works for reasonable private use or to copy for one's own use items, such as CDs, that have been purchased on to a computer or mobile devices (though the UK is an exception here – see Gowers, 2006). This has led to a certain amount of confusion in a situation in which it has anyway been difficult to persuade people that just because it is easy to download music, and 'every body does it' did not mean that it was, therefore, legal to do so; this problem was exacerbated during a crucial period in which the music industry attempted to rely on law enforcement rather than developing legal means for consumers to download music, which lost them the initiative (Bakker, 2005). With so much material being offered for free over the Internet by people who did not care or about copyright and even with the encouragement of some professional artists, in retrospect, it is hardly surprising that this happened. It is notable that the film industry is trying to avoid these difficulties.

Unauthorised downloading has the result that no arrangement is made for payment to rights holders – creators and distributors; however, to overcome the problem exceptions and limitations have been institutionalised in some countries through compulsory licensing, for which there is equitable remuneration. Under the EC Rental Directive (1992), all EU member states were required to collect remuneration for the public performance of sound recordings to be distributed by collecting societies to performers and sound recording makers (Towse, 2001). There are other compensatory schemes, such as lump sum levies or taxes on equipment, such as computers and blank CDs (Farchy and Rochelandet, 2002). The money so raised is then handed over to the collecting societies for distribution. These schemes are regarded by some as very blunt instruments in terms of the efficiency of their administration and the fact that they can only approximately reward individual creators for the use of their works and some countries oppose them (the UK is a case in point; see Gowers, 2006). Unsurprisingly, computer and software manufacturers object to these taxes and levies and this objection and others concerning administration by collecting societies has become a hotly debated issue in the EU.

Changes to copyright law due to the Internet

Digitalisation and the Internet are treated by copyright law as further manifestations of technological progress capable of being encompassed within the scope of copyright. As with previous technical developments, the law has had to be changed to cope with their effect on the legal rights and economic position of rights holders. It comes into question, though, whether the nature of these new technologies and the vastly increased ease of copying and distribution that they make possible can be dealt with within the spirit of copyright law, in terms of both the protection it offers authors and other copyright owners and of the public interest in having 'fair use' access to copyrighted works (Schneider and Henten, 2005). The changes to copyright that are deemed to be universally necessary to extend the law for the era of the Internet and digital content were negotiated and laid down in the 1996 World Intellectual Property Organisation (WIPO) Copyright Treaty (WCT) and the WIPO Performances and Phonograms Treaty (WPPT) – the so-called 'Internet' Treaties. They required national legislatures bring in measures to incorporate the following into their copyright law: a new exclusive right in favour of copyright owners, including sound recording producers and performers, for making their works available online to the public (known as the 'making available right'); prohibiting the circumvention of technical means of protection (known as technological protection measures, TPMs); and prohibiting tampering with DRM.

In Europe, the EU signed the WIPO Internet Treaties on behalf of its member states and subsequently issued Directive 2001/29/EC *On the harmonisation of certain aspects of copyright and related rights in the information society*, the so-called 'Copyright Directive' (EC 2001) requiring member states to reform their national copyright laws to comply with the Directive and the WIPO Treaties. Consequently, all EU states now have these features incorporated in their laws. Some of these features, however, have been controversial, even among those individuals and groups who in general support the principle of copyright (and there are those who do not). Many are concerned about the potential restriction of 'fair use' limitations and the 'locking up' of works in the public domain that DRM and TPMs could bring about. The concern is that the law can be used to promote monopoly control that exceeds that needed solely to protect copyright: a case in point is the lock-in of iPod and later iPhone to iTunes using FairPlay copy protection (Stross, 2007). Moreover, some are concerned that DRM and TPMs are included in copyright law at all since they are means rather than ends and have nothing to do with author's rights. On the other hand, firms in the media industries, especially the sound recording and film industries, argue that without such measures they cannot develop online services that offer legal alternatives to music and film piracy.

The impact of the Internet on copyright law

These issues again raise the question of whether the advent of the Internet and digitalisation, two sides of the same coin in this context, is unprecedented in its impact or whether it is not just another step along the road of technical progress that, in this arena, began with the invention of the printing press and has simply gathered speed. Digital technologies have made considerable changes to the economics of the media content industries. They enable creators to produce multiple perfect copies of the master copy at very low cost. They also enable users to quickly reproduce copies at a very low cost once they have purchased the necessary equipment (computers, camcorders, DVD players, CD burners, digital cameras and the rest) that are available at prices easily affordable by a majority of families in most developed countries. Any digital material that is published, legally or not, on the Internet can be copied more or less speedily with broadband connections for the copiers' own use or for that of others. What is different in this world from the former one – that of VCRs and photocopiers – is that it is not only much faster and cheaper to copy but it is also possible to upload and distribute works that have been copied. And once a copy is 'out there', anyone can copy it. Property laws can only be implemented with fences to keep trespassers out and copyright can only be implemented with something – at present TPMs – fencing it in.

Thus, we may say that the Internet has presented a strong challenge to copyright law, one it has met by extending the same principles but doing so possibly in ways that change the nature of the long-established fundamental freedom to use protected works for private purposes; TPMs may also effectively extend the duration of copyright if works in the public domain are delivered in digital form packaged with protected works. It is widely held that the duration of copyright is a trade-off between the period of protection needed to provide an incentive to create and distribute content and the cost to users that this imposed by the copyright, which inevitably increases with the duration of the term. Private digital copying, however, challenges the economic viability of content creators unless some further measure of protection is adopted. It is too easy to evade the law and too difficult and expensive to pursue all offenders to be able to enforce copyright law. The problem society has to face is the age-old one perceived by the economic interpretation of copyright: finding the balance between incentives to authors to create and publishers to market their works and the public interest in having access to those works. The laws mandated by the 'Internet Treaties' place what many people feel is excessive trust in DRM that is not fully proven and not yet standardised. We may ask if emphasis in the law on DRM and TPMs is the best way to do it and whether some copyright holders, such as multi-national media conglomerates, are not in a better position to not only gain from the law but to lobby for stricter legislation.

There seems to be no simple solution to the problem of how to encourage creativity when one click can send an author or performers' work all over the globe in a split second. Copyright is, after all, a system for getting users to finance creativity. For some, rewards can be appropriated indirectly: free distribution of your music can act as advertising for your concerts at which you can exclude anyone who does not want to pay for entrance, but that does not apply to other artists; writers, for example, do not have such means available. However, strong enforcement may invade privacy and alienate and criminalise ordinary people, most problematically children. This could have a greater social cost than is gained by the copyright incentive and protection of authors. These are the difficult social choices that digitalisation and the Internet in combination with copyright law present to national governments everywhere. Copyright law seems to be one area in which the Internet has had a notable impact.

Conclusions

From the above analysis of these three areas of policy, it appears that the Internet presents a major challenge to traditional approaches to securing media pluralism and diversity and to protecting the creation and distribution of media content. Digital convergence makes it harder to sustain existing mechanisms for delivering public service broadcasting and for applying competition and content rules designed to facilitate the expression of a range of voices and perspectives. Yet it is equally clear that the Internet has had a discursive as much as a material impact on policy and that it has been used as an excuse for a broad range of liberalising and re-regulatory measures that are reshaping the current media environment. So while broadband is highlighted as an innate source of pluralism – lowering costs of market entry, facilitating new sources of news and information, generally increasing competition and minimising monopoly concerns, there is less detail about the precise ways in which the Internet requires significant policy shifts.

For example, while the EC justified its revision of the TVF Directive with reference to the impact of the Internet on a changing broadcasting ecology, many of the EC's subsequent documents on audio-visual policy and the Directive barely mention the Internet, convergence, nor broadband and are much more concerned by the challenge to terrestrial television presented by digital, satellite and cable systems. The UK communications regulator Ofcom, in its phase two review of public service broadcasting (Ofcom, 2004) argues for new broadcasting structures and modes of finance because of the declining value of analogue spectrum and the prospect of digital switchover. Yet, the Internet features in this argument as only one part of a broader *digital* challenge to current forms of regulation and governance alongside mobile telephony, PVRs and cable and satellite systems.

None of this is terribly surprising. That emerging communication technologies like digital platforms and the Internet are not able to escape entrenched economic problems affecting other media technologies has been long predicted. Writing in 1997, the economist Andrew Graham argued that the Internet, despite its public origins and pluralistic tendencies, was likely to be absorbed into corporate structures and governed by commercial logic. High-quality multimedia content, he argued, shares the same tendencies as other forms of media content in that: 'it is expensive to produce in the first place and yet, once commissioned and created, relatively cheap to edit or to change and trivially cheap to reproduce' (Graham, 1997: 16). He concluded that Internet content: 'has high fixed costs and low marginal costs – and these are the natural creators of monopolies' (ibid). Digital technologies, far from undermining the need for regulation, pose three specific problems for public policy (Graham in Seaton, 1998):

- an intensification of economies of scale and the emergence of new types of scarcity (of talent) and monopoly (bottlenecks controlled by private suppliers);
- an intensification of economies of scope because of convergence and cross-promotion; and
- economic benefits of being in a network leading to further concentration and not 'a world of free competition'. (33)

It seems rather obvious after all that if we are still committed to policy objectives concerning innovation, creativity, pluralism and diversity, then there is little point in junking the traditional mechanisms for achieving these outcomes simply because we are faced with *different* technologies. As Gibbons points out (2000: 312): 'the public interest in media activity is not rendered less relevant by the media's form'.

Conclusions about the revolutionary power of the Internet are, therefore, politically and economically driven rather than the inevitable result of technological innovation. Perhaps we should not be asking about the impact of the Internet on traditional media but about the relevance or resilience of existing media structures as well as policy approaches on the development of the Internet. As Robert McChesney argues:

To the extent that the Internet is incorporated into the overall media system, traditional media policies governing that system will go a long way toward shaping the Internet as well. Which is another way of saying that policies surrounding media ownership and support for public media will be central to determining the future of the Internet (McChesney, 2004: 224).

References

Anonymous (2006). 'YouTube: a quick profit, an opportunity and possible problems for copyright owners', *Music & Copyright* No 330 October 25, 2006 Informa Publishing, London 2006.

Anonymous (2007). 'Sex sell, but maybe not for Blue Ray', News Feed Researcher 14 January 2007. Available at http://newsfeedresearcher.com/data/articles_t3/idt2007.01.14.12.26.20.html (accessed on 27 January 2007).

Bakker, P. (2005). 'File-sharing – fight, ignore or compete: Paid download services vs. P2P-network'. *Telematics and Informatics* 22 (1–2); 41–55.

Blomqvist, U. et al. (2005). Broadband technologies transforming business models and challenging regulatory frameworks – lessons from the music industry, Music Lessons project, KTH, Stockholm, available at http://w1.nada.kth.se/media/Research/MusicLessons/Reports/MusicLessons-DL2.pdf (accessed 24 February 2006).

Burgelman, J.C. (2000). 'Regulating access in the information society: the need for rethinking public and universal service', *New Media & Society* 2(1): 51–66.

Collins, R. and Murroni, C. (1996). *New Media, New Policies*. Cambridge: Polity.

Congdon, T. (1995). 'The Multimedia Revolution and the Open Society' in T. Congdon et al., *The Cross Media Revolution: Ownership and Control*. Luton: John Libbey: 11–24.

Coonan, H. (2005). 'The New Multimedia World', Address to the National Press Club, Canberra, 31 August 2005.

Council of Europe (1990). 'The role of communications technologies in the safeguarding and enhancing of European unity and cultural diversity', COM (90)1a, Strasbourg, 7 August.

DTI/DCMS (2000). *A New Future for Communications*, communications white paper. London: DTI/DCMS.

DTI/DCMS (2001). Consultation on Media Ownership Rules. London: DTI/DCMS.

EC Directive (1992). On Rental Right and Lending Right and on Certain Rights Related to Copyright in the Field of Intellectual Property. Luxembourg. 92/100/EEC.

EC (1994). *Europe and the Global Information Society, The Bangemann Report*. Brussels: European Commission.

EC (1997). *Green Paper on the convergence of the telecommunications, media and information technology sectors and the implications for regulation – towards an information society approach* COM(97)623, available at http://aei.pitt.edu/1160/01/telecom_convergence_gp_COM_97_623.pdf (accessed 24 February 2006).

EC (2000). *Statement of Objections, Case COMP/M.1852, Merger Procedure*. Brussels: DG Internal Market.

EC (2001). *Directive 2001/29/EC on the harmonisation of certain aspects of copyright and related rights in the information society*, Brussels.

EC (2003a). *New Regulatory Framework for electronic communications infrastructure and associated services*, available at http://europa.eu.int/information_society/topics/telecoms/regulatory/new_rf/index_en.htm.

EC (2003b). *The Future of European Audiovisual Regulatory Policy*, COM(2003) 784 Final, available at http://europa.eu.int/eur-lex/en/com/cnc/2003/com2003_0784en01.pdf.

EC (2004a) *Statement of Objections, COMP/M.3333 (Sony/BMG), D/202145*, 24 May. Brussels: Competition Directorate.

EC (2004b). *Commission Decision, COMP/M.3333 (Sony/BMG) C(2004) 2815*, 19 July. Brussels: Competition Directorate.

EC (2005). *Liverpool – Final report of the working group 1: Rules applicable to audio-visual content services*, September (available at http://www.europa.eu.int/comm/avpolicy/revision-tvwf2005/2005-conference.htm).

Farchy, J. and Rochelandet, F. (2002). Copyright protection, appropriability and new cultural behaviour. In Ruth Towse (Ed.) *Copyright in the Cultural Industries*, Cheltenham: Edward Elgar.

Freedman, D. (1996). 'Political Consensus on the Information Superhighway', *Communications: The European Journal of Communication Research*, 21(3), 273–290

Garnham, N. (1998). 'Media policy'. In A. Briggs and P. Cobley (Eds) *The Media: An Introduction*. London: Longman.

Gibbons, T. (2000). 'Pluralism and the New Media'. In C. Marsden (Ed.) *Regulating the Global Information Society*. London: Routledge.

Gore, A. (1994) Speech to the International Telecommunications Union, Buenos Aires, 24 March, available at http://www.goelzer.net/telecom/al-gore.html (accessed 24 March 2006).

Gowers, A. (2006). *Gowers Review of Intellectual Property*, London: The Stationery Office. http://www.hm-treasury.gov.uk/media/583/91/pbr06_gowers_report_755.pdf

Graham, A. and Davies, G. (1997). *Broadcasting, Society and Policy in the Multimedia Age*. Luton: John Libbey.

Graham, A. (1998). 'Broadcasting policy and the digital revolution'. In J. Seaton (Ed.), *Politics and the media : harlots and prerogatives at the turn of the millennium*. Oxford: Blackwell.

Hutchison, D. (1999). *Media Policy: An Introduction*. Oxford: Blackwell.

Stross ,R. (2007).'Copy protections handcuffs music buyers'. *International Herald Tribune International Herald Tribune*, 15 January.

Koelman, K. (2004). 'Copyright Law and Economics in the Copyright Directive: is the Droit d' Auteur Passe?'. *International Review of Intellectual Property and Competition Law*, 6; 603–38.

Leadbeater, C. (1999). *Living on Thin Air*. Harmondsworth: Penguin.

McChesney, R. (2004). *The Problem of the Media: U.S. Communications Politics in the 21st Century*. New York: Monthly Review Press.

McQuail, D. (1992). *Media Performance*. London: Sage.

Monti, M. (2004). 'Access to content and the development of competition in the New Media Market – the Commission's Approach', Speech 04/353, Brussels, 8 July, available at http://www.ebu.ch/CMSimages/en/BRUDOC_INFO_EN_135_MONTI_SPEECH-04-353_EN_tcm6-13650.pdf.

Murdoch, J. (2005). Speech to the 2005 European Audio Visual Conference, Liverpool, 21 September, available at http://www.culture.gov.uk/about_dcms/eupresidency2005/broadcasting.htm#documents (accessed 18 October 2005).

Napoli, P. (2001). *Foundations of Communications Policy*. Creskill, NJ: Hampton Press.

Negroponte, N. (1995). *Being Digital*. London: Hodder and Stoughton.

Ofcom (2004) *Ofcom review of public service television broadcasting*, phase 2. London: Ofcom, available at http://www.ofcom.org.uk.

Powell, M. (2003). 'Should limits on broadcast ownership change?' *USA Today*, 21 January, available at http://www.usatoday.com/news/opinion/editorials/2003-01-21-powell_x.htm.

Quah, D. (1996). *The invisible hand and the weightless economy*. London: Centre for Economic Performance, London School of Economics.

Schneider, M. and Henten, A. (2005). 'DRMS, TCP and the EUCD: technology and law'. *Telematics and Informatics* 22 (1–2) 25–39. Tunstall, J. (1977). *The Media Are American*. London: Constable.

Towse, R. (2001). *Creativity, Incentive and Reward: an economic analysis of copyright and culture in the information age*, Cheltenham, UK and Northeampton Mass., USA, Edward Elgar Publishing.

Wallis, R. (1998). 'The Bumpy Road towards Convergence'. In R. Picard (ed.) *Evolving Media Markets: Effects of Economic and Policy Changes*. Turku: Turku School of Economics.

Warner Music Group (2007) 'Statement regarding Potential Warner Music Group Corp. Proposal to Acquire EMI Group plc' February 20th 2007 http://www.wmg.com/news/article/?id=8a0af81210c2b40b0110df66b1ed2939 (accessed on 25th February, 2007).

Williams, G. (2005). What is the *Television Without Frontiers* Directive? *Free Press*, October.

7

THE IMPACT OF THE INTERNET ON MEDIA ORGANISATION STRATEGIES AND STRUCTURES

Lucy Küng, Nikos Leandros, Robert G. Picard, Roland Schroeder and Richard van der Wurff

This chapter explores the effect on the Internet on organisations in the media sector from the perspective of theories of strategy and organisation. By extension its focus is the media organisation itself, specifically the inter-related phenomena of strategy, structure, processes and business models. As such it covers a terrain that is at once very broad and also very fragmented, and full analysis of each of these issues and their inter-relationships is not feasible. The chapter, therefore, explores broad generic developments common to all sectors and affecting all organisations in them to varying degrees.

Incumbent versus insurgent – different contexts, different challenges

An important distinction in management theory is between incumbent, or established, organisations and new firms (insurgents as they were called at the height of the first dotcom boom). One reason for this is that the internal and external contexts implicit in these two contrasting situations give rise to different management priorities. Chief among these is that incumbent firms must not only develop an appropriate response to a changing strategic environment, but also find a way of implementing this and circumventing the hurdles presented by 'legacy' systems and processes. A book exploring the impact of the Internet on the existing mass media will inevitably have as its focus the established media firm.

First Internet era

The chapter, therefore, distinguishes between incumbent and new organisations, unavoidably focussing on the former. It draws a second important distinction, between the first Internet era, characterised by a breathless enthusiasm and predictions of profound transformation, and the second Internet era, which with far less fanfare, is quietly bringing the extreme changes promised by the first.

The first Internet era took place roughly between 1995 and 2001. Although it dates back to the late 1960s, the Internet developed into a mass medium in the mid-1990s, once the related developments such as the Web, Netscape Navigator and affordable home PCs (see Chapter 2 for discussion of these factors) rendered it useable by the general population. Thereafter, it became the world's fastest-growing communications medium (US Department of Commerce, 1998).

The arrival of the Internet placed incumbents under a pressure to move online that with hindsight appears extreme. A major cause was the financial markets' enthusiasm for the Internet sector. From the mid-1990s to the early 2000, very high valuations were placed on Internet-businesses, especially content-related ones. This led shareholders and executives, on the one hand worried by predictions of the death of their existing businesses, and on the other thrilled by the high valuations placed on the 'dotcoms', to push for a move into Internet and e-commerce. Another factor driving incumbents into the Internet field was a belief that the Internet domain was characterised by significant order of entry advantages. It was commonly held that 'first movers' would develop impregnable market leadership positions (often based on network externalities) that later entrants would never be able to emulate. As a result the Internet became a strategic priority for incumbent media firms, and many made very significant financial commitments to the field (for example, in the first quarter of 2000, Reuters announced budgeted investments of £500 million over the next four years, Reed Elsevier £600–700 million over the next three years and BSkyB £250 million over the next 18 months).

From a management perspective, the Internet created a new strategic environment that emerged and usurped the existing one with surprising speed. Environmental change is not new for the media industries. The sector owes its existence to technological advance, and from the 1980s onwards it had been confronted with a number of developments that have necessitated strategic adaptation – the introduction of the CD-Rom, of new transmission technologies such as cable and satellite, a gradual shift from collective to individual payment systems for broadcasting, the gradual adoption of PC-based content production methods and so on. But from a strategic perspective each of these developments constituted incremental changes to the status quo. Satellite and cable were new distribution systems for existing programming formats. PC-based production techniques presented new ways to produce existing media products such as books, magazines and newspapers. As a result, although these developments amounted to significant alternation for the industry, the environment remained what strategists would term 'mature'.

Mature contexts are characterised by slow growth, intense competition between a known group of players, and knowledgeable customers (Porter, 1980). The Internet created an 'emergent' strategic environment. Such environments are typical to the high-tech or biotech industries and are characterised by high levels of uncertainty: industry boundaries are unclear, business models evolve rapidly, consumer preferences are unknown and competition comes from hitherto unknown players (Eisenhardt and Brown, 1998; Robins and Wierserma, 1999). Emergent contexts present a complex management challenge, particularly for incumbents encumbered by legacy systems and processes.

Strategic responses to first Internet era

The established media organisations came under heavy fire during the first Internet era, accused of failing to appreciate the potential of the new media at first, and then of reacting too slowly and too cautiously once they had. This had serious ramifications. The stock price of Reuters, a blue chip European media company, plummeted when its CEO admitted the company had no Internet strategy (a reason for the subsequent major investment described earlier in this chapter). The share price of Time Warner, the world's largest media organisation that owned some of the best-known brands in the industry, including *Time* magazine, Warner Bros music company and CNN, fell dramatically when it's Internet strategy collapsed. This led it to be acquired in 2000 by AOL, an Internet service provider whose share price was soaring.

For incumbents, the Internet was challenging the very fabric of the media world they knew. The value of their 'old' media assets had fallen dramatically. Like Time Warner, their depressed share prices made them vulnerable to acquisition by Internet companies with high valuations (Google and Yahoo were the most feared predators, and their names were regularly linked with old media 'brides' in the business and financial press).

Incumbents' hesitation about the Internet was understandable. They had reservations about cannibalising their core cash-flow-generating businesses by making their media products available free of charge on the Internet. For European media businesses the fragmentation of the advertising and retail markets complicated pan-European offerings and constrained network effects and first mover advantages. The corporate structure of many family owned or privately controlled media companies prevented them from offering the stock options that were important to attracting talent.

However, the Internet also offered strategic advantages. The AOL/Time Warner merger had demonstrated the potential that might result from the combination of content and distribution. Rapid advances in digital transmission systems for cable, satellite and terrestrial television as well as high-speed telecoms links using DSL technologies meant that opportunities for rapid digital download of media content were increasing.

The Internet, therefore, offered a 'carrot and stick' inducement to incumbent media firms. This combination, coupled with the new medium's inescapable momentum, led once hesitant incumbents to move with surprising speed and verve into the online world (Waters, 1999; Harding, 2 February 2000), giving rise to a radical series of strategic reorientations. Below, the Internet responses of the then four of the biggest media organisations – Bertelsmann, Disney, Time Warner and Vivendi – are summarised.

Three aspects of these strategies are notable. First, they were not natural extensions of current activities, but rather new strategic paths that brought them out of known sectors into emergent ones, out of the media industries into neighbouring sectors of IT, telecoms and consumer electronics. They, therefore, provide some evidence of convergence. The second is the lack of success of these strategies, despite the high strategic priority placed on them, the calibre of advice these organisations sought in drawing up these strategies (these organisations were advised by leading management consultancies) and the attendant resource commitments made. Third is the high turnover of chief executives, partly as a result of these strategies. By the end of 2002 three of the CEOs discussed here had lost their positions (Bertelsmann's Thomas Middelhof, Time Warner's Gerald Levin and Vivendi Universal's Jean Marie Messier, not to mention Steve Case, Chairman of AOL Time Warner).

Bertelsmann

The Internet led to a major strategic reorientation for Bertelsmann. The conglomerate set itself the ambitious goal of becoming the number one Internet player in the media industries. It planned to do this by dominating three levels of Internet activity – content businesses, portals and direct-to-customer sales businesses.

To realise this strategy Bertelsmann both developed internally, and acquired externally a range of Internet businesses (primarily in e-commerce). These were concentrated in a new division, the 'Direct Group'. The Direct Group businesses included Bertelsmann's stake in AOL Europe, BOL.com – a European online book and music retailer, CDNow.com – a US online music retailer, Barnes&Noble.com – an online bookseller – and Getmusic.com – a joint venture with Vivendi Universal.It also, controversially, rescued the disputed music downloading site Napster from bankruptcy, intending to use this as the kernel of an online music subscription service.

Overall, this strategy was not successful. The DirectGroup sustained $123 million in Internet start-up losses in second half of 2001[1], and lost a further $125 million in first half of 2002, although this poor financial performance was alleviated by the sale of its 50 per cent stake in AOL Europe back to its parent company at the height of the Internet bubble for $9.12 billion, generating $7 billion cash. Its Internet activities were folded back into the core businesses. CEO Thomas Middelhof left in July 2002, although this appears to have been due to a combination of factors. His expensive and unsuccessful Internet forays played a role, but so too did conflicts with the owning family over his leadership style and desires to take Bertelsmann public.

Disney

Like Time Warner (see below) Disney was an Internet pioneer, launching two of the first branded consumer websites, ESPN.com and Disney.com, in 1995, and establishing ABC.com in 1999. Disney's stated online strategy was to use the strength of the Disney brand to draw consumers to these sites, generating revenues from advertising sales and transaction fees. Intended transactions included sales of Disney's extensive merchandise lines, subscriptions to online magazines and tickets to theme parks[2].

A major strategic move came in 1998 when Disney bought a majority stake in Infoseek.com, a portal. This was followed by outright purchase of the site in 1999. Disney then consolidated Infoseek with its other Internet sites into a new 'umbrella-site' portal which it called Go.com. Go.com failed to reach Disney's strategic objectives and was closed in 2001 at cost of $862 million[3], at which point the various Internet businesses were reintegrated into the parent.

Time Warner

Ironically, in view of the fact that its subsequent merger with AOL was the result of its lack of Internet activities, Time Warner was one of the first of the media majors to embrace the Internet. In 1994 it created Pathfinder.com, an umbrella-site that consolidated all the various sites that had been created for its content properties, particularly for magazine titles. Pathfinder never became a success and the site was closed finally in 2001. This failure was attributed to a combination of being too early a mover (before mass market adoption of the Internet) and an ill-judged branding strategy (using a new name, Pathfinder, rather than those of its existing media products).

Time Warner's lack of Internet presence created pressure from the financial markets, and was a major contributory factor in its being taken over by (or merged with, depending on perspective) AOL in 2000. The strategy was to create a hybrid old and new 'converged' media firm that allowed media products to sold across as many platforms as possible. AOL Time Warner failed to realise this strategy and in 2002 a $45 billion goodwill write-down led to the largest corporate loss ever of $98.7 billion.[4] Chief architect of the merger from the Time Warner side, Gerald Levin retired a year early in April 2002, and his counterparts on the AOL side, Steve Case (Chairman) and Bob Pitman (COO) both resigned in 2003.

Vivendi Universal

Vivendi's strategy for the Internet was dramatic and far-reaching. It sought to unite a combination of communication (rather than simply media) infrastructures (telephones, Internet, television) with a varied range of content (images, sound, information, services) in a single firm. Vivendi concentrated its Internet activities in a new division, Vivendi Universal Net umbrella division. This housed Vizzavi (a multi access portal which was a joint venture with Vodaphone), MP3.com and Education.com.

Like its peers, Vivendi had little success with its ambitious Internet plan. CEO Jean-Marie Messier lost his job in 2002 and left a €19 billion debt, the largest loss in French corporate history. A subsequent liquidity crisis led to a $16 billion disposal programme, which involved unwinding many of the assets acquired from 2000–2002[5].

Strategic responses to the second Internet era

With hindsight, these strategies were dramatic responses to a dramatic context. The collapse of the dotcom economy, combined with a steady progress in Internet penetration, provided incumbents with an opportunity to reflect on the recent past and develop more measured responses to the rapidly maturing medium the Internet represented.

However, it was nonetheless clear that despite the cooling of the initial Internet frenzy, the new medium was bringing fundamental and irreversible change for the media industries. The Internet as a media and communications medium was becoming part of the fabric of life for more and more of the population, and its disruptive force, while no longer a subject for newspaper headlines and industry conferences, was becoming more pronounced and irreversible. As penetration of broadband and wireless technologies continued, as file sharing and digital downloading markets matured, as participatory and peer-content sites became more mainstream, mass media firms began to recognise that the long-term erosion of traditional media products by new media ones was inevitable (Picard, 2003).

The second Internet era saw the established media industries finally adjusting to the Internet as a fact of life. Dedicated 'online' units became closer and closer to core activities, and in many companies the distinction evaporated entirely. An increasing number of content creators worked for offline and online products at the same time and without complaint. Those within media firms came to see offline and online as synergistic, rather than competing spaces.

Media firms developed different types of strategic responses to the second Internet era. Two stand out in particular – coopetition and cross-media strategies.

Coopetition strategy

Developments of new types of media and content services have lead many firms to engage in cooperative ventures rather than to maintain independent activities. This type of activity – called coopetition – involves business arrangements and strategies in which rival companies that normally compete establish cooperative activities through alliances, partnerships, sharing arrangements and networks. It is based on the view that competitors need not always fail for others to be successful and is a voluntary action based on common interests and desires to share mutual benefits (Brandenburger & Nalebuff, 1996). Coopetition creates cooperation in some activities while maintaining competition in others.

Coopetition stabilises competition by differentiation and niche recognition, by seeking organisational effectiveness through flexibility, adaptation and limiting expenditures, by seeking to improve the positions of cooperators against a common threat or in exploring a risky opportunity. It is most likely to develop when profits are decreasing when the participants' markets are stagnant or decreasing and when new activities for each firm are involved. Coopetition presents a means of achieving benefits of synergies without acquisition of competitors or heavy investments in joint ventures, typically by using existing resources that require little reconfiguration or upgrading, and by providing the ability to share media platforms without conflicting with ownership policies and law. Such synergies are being sought in the coopetition in local classified advertising between Yahoo! and 176 US newspapers begun in 2006. Yahoo! is providing technology that allows advertising placed in the papers to also appear on the portal's classified sites and the newspapers' own sites, with the Internet firm and papers splitting revenues.

Its primary advantages are risk reduction, cost savings, asset sharing, access to learning without making significant investments and increasing the speed of learning and product development. Disadvantages include the potential for knowledge and skill gaps among partners, organisational resistance, poor integration of the activities involved in coopetition and the potential for poor returns or financial losses.

When coopetition is involved, strategic clarity must surround the purposes and goals of the joint activity and the amount of involvement and effort to be included. Transactional issues involving the contractual bases for the cooperation and the extent to which exclusivity is involved must be determined. Companies engaged in coopetition must solve a variety of operational issues involving the nature of their individual contributions, types of resources involved and how they are shared, the extent to which different types of information will be exchanged and a variety of challenges related to trust, coordination and incentives for collaboration (Bamford, 2002; Falk & De Rond, 2002; Segil, 2002).

Companies engaged in coopetition need to work to maintain competition in areas of core competency and value creation and seek joint activities involving areas in which the firms are not strongly competitive. Typically, one partner must have strong needs that promote the coopetition and geographical proximity is needed if physical exchanges are involved. Ultimately, the results of the coopetition should lower the financial risks of individual action and improve the activities of both firms and fit within their activities.

Because coopetition involves outside parties, the extent to which the individual parties control the joint activities are limited and there is a need to continually build and maintain common ground and common goals. It is also important for participating parties to continually evaluate the effectiveness of the arrangement and to ensure that the incentives to participate remain in place.

Although coopetition presents organisation challenges, it permits organisational learning, reduces investments and competition, avoids the unprofitable dividing up of a small emerging between among dominant players, helps avoid the winner-takes-all risks inherent in direct competition in emerging activities and creates win-win situations through cooperative advantages.

Cross-media strategies

The development of the Internet and its adoption by mass media organisations as a new means of reaching audiences has led many companies to believe that synergistic advantages will be produced through cross-media activities – that is, exploiting content assets across as many platforms as possible, but in particular offline and online. The logic is that these centrally coordinated activities will produce greater added value than separate independent activities, that systemic effects from coordination and fusion of activities will reduce costs and increase revenues, and that shared resources and knowledge and competence transfer among the operations will produce additional benefits.

The economic advantage from cross-media activities stems from the additional use of existing content that creates scale economies and better average costs for their use, from transaction cost reductions arising from the simplification and reduction of the costs of the acquisition of content and other resources, and from economies of scope produced by leveraging the market recognition of established firms so that lower marketing expenses are required for new activities, by exploiting existing audience and advertiser relationships and by creating opportunities for additional revenue without the concurrent need for full resources required by independent creation and distribution.

However, the benefits derived from cross-media activities are constrained because these tend to be greatest at firm level rather than business unit level, and thus corporate owners and corporate centre managers gain more advantages than do divisional and business unit level managers.

Cross-media activities also make strategy development and implementation more complex, giving rise to tensions concerning where to locate activities within the company structure (see below), in terms of authority and control issues, and of establishing incentives and benefits to business units. All of these factors reduce the benefits flowing from cross-media strategies, since as the complexity increases, so too does internal resistance, inefficiencies and the increased costs of coordination due to expenses of linking and coordinating a number of different systems and additional managerial time and effort.

This problem is illustrated in what seems to be the simple question of where online activities should reside within a company. In addition to the 'meta-level' strategic issues discussed above, there are significant challenges from a cross-media perspective because business units have their own interests, strategies, priorities and control desires and make their own investments/divestments. These problems are compounded because reward systems are based on divisional or business unit performance and there are difficulties in evaluating their actual contributions to cross-media synergies. This leads to increased conflict within the organisation and the need to create better and new conflict resolution methods. In addition, issues of company culture and desire to engage in cross-media activities may affect the decision of where to locate the operations.

The issues of authority, strategy, coordination, incentives become even more complex when subsidiary companies or unaffiliated companies are involved – for example, joint venture partners. Such external cross-media activities can raise strategic difficulties; purposes, goals and levels of involvement can differ. There can be transactional challenges arising from the contractual bases of the relationship and issues around the exclusivity of content. Operational issues such as levels of contributions and resource sharing among the parties, information exchange and constraints, degree of content exchange, competitive distrust, coordination methods and staff incentives can also pose significant challenges.

Because of the challenges of operating both internal and external cross-media activities, it appears that such activities create advantages for well-established, dominant players with high incumbent advantages. These have the ability to rapidly deploy cross-media products, to use proprietary content assets, to leverage existing brands and customer relationships and to make investments in coordination and management that are necessary. Opportunities for new players are limited to a few-well funded entrants. Smaller existing media firms without the advantages of larger firms must generally confine their cross-media activities to local or niche markets. These factors create a tendency for cross-media operations to extend the dominance of leading players in print and broadcasting, thus increasing concentration and market power, and to lead to joint activities among competitors that raise issues of market power and collusion. This process is illustrated by *Financial Times Deutschland*, which is using its strength in print financial news to provide financial news to dozens of radio stations, as well as to operate a financial news website and to provide mobile phone news services and news notification services.

The requirements and effects of cross-media activities lead to the question of how cross-media activity will alter the structure of the media industries over time. If one considers the development of the computer industry, it was characterised by a vertical industry structure with integrated product architecture and production until the mid-1980s when modularisation of production became the norm and created a horizontal industry structure. Today, media industries tend to have vertical organisation patterns, but cross-activities are leading to a modularisation of production and other media activities. This has the potential to produce a horizontal industry structure in the future that would significantly alter existing structures and relationships.

The issue of the how the Internet affects the strategies of incumbent media firms then must be understood within its broader context of how it affects internal and external organisation structures, operations and relations, and how it will affect overall industry structure in the long-term. Because the Internet has been having significant effects for only a decade, it is not possible fully and conclusively to document all its organisational effects, but the experience of the decade indicates that effective operations require organisational change and restructuring. These changes are more significant for some types of media than for others, for companies that already operate in many media fields than those that are more focussed, for companies of different sizes and for companies with differing internal structures. These structural changes are the subject of the next section of this chapter.

Structural changes

That the Internet is changing the structure of media firms is indisputable, but the changes underway display a wide degree of variation. While it is hard to make conclusive observations, it is clear that large, vertically integrated, hierarchically managed structures are coming under pressure. It is also clear that there is no single solution concerning the most appropriate organisational form in the mass media industries as they go forward in the second Internet era. The emerging strategic environment presents the media organisation with a number of competing requirements: for speed and flexibility *and* economies of scale and scope, for first mover versus incumbency advantages, for in-house activities versus outsourced and for integration and control versus separation and autonomy. The resolution of these dilemmas is a central task for strategy-makers.

In classic management theory, structures provide a means of anchoring core processes into the wider organisation and for the parts of an organisation to relate to each other. The structure of an organisation also represents one aspect of its response to its internal and external environment. Since environments are far from static, this process is continuous and restructuring is likewise a continuous process.

The emergence of the Internet, and closely interrelated developments such as digitalisation and new distribution platforms, have given rise to a broad span of alterations to the structure of media firms, including alliances, mergers, acquisitions, spin-offs and the creation of network structures. These developments are not mutually exclusive: a media organisation can acquire one company, establish a number of alliances, spin off a division operating in a new area and be networked into other key players in the media and related sectors; nonetheless, this chapter will attempt to disentangle these developments and explore each in turn.

Alliances and partnerships

Strategic alliances are normally understood as cooperative arrangements between two or more potentially competitive firms, but the term can encompass many different types of inter-organisational arrangement ranging from strategic link-ups between major players (for example, the Sony-BMG joint venture), to short-term partnerships (such as the BBC's fleeting link up with Yahoo! to supply Internet news content for mobile devices) (alliances can be used as a test phase for a full merger or acquisition).

Alliances are a well-established tool for strategic growth in the media industries. For example, the globalisation process that has been ongoing in the television industry since the mid-1980s was achieved in large part through numerous cross-border collaborations involving financing, production, distribution and programme formats.

Alliances are also a long-standing tool used in the technology and communications sectors, where the size, scope and complexity of the fast-changing landscape mean that no single organisation, however substantial and well-resourced, can ever hope to track all developments or cover all options. As with other phenomena described in this chapter, the media industries' increasing shift towards alliance-based growth echoes an established pattern in technology markets. As noted above, such structures are well-suited to the media industries, which have a long tradition of alliance-based work and a good understanding of working within such structures.

The new technical possibilities to produce different media formats from one single data source and the increasing use of a common infrastructure for the distribution of content across different channels have on the one hand spurred merger and acquisition activity, but on the other led to a ubiquitous trend for collaborative structures of all types, including international partnerships. Cross-border acquisitions or link ups with companies with local market knowledge have been common over the past years and many media companies now have publications, other media outlets, content producing companies and various other activities in different countries (Chan-Olmsted & Albarran, 1998; Chan-Olmsted & Chang, 2003; Hollifield, 2004). A particular hallmark of alliances during the first Internet era was their transitory nature. Many were informal and open-ended agreements which disintegrated almost as quickly as they were established. These arrangements, known as 'alliances du jour', were in essence low commitment vehicles for tentative business development.

Inter-organisational partnerships have been found to be the preferred strategy for entering the Internet, broadband or wireless market (Chan-Olmsted and Kang 2003). These moves are driven by a variety of motives, including gaining access to competencies, expertise, talent, knowledge and technologies, to achieve faster market entry, to reduce the risk entailed with experimental new products or services, to reduce entry barriers (for example, the need for strong brands or to achieve scale economies) or to defray the cost of significant content investments. An alliance can also serve as a precursor to a full-blown acquisition or merger.

While many alliances are between actors in the media industries, there are also numerous examples of inter-organisational ventures between players in converging sectors (for example, CBS' project to distribute old episodes of television programmes via Google). Thus, the trend towards alliances in the media sector arising from the emergence of the Internet can be viewed as furthering the process of convergence between this and the neighbouring industries of telecoms, information technology and consumer electronics.

While the logic behind an alliance may be straightforward, they can be extremely challenging to manage. A high profile example of this is the 50/50 joint venture between Sony's recorded music business and that of Bertelsmann. This partnership was a response to the intense pressure of music sales and the growth of digital downloading and file-swapping on the Internet. This did allow some savings through combining duplicated activities, but these were outweighed by legal costs, accounting charges and operating profits declined overall. Specific problem areas included disagreements over leadership, cultural tensions and different performance targets on the part of the parents.

Networks

When an organisation is involved in many alliances with different partners, a network structure can emerge. This is not a new development for the media: Hollywood has operated on the basis of co-dependent systems where films have been created by assemblies of independent talent (actors, screenwriters, producers, directors, etc.) since the break up of the studio system in the 1940s. However, a gradual shift that has taken place whereby the large complex multidivisional organisations that have become the norm for the largest global media firms (Eisenmann & Bower, 2000) have become enlarged further through the addition of a rich variety of complex collaborative arrangements that allow the central media organisation to experiment or engage in activities on the fringes of its 'established' value chain, particularly outside its traditional geographic borders. These enterprises evolved from the combination of various networking strategies: the internal decentralisation of large corporations, the cooperation between SMEs, the linkage between these small and medium business networks and the strategic alliances and partnerships between large corporations and their ancillary networks (Castells, 2001). A classic example of such an arrangement, one that predated the Internet and that has now been replaced by a full merger, is the Disney-Pixar alliance which stood at the centre of a complex network structure involving partners as diverse as McDonalds and Industrial Light and Magic.

Many theorists expected that the advent of the Internet would also herald the adoption of the network as the dominant organisation form both within the media industries and in business in general. The Internet would lead to a 'de-integrating' of industrial structures, to a shift from large, complex and stable hierarchies to more flexible, fluid and laterally coordinated ones characterised by high levels of collaboration. Thus, Castells argued that traditional vertically integrated large corporations were on the wane as a default structural model and that the emergence of the Internet as a 'fundamental medium of communication and information-processing' would be the trigger for business to adopt 'the network as its organisational form' (Castells, 2001: 66), primarily because it would reduce transaction costs, boost price transparency and increase pressure to outsource activities to small and medium-sized firms that were more dynamic and innovative.

This expectation arose from the breadth and complexity of emerging media and communications industries – networks do well in complex environments. The benefits they provide relatively fast access to scare resources, capabilities, information, technologies, new markets and so on, can reduce risk and competition and allow economies of scale and scope.

Mergers and acquisitions

Mergers and acquisitions have been a familiar feature of the media industries since the 1980s and peaked around 1998 when the media sector took third place in the US M&A league tables. The key driver here was the spectre of convergence. Technological developments (the 'digital revolution'), deregulation and globalisation created to a raft of new opportunities for media organisations. These developments massively increased both the opportunities for and attractions of consolidation. Digitalisation allows different forms of media to be converted into a common format and to be moved rapidly around the globe. The convergence of the underlying technologies of telephone, computing and media created opportunities for media firms to move into new fields, and compensate for actual or anticipated decline in core businesses. Thus there were more platforms for media content, more formats into which content can be packaged, more markets in which products could be sold and new ways to deal directly with audiences/consumers worldwide, especially using Internet and telecommunications-based communication platforms. This increased a media organisation's potential for economies of scale and scope, making a global scope more feasible and financially attractive for many more media organisations (motion picture distributors and music companies had dominated the world market for decades before these technologies). The result was a wave of structural changes spanning expansion, diversification and concentration of ownership (Doyle, 2002).

It is by no means evident that the wave of horizontal, vertical and cross-industry acquisitions has benefited protagonists in all cases. Many of these organisations have found themselves over-extended and are now looking at demerger or disposals. Synergies are not easily realised and coordination is difficult to implement. Cultural and organisational conflicts within the merged companies may also appear leading to disappointing results (Ozanich & Wirth, 2004). The classic example is the AOL/Time Warner merger, discussed earlier in this chapter, which was hailed as: 'a strategic merger of equals to create the world's first fully integrated media and communications company for the Internet century in an all-stock combination valued at $350 billion dollars'.[6]

The troubles that some of the merged companies have been facing lately has led to a broad discussion about whether synergies are achievable or even desirable. Recent changes in the strategy of media giants such as Time Warner, Bertelsmann and Vivendi suggest a return to a more focussed approach and greater emphasis to flexible forms of cooperation.

Spin-offs

hardly a week goes by without news that a media company may sell shares in an online operation[7]

During the first Internet era there was a marked trend for media organisations to carve out the high-growth Internet-related activities and spin these off. In this structural option they were following the lead of the high-tech sector, where since the mid-1990s companies had divested those parts of the business that offer the greatest potential for growth, even if those divisions performed essential components of their operations. Thus, in 1996 AT&T spun off Lucent Technologies and NCR, and in 2000 its wireless activities. In the media industry, in 1998 the Fox Entertainment Group was spun off from News Corporation and Infinity Broadcasting from CBS.

The spin-off option was favoured by investors since it allowed capital markets to value the online business as a pure play. Further, it allowed the parent to capitalise on the high valuations placed on high-tech businesses, particularly internet-related ones. The returns from some of the early activities, whether in equity or cash, were spectacular. In the examples cited above, AT&T, News Corporation and CBS each acquired close to $3 billion for their spun-off divisions. Dow Jones, publisher of the *Wall Street Journal*, admitted that their decisions on whether or not spin-off the publication reseted mainly on its likely affect on valuation (Waters, 2 December 1999).

An Internet listing also provided access to a pool of cheap capital, which generated 'acquisition currency' to rival the expansionist Internet companies (Deutsche Bank, 2000) and gave incumbents the chance to make acquisitions without diluting the earnings of underlying shares. Internet equity was also important as a means to attract and reward key management and technological talent, an important consideration in view of the talent exodus from old to new economy companies. In addition, the success of the spin-off in the stock market reflected positively on the parent company's stock and there was often a surge in both prices. The newly formed company also benefited: armed with fresh capital the spin-off enjoyed the freedom to operate as an entrepreneurial venture and develop its own business model. But motives were also defensive. Internet businesses represented significant risks for parent organisations: simply staying in the game required enormous injections of capital and could incur huge losses, both of which were unpopular with shareholders. This trend started in the US but spread to Europe. Bertelsmann, Canal Plus, Pearson, EMAP, RTL, Reuters and many others were all at some point actively developing Internet-related businesses to take public. In all cases they sought to capitalise on a tremendous revenue opportunity, either by leveraging offline brands in the online space, or by freeing up new media activities from the constraints of existing offline business models.

New media investment funds

BskyB has tripled its market capitalisation in three months by making Internet investments and thus repositioning perception of itself (Makar, 2000)

Another strategic/structural option adopted by the media industry during the first Internet era, again one long-favoured by the IT industry, was the creation of investment funds to acquire minority stakes in Internet and digital media companies. Time Warner invested $500 million in digital infrastructure and websites, making minority investments of $5–20 million. Bertelsmann invested DM 150 million in Bertelsmann Ventures which backed young Internet companies in e-commerce, content and community services. Reuters established a Greenhouse Fund in 1996 to gain better understanding of how the Internet would develop and invest in promising web-based businesses.

For the IT and telecoms sectors, the rationale for investing in start-ups as a growth route was that even the most technologically advanced companies were under pressure from the speed at which the technological landscape was changing. Companies found that by establishing inhouse venture capital funds they could track fast-changing communications and Internet technologies, enter new fields quickly, boost demand for their products and, hopefully, make good returns on their investments. Cisco, Microsoft, Intel, Lucent, Microsoft, MCI WorldCom and Oracle all created their own venture capital organisations during the 1990s.

Location of Internet activities in established media firms

A particular structural issue that incumbent mass media organisations faced during the first Internet era concerned deciding where to house their

Internet businesses. This may seem like a mere detail in orchestrating a strategic response, but it received almost obsessive attention, due to the prevailing assumption that the conservatism of traditional media 'dinosaur' businesses would nip off nascent Internet businesses in the bud.

This discussion tapped into a long-standing discussion in strategy literature, namely how to resolve the intrinsic tension between entrepreneurial new activities and mature old ones. There is no consensus concerning how this should be handled. For some researchers, a new venture tasked with responding to a disruptive technological innovation needs to be granted autonomy from the parent (see, for example, Christensen, 1997; Christensen and Overdorf, 2000). This arrangement should ideally be permanent, despite pressures to the contrary. Gilbert, in his study of US newspapers' Internet initiatives noted that once the new venture and its market have matured, pressures to integrate grow as the parent identifies 'increasing opportunities … to leverage resources between the old and new businesses' (Gilbert, 2002:8). These should be resisted, but should integration become inevitable it must be approached in a modular way, whereby there is collaboration in focussed areas, but the systemic autonomy of the two organisations remains intact.

Gulati and Garino (2000:108) who concentrated explicitly on the issue of whether Internet businesses should be integrated with non-Internet parents suggested that: 'the benefits of integration are almost always too great to abandon entirely'. They argue that the critical issue is not whether integration should take place, but rather its degree.

From a practitioner perspective, established media firms displayed considerable similarity in terms of how they handled their Internet divisions, which involved a three-stage cycle moving from integration, through autonomy and back to re-integration.

First experiments with the Internet were in the main conducted within existing 'old' media divisions. This was because at that point the new media products were in general extensions of existing old media ones. However, early success with these Internet products, and the explosive growth of the Internet sector as a whole, led to the establishment of independent new media divisions. Not only would this allow an increase in volume and diversity of new media activities, but autonomous units could create expertise in 'hothouse' environments, and because they stood outside of the parent's legacy systems and bureaucracy, would be able to grasp market opportunities more quickly. Stand alone units could also be spun off, creating 'Web currency' to fund further Internet-related acquisitions. The final stage in the cycle was for the new media divisions to be reintegrated into the parents – thus CBS brought cbs.com and cbsnews.com back into the broadcast division, News International disbanded its News Networks division and Bertelsmann integrated its Internet activities back into the corporate centre. The reason for reintegration was essentially a change in context. The collapse of the Internet economy meant spin-offs were no longer feasible, and it was necessary to rein in costs, especially since revenues were still largely absent. An additional issue, however, was tensions between the core and the new media divisions. Disputes over shared customers, resources and revenues were costing management time and causing delays in market entry.

Changes to media firm processes

At its simplest, strategy is concerned with finding an optimum match between an organisation and its competitive environment. In reality, the picture is far more complicated, with a plethora of competing schools and approaches suggesting how this may be achieved. Within strategy literature an important distinction is drawn between what is known as strategy content and strategy process (Chakravarthy and Doz, 1992).

Analysis concerned with the content of strategy is focussed on the under-standing the nature of the strategic environment, assessing the organisation's strengths and weaknesses relative to this, and then developing goals or plans to reach strategic goals. Its tools include a range of analytical models that map the economics of business cycles, identify the attractiveness of particular sectors or products, and strengths relative to competitors that will lead to optimal performance. The analysis presented in this chapter so far concentrates on the content of media firms' responses to the Internet.

Approaches concerned with the 'process' of strategy look at how an organisation adapts in step with a changing environment, and at how effective strategies are shaped and then implemented from an internal firm perspective. The focus is on ensuring that processes, structures and systems allow firms to survive in complex and uncertain environments.

Impact on value chains

The value chain (Porter, 1985) is an analytical construct with roots in theories of the industrial organisation and microeconomics. It uses the concept of 'value' from an economic perspective, and assumes that organisations employ a variety of resources to create products and services that are made available in the market. Successful companies combine those resources in a way that creates products and services with more value than the combined value of the resources used. This surplus value represents profits or earnings.

The value chain disaggregates the activities of a firm into a series of sequential processes stretching from the supply side to the demand side, from inputs to outputs. These processes together make up the set of tasks performed to create and distribute goods and services. Each of these is reviewed from the perspective of the 'value' it adds to the final product or service (margin). The more competitive the value chain of an organisation, the more the overall product's value exceeds the sum of its parts, the more overall margin that can be realised as profits. Thus the model implicitly assumes that competitive advantage is created through scale, through vertically integrating as much of the value chain as possible.

Value chain analysis has been a tool of preference for those analysing the impact of the Internet on the media industries – at both sectoral and firm level – for practitioners, consultants and academics (see, for example, Tapscott, 1996; Yoffie, 1997; Downes & Mui, 1998). This is perhaps because it provides an easy to grasp visual representation of the changes underway.

Before the advent of the Internet and associated technological changes, businesses in the mass media industries had relatively straightforward value chains (normally comprising a variant of the following stages – developing content, packaging content, distributing content and reception of content) and high levels of control over each of these stages. Figure 7.1 shows a value chain analysis of the movie industry.

Since then, a number of significant changes have taken place in the value chains of the various sectors that collectively comprise the mass media industries. These fundamental changes to value chains led media organisations to engage in a raft of changes to their strategies, structures and business models, and can be viewed as the underlying driver for the changes to structures and strategies discussed in this chapter. The changes fall into four broad categories:

- Disintermediation or unbundling: Disintermediation was *the* buzz word during the first Internet boom. While never definitively defined, it concerns a group of related developments that together made it feasible to unbundle specific stages from hitherto

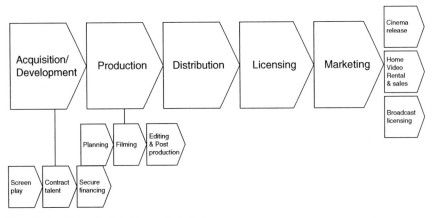

Figure 7.1 Value chain in the movie industry

vertically integrated chains and led to the break up of long-established value chains – especially those controlled by key players. These developments included technological advances, the deregulation of markets and the availability of venture capital during the first dotcom wave that encouraged start ups.

The newspaper industry provides a good example of value chain unbundling as a result of the Internet. The long-standing business model for the newspaper industry was driven by the fact that both the first copy costs of producing daily newspaper content and the fixed costs of printing and distribution are high. Publishers can, therefore, only produce newspapers at mass market prices if they realise economies of scale and combine different revenue sources, that is, print and distribute as many identical newspaper copies to as many readers as possible, generating per-copy revenues from readers, and in addition to sell access to these audiences to advertisers, generating income from those advertisers. Advertisers in turn are willing to buy advertising space, because this enables them to reach major groups of customers more cost-effectively than by producing and distributing information to major audiences themselves. Thus newspapers developed into bundles of different types of content, including different types of advertising, which offered something for broad generic swathes of public tastes.

The Internet and digitalisation have reduced the costs of reproduction and distribution. It is now economically viable to unbundle and distribute different combinations of newspaper content to different audiences (a process sometimes termed customisation). The Internet has also brought new competitors. Advertisers have a far greater range of vehicles – from niche publications to online sites such as Google and eBay – to reach potential customers. Further, non-news companies may buy news from news agencies and enter the (online) news market, too. These unbundled products, customised for target audiences, are better positioned to serve customer needs than traditionally bundled products that provide something for everyone.

- Fragmentation: This can arise from the unbundling of stages into a number of discrete activities (for example, rather than simply producing content to be distributed by an own distribution network, many media companies now produce their own content, but also aggregate content from other sources). Fragmentation can also occur because a stage that once involved a single activity – say the distribution of content over a single platform – now takes place over a number of different platforms, for example, newspaper content being distributed in both paper and online versions.
- Extension: This involves the addition of new stages. Examples include the provision of individual episodes of television series over the Internet, or for replay on a video iPod, both of which are new stages in the television industry's value chain (and also the addition of additional distribution window). Similarly, when the music industry engages in digital distribution new stages such as billing, transaction management, access/connection are added to the value chain. However disintermediation and extension, when occurring together, can result in 'reintermediation' which is understood as the introduction of new stages to a value chain that has had stages removed from it.
- Non-linear or reverse value chains: these types of changes can arise through the creation of direct links between stages that were hitherto unconnected, leap-frogging existing stages. An example is record companies that use the Internet to discover new artists and then distribute their work over the Internet, bypassing standard production

and distribution processes. Reversals in traditional value chains can take place when musicians post tracks online, garner a fan base – perhaps through the use of blogs – and as a result of their success are signed up by a record label.

Impact on journalistic work processes

The Internet and the application of information technologies have caused far-reaching changes within work processes and routines in most industries around the world. The digitalisation of value chains and content has created a demand for a strategic change in perspectives within the media and communication industries (Zerdick, Picot, Schrape, et al., 2001). Procurement, supply, sales, payments and even delivery are increasingly managed online: the higher the Internet penetration in a country, the higher the number of customers using online technologies. In 2006, most European countries accounted for a penetration rate of more than 50 per cent of the population (Internet World Stats, 2006). Aside from drastic effects on the economy and business organisations, these developments result in radical changes for the employees and their work processes and routines.

The media industries are also strongly affected by these developments as content production and publication processes increasingly turn digital: a journalist, for instance, will create digital text, photos, audio or video files. Modern newsroom technology will allow the content publication through content management systems (CMS) via the Internet from practically every place equipped with an Internet access. Idealistically, the production follows the strategy 'One Source, all Media', whereby a journalist creates the content once and then publishes it in a newspaper, for broadcast or online without alterations.

These sometimes radical changes have had a range of effects on content production or research behaviour. Castells (2000: 77) referred to the new economy as: 'informational, global and networked' and underlined that a crucial determinant for productivity and competitiveness would be the efficient application of knowledge-based information. Aside from describing the effects on a global economy, Castells (2000: 260) also focussed on how the work is affected by a network economy. He classified employees by their access to networked information and their role in decision-making processes, and identified three categories of employees:

- 'the networkers' who set up connections on their initiative (for example, joint engineering with order departments or companies), and navigate the routes of the network enterprise;
- 'the networked' who are online but without deciding when, how, why or with whom;
- 'the switched-off workers' who are tied to their own specific tasks, defined by non-interactive, one-way instructions.

Applying these categories to the work processes of journalists, we see that they are active at two levels of decision-making processes: (a) as 'the networked', in that production routines are defined and predetermined by the structures of the CMS and do not allow journalists to apply individual methods; and (b) as 'networkers', since in order to research, communicate, write and select a news story the journalist clearly connects to a network according to personal initiative.

One of the first scholars to research the interface between journalism and new media technologies in a structured way was Pavlik. He suggested that (2000: 230):

technological change influences journalists in at least four ways. Technological change affects: (1) the way journalists do their job; (2) the nature of news content; (3) the structure and organization of the newsroom; and (4) the nature of the relationship between and among news organizations.

A number of empirical studies in recent years have sought to understand the impact of the Internet on the role of the journalist and their work routines. All conclude that the Internet and online communication has drastically changed the journalist's work routines, chief among these being that the Internet has become a major source of information. Keel and Bernet (2005) analyzed the Swiss-German journalist community from all media genres. They found that journalists create a hierarchy of credibility for online information, with the websites of public administration units, universities, news portals and NGOs being trusted the most. In 2002, a study by *news aktuell* (2002) in Germany found that the evaluation of credibility and trust of online information still represents the biggest challenge for journalists.

Conclusions

Incumbent media organisations have clearly been transformed as a result of the Internet. That transformation has, however, followed a process very different to that predicted by management researchers when the new medium burst on the media scene. Taken together, the two Internet eras have led to a transformation process that has been far from instantaneous, disjointed and often painful, especially for the architects of the more ambitious strategies and the staff recruited to realise these. In the main violent new strategic directions have been abandoned in favour of a gentler path of adaptation, absorption and combination of old and new media activities. But value chains have become more complex and more expansive, and organisation boundaries have blurred as an increasing number and variety of collaborative ventures. As a result, the management task has become commensurately more complex and challenging for those tasking with leading media firms in the post-Internet era.

Notes

1. Wall Street Journal Europe, 21 July 2002.
2. Sims, D. Hollywood says entertainment – not tech – will rule the net. http://www.techweb.com/wire/story/TWB19980113S0008 (accessed 06.06.01).
3. Walt Disney Company Financial Statement 2001.
4. *Television*, July/August 2002.
5. *Financial Times*, 25 November 2002.
6. Time Warner Inc, Press Release, p.1, 10/1/2000.
7. Waters, R. 'Going out on a limb', *Financial Times*, December 1999.

References

Bamford, J.D. et al. (2002). *Mastering Alliance Strategy*. San Francisco: Jossey-Bass.

Brandenburger, A.M. & Nalebuff, B.J. (1996). *Co-opetition*. New York: Doubleday.

Chakravarthy, B. S. & Doz, Y. (1992). 'Strategy Process Research – Focusing on Corporate Self-Renewal'. *Strategic Management Journal*, 13: 5–14.

Castells, M. (2000). *The Rise of the Network Society*, (2nd Edn.). Malden, MA: Blackwell Publishing.

Castells, M. (2001). *The Internet Galaxy*. Oxford: Oxford University Press.

Chan-Olmsted, S. and Albarran, A. (1998). 'The Global Media Economic Patterns and Issues'. In Albarran, A. and Chan-Olmsted, S. (Eds), *A framework for the Study of Global Media Economics* (pp. 3–16). Ames: Iowa State University Press.

Chan-Olmsted, S. and Chang, B. (2003). 'Diversification Strategy of Global Media Conglomerates: Examining Its Patterns and Determinants'. *Journal of Media Economics*, 16(4), 213–233.

Christensen, C. M. (1997). *The Innovator's Dilemma: When New Technologies Cause Great Firms to Fail*. Boston: Harvard Business School Press.

Christensen, C. M. and Overdorf, M. (2000). 'Meeting the Challenge of Disruptive Innovation', *Harvard Business Review*, March.

Downes, L. and Miu, C. (1998). *Unleashing the Killer App. Digital Strategies for Market Dominance*. Boston: Harvard Business School Press.

Doyle, G. (2002). *Media Ownership*. London and Thousand Oaks: Sage.

Eisenhardt, K. M. & Brown, S. L. (1999). 'Patching: Restitching Business Portfolios in Dynamic Markets'. *Harvard Business Review*. May–June: 72–82.

Eisenmann, T. R. & Bower, J. L. (2000). 'The Entrepreneurial M-Form: Strategic Integration in Global Media Companies'. *Organization Science*. 11 (3), May–June, 348–355.

Falk, D. & De Rond, M. 8 (2002). *Cooperative Strategy: Economic, Business, and Organizational Issues*. Oxford: Oxford University Press.

Gilbert, C. G. (2002). 'Can Competing Frames Co-exist? The Paradox of Threatened Response'. Working paper from the Harvard Business School Division of Research.

Gulati, R. and Garino, J. (2000). 'Getting the Right Mixture of Bricks and Clicks'. *Harvard Business Review*, May–June: 107–2000.

Hollifield, A. (2004). 'The Economics of International Media'. In Alexander, A., Owers, J., Carveth, R., Hollifield, A. and Greco, A. (ed.), *Media Economics. Theory and Practice (pp. 69–84)*.London: Lawrence Erlbaum Associates.

Internet World Stats (2006). *Top 32 Countries with the highest Internet Penetration Rate*. Retrieved October 14, 2006 from http://www.Internetworldstats.com/top25.htm.

Keel, G. & Bernet, M. (2005). Journalisten im Internet 2005. Eine Befragung von Deutschschweizer Medienschaffenden zum beruflichen Umgang mit dem Internet. Retrieved October 14, 2006 from http://www.iam.zhwin.ch/download/Studie_2005.pdf.

Makar, I. (2000). 'To him that hath shall be given … new developments and old players'. Speech to *Financial Times* New Media and Broadcasting Conference. London.

news aktuell (2002). *Media studie 2002 Journalisten online – die Folgestudie*. Retrieved October 14, 2006 from http://www.newsaktuell.de/de/download/ms2002-d.pdf

Ozanich, G. & Wirth, M. (2004). 'Structure and Change: A Communications Industry Overview'. In Alexander, A., Owers, J., Carveth, R., Hollifield, A. and Greco, A. (ed.), *Media Economics. Theory and Practice (pp. 69–*84).London: Lawrence Erlbaum Associates.

Pavlik, J. (2000). The Impact of Technology on Journalism. *Journalism Studies*, 1 (2), 229–237.

Picard, R. (2002). *The Economics and Financing of Media Companies*. New York: Fordham University Press.

Picard, R. (2003). Cash Cows or Entrecôte: Publishing Companies and Disruptive Technologies. *Trends in Communication,* 11 (2), 127–136.

Porter, M. E. (1980). Competitive Strategy. Techniques for Analyzing Industries and Competitors. New York: Free Press.

Robins, J. A. & Wiersema, M. F. (2000). 'Strategies for unstructured competitive environments: Using scarce resources to create new markets'. In Bressler, R. K. F., Hitt, M. A., Nixon, R. D. and Heuskel, D. *Winning Strategies in a Deconstructing World*. Chichester: John Wiley and Sons.

Segil, L. et al. (2002). *Partnering: The New Face of Leadership.* American Management Association.

Tapscott, D. (1996). *The Digital Economy: Promise and Peril in the Age of Networked Intelligence*. New York: McGraw Hill.

US Department of Commerce Secretariat on Electronic Commerce (1998). *The Emerging Digital Economy*. Washington.

Yoffie, D. B. (ed.) (1997). *Competing in the Age of Digital Convergence*. Boston, Massachusetts: Harvard Business School Press.

Zerdick, Axel, Picot, Arnold, Schrape, K. et al. (2001). *Die Internet-Ökonomie. Strategien für die digitale Wirtschaft* (Rev. ed.). Berlin: Springer.

8

THE IMPACT OF THE INTERNET ON BUSINESS MODELS IN THE MEDIA INDUSTRIES – A SECTOR-BY-SECTOR ANALYSIS

Marko Ala-Fossi, Piet Bakker, Hanna-Kaisa Ellonen, Lucy Küng, Stephen Lax, Charo Sadaba and Richard van der Wurff

The previous chapter worked at a fairly high level of abstraction, analysing broad developments in terms of strategy, structure and process common to all sectors of the media industries. However these 'generic' developments have clearly affected the different constituent sectors of the industry in different ways. This chapter, therefore, provides an analysis of the impact of the Internet on the business models of the media industries' various constituent sectors on a case by case basis.

The term 'business model' is particularly common in practitioner literature, and an essential component of any documentation involved with financing new ventures or takeovers. Like many terms connected with the 'new economy', while frequently used, a commonly agreed definition never really emerged. The term is most commonly used to capture the essential aspects of a business, either the means by which income will be generated from a product, or a summary of the core processes involved in the production of that product. However, it is important to note that those with information technology backgrounds use the term to describe a product's process architecture.

Newspapers

The general assessment in the first Internet era, when most newspaper publishers jumped online, rushing to add websites and online newspapers to their print flagships, was that newspapers and newspaper business models were being threatened to the core by the rise of the Internet. Traditional print newspapers and traditional reporting would become obsolete in no time, and publishers had to adapt to 'the new digital realities' (Lasica, 1996: 20). Since that time, we have entered a second, calmer era of Internet growth. Newspaper publishing still remains, for the time being, a profitable business. The threats posed by the Internet need some time, perhaps even a generation, to materialise in full. At the same time, the Internet experiments of publishers and editors in the first era have shown that newspapers – in business and editorial terms – are slow-moving entities, deeply embedded in a print culture. They need time to adapt to a future in which the Internet, in still unforeseen ways, has become a standard ingredient of media consumption.

Beginning with the threats posed by the Internet to the newspaper industry: the Internet provides an ominous substitute for print newspapers for readers, especially younger ones, and for advertisers, at a time when the print newspaper market is stagnating anyway (Picard, 2003). Print newspapers are at best mature products that face a shrinking reader market and a declining share of the advertising market. They are not succeeding in attracting young readers who could compensate for the natural decline in older readers. Instead, a new Internet-savvy generation is emerging that has not and will not acquire a print newspaper reading habit (Lauf, 2001).

Online, newspaper publishers face a wide range of new competitors. The low entry barriers of Internet publishing enable public broadcasters, magazine publishers and Internet service providers, amongst others, to become online news providers. Since news is not the core business of these new players but rather a means to attract recurring visitors, they offer online news for free. Examples include CNN, BBC and Yahoo! news. Newspaper publishers have followed suit, but have had to be careful that their free online newspapers did not cannibalise print revenues.

Online competitors profit from opportunities, discussed earlier, to 'unbundle' the newspaper. They distribute different combinations of what used to be newspaper content to different audiences. Examples include personalised news services that provide individual readers with specifically requested news articles, and electronic markets and job sites that replace newspapers' classified and employment advertising pages. These unbundled products, customised for specific needs and audiences, generally serve customer needs better than traditionally bundled products that provide something for everyone (Evans & Wurster, 2000; Weber, 2006).

Last but not least, the Internet threatens the traditional editorial role of newspapers. The role of journalists as gatekeepers who select and report 'the news' is more difficult to maintain in an environment where customers in principle have access to similar sources as journalists, and users become important originators of content, too. Like the decline of newspaper readers, this is not a new trend – civic journalism has been a key issue in journalism for some time – but the Internet works upon and reinforces the existing trend, bringing it to a new level.

In response to these threats and challenges, publishers have devoted enormous amounts of strategic attention to the Internet and the opportunities it offers. The majority of newspapers have some kind of online edition, there is little in a newspaper that is not also on the Internet site, and newspapers increasingly recognise that branded websites with good content, and discussion areas, are crucial to their survival. However, few publishers earn sufficient online revenues to cover online running expenses, let alone to recover online investments or compensate for declining print revenues (Brook, 2006; Harvey, 2004). Online newspapers are, therefore, in business terms, still experiments – experiments that are developed as learning-by-doing, and that so far do not come close to the high expectations of the enthusiasts of the first Internet era.

One of the advantages of the Internet for newspaper publishers is that online delivery of electronic news is much cheaper than manual delivery of printed newspapers. This is important for an industry in which costs of paper, ink and printing presses make up an important share of variable and total costs. Another advantage is that digital distribution enables publishers to expand readership. They may attract new demographic groups that are interested in online but not in print news, and they may serve readers from overseas and in other long-distance markets. The online edition of the *Wall Street Journal*, for example, is now accessible in the smallest village in Europe; and Dutch religious newspapers are electronically delivered to expatriates around the globe.

Obviously, newspaper publishers profit from the same opportunities for unbundling and customisation as other online news providers. Publishers, too, can service particular audience segments with customised combinations of news, information and/or advertising. That may not only attract new specialist readers, but more generally enables newspapers to respond to the growing individualisation in society, which makes demand for news and information more heterogeneous, and cause advertisers to shift from mass to target advertising (Silk, Klein & Berndt, 2001). Likewise, publishers, too, can use the interactive properties of the Internet to involve users in news production. User-generated content and news 'from around the corner' are among the features that are expected to interest and attract new, young readers. Besides, offering new services and 'micro content' about developments in local communities is expected to deepen relationships with existing readers.

The major challenge that publishers face, however, is raising online revenues. Basically, publishers can draw upon three types of online revenues: advertising, news sales and sales of other products (Gallagher et al., 2001; Ihlström & Palmer, 2002).[1] Advertising is the most frequently tapped revenue source of these three. Online advertising is growing rapidly, but online advertising revenues nevertheless remain small – in the vicinity of 5 per cent of total advertising revenues for US newspapers in 2005 (2006; Harvey, 2004), and increases in online newspapers' advertising revenues are dwarfed by those of portal such as Yahoo!, Google, AOL and MSN.

Selling online news – the second revenue source – is usually recommended for a few newspapers only that operate in the high-end financial/business segment (Hayward, 2002). But studies indicate that general online newspapers, too, may earn money by selling (access to) searchable archives and customised news (Ihlström & Palmer, 2002). In the past, publishers have experimented with different payment models, and a weak current trend is towards premium models, in which part of the online offer is for free and premium services are charged. Nevertheless, many online newspapers still continue to be free. Instead of charging money, they require registration (Schiff, 2006), and use the collected user data to offer better-targeted advertising or to sell additional products to visitors.

Non-news sales, thirdly, encompass primarily small-scale activities as the sales of crossword puzzles, horoscopes and (personalised) health and beauty tips (Harvey, 2004). Non-news sales may grow if newspapers focus more on brand-extensions (INMA, 2006) or affiliate programmes (where buyers are directed to online stores of other suppliers) (Gallagher et al., 2001:1166).

What is the implication of these changes for newspaper business models? Against the background of these threats, challenges, opportunities and uncertainties, publishers are experimenting with online editions of their print newspapers. Some publishers adopt a cautious approach because they believe in the viability of the good old print newspaper and are reluctant to take risks, or simply lack the resources for sweeping experiments. Others follow a more ambitious strategy, for the opposite reasons. They believe in an online future, are more inclined to experiment or have more resources to do so. These differences in strategic ambition give rise to different online strategies and business models for print newspaper publishers.

A simple and low-risk online strategy that newspaper publishers have adopted in the past is to use the Internet as a marketing tool, in particular to attract new (young) readers. Especially in the early days of the Internet, online marketing was strongly recommended for all kinds of businesses. With the exponential growth of the Internet, however, it is becoming more and more difficult to reach potential customers, making it more difficult and costly to develop a successful online marketing strategy.

A more ambitious strategy, in which the print product still remains key, is to use the Internet to strengthen the newspaper's relationships with existing (print) customers, a customer relationship manager (CRM) strategy. Newspaper websites using a CRM strategy create a dialogue with customers in order to gain reader information and input, and offer at least one valuable service or application that attracts print readers regularly to the website.

Both the marketing and the CRM strategy imply that the costs of the online edition are paid for by (hopefully increasing) print revenues. That is but one reason why the future will involve other business models. Incidentally, in these business models, the Internet will be just one channel among others through which news providers serve their customers.

One option for the future is the development of a paid content or news portal model, in which providers offer a range of (premium) services to selected readers that are willing to pay for customised or personalised news and additional information services (Picard, 2000; Schiff, 2006). Providers may additionally sell access to their selected audiences to interested advertisers at premium rates. So far, this strategy has been adopted by major financial and business newspapers. In the future, providers adopting this business model will complement print and online news with mobile, e-mail and SMS premium services.

A second option is to elaborate the CRM strategy and develop the online newspaper into local portals or e-commerce platforms. This seems to be the strategy of choice of local newspapers in the US, whose primary strength is their local coverage and who see great potential for advertising and e-commerce in their local markets (Chyi & Sylvie, 2000). In Europe, on the other hand, building a strategy around an e-commerce platform might be taking things too far for readers who still perceive the newspaper primarily as a news medium (Ihlström & Palmer, 2002).

A third option is the crossmedia narrowcasting model. Providers adopting this model distribute news and advertising via multiple distribution channels and networks to a range of specific audiences, such as visitors in sports stadiums or air passengers. The main source of revenues is advertising. The Telegraaf Media Groep, for example, publisher of *De Telegraaf*, the most popular newspaper in the Netherlands, is directly or indirectly involved in narrowcasting news, employment ads (or both) to McDonalds outlets and on public transport (buses, subway and so on). Whereas the news portal and e-commerce business model are typical Internet business models, the narrowcasting option goes beyond the Internet and reflects the impact of the wider development of digitalisation on the newspaper business.

Of course, elements of different business models can be combined. In that sense, every business model of a company is unique. The main development, however, is clear. The Internet is taking over some functions from newspapers. Publishers consequently are challenged to redefine the particular niche on the news and advertising market in which they have or may develop a competitive advantage. It is more than likely that publishers will combine different media, including print, Internet and other digital media, to enlarge the overall niche for their brands and to serve selected customers as best and cost-effectively as possible. The outcome of this process depends to some extent on the technical characteristics and cost structures of the media involved, but first of all on strategic prowess (and a little luck).

Magazines

Historically viewed, the Internet has been the source of the most significant changes in decades to the magazine industry (the previous one having been the development of new digital printing technologies that lowered barriers to entry). The Internet has contributed to a wholesale alteration to business models, although these developments need to be viewed against a number of other developments that are not directly attributable to the Internet, notably an increase in specialist titles aimed at niche segments and a simultaneous decline in the appeal of generalist titles, in particular, magazines devoted to news and current events. In the main, these developments have been painful for the sector – a number of titles have disappeared and revenues have declined as advertising has migrated to the Internet. However, some insiders argue that these developments were long overdue, and that a 'clean up' of inferior titles was necessary. They argue that the strongest titles, the most powerful brands, have survived and perhaps even prospered as a result of the changes the Internet – an example of Schumpeterian creative destruction.

On average, consumers spend about as much time on print media today as they do on the Internet, however, the time spent on the Internet is growing faster than time spent on other media, and this trend is likely to continue. Further, magazine advertising spending is stagnant, while the Internet shows strong growth. From an advertising perspective there is an equivalent threat. The search engines that serve the ads on many content sites take a portion of the revenue so while magazines and others are playing online as well, they still may not benefit fully from Internet advertising. However, magazine publishers believe that advertisers value the combination of online and offline advertisements, and a majority of publishers have attracted new advertisers for purely online campaigns (FIPP, 2005).

Thus, as with other sectors, one major challenge posed by the Internet in relation to magazines is simply that it has diverted consumers' and advertisers' attention and spending. On the other hand, it could be argued that given the general trend of media fragmentation, the Internet gives magazines a means to communicate with their target audience on a daily basis including between the monthly issue and thus helps magazines to maintain competition for readers' and advertisers' time and money.

To date, many predictions concerning the impact of the Internet on the magazine sector have not held true. Internet has not had a disruptive impact on magazine publishing, nor have magazines shifted wholesale from paper to online versions, and the spate of online-only magazines has largely subsided, with only a few notable examples such as *Salon* and *Slate* surviving. While the Internet and digitalisation speed up processes and alter ways of communication, the Internet has not, at least not yet, significantly changed the five forces as identified by Porter that shape the nature and state of competition in the magazine publishing industry (Porter, 1985, 2001). Nor has the Internet challenged the core competence of magazine publishers. Whether publishing in print or on the Internet, sensing customer needs and packaging segmented content under the magazine brand concept are still key business strategies.

Instead of radical change, a number of subtler developments have taken place, which represent a more gradual evolution of the magazine industry. Virtually all magazines now have an online presence and some have achieved leading positions within their categories. The majority of magazine publishers have embraced the Internet as part of a multi-platform strategy that has moved them into higher-value information and extended their offering and brands across different platforms that range from traditional print activities through the Internet into mobile media and live events.

In terms of the magazine concept, it seems that magazine Web pages are currently considered to be on an equal footing. According to an international survey by The International Federation of the Periodical Press (FIPP, 2003), the main goal for the magazine websites in 2003 was to attract new readers to the print version. However, by 2005, the main goal was to expand the magazine audience by creating an online readership (FIPP, 2005). Most publishers also aimed at creating revenue streams and profits online in the long term, and planned on building a community around the magazine brand.

The Internet does, indeed, support the communal aspect of magazines. Being targeted for a segmented target groups that already share common interests, virtual communities on magazine websites provide a fruitful platform for ongoing customer–interactions. In fact, a study commissioned by the UK periodical publishers association (PPA) proposes that magazines could take a new role as bridges to interactivity (2004). Interactive media helps to promote a stronger relationship with other brand users. These ongoing interactions with the readers also help the magazines to incrementally develop and strengthen their offerings in line with customer feedback and developments in the competitive environment. Moreover, close customer interactions support brand loyalty which could be considered of strategic importance in the fragmenting media landscape.

Thus, while the Internet poses a threat to advertising and circulation income, magazine groups also see it as a path to growth, cost reduction, differentiation and innovation. For example, some magazine publishers have expanded their online operations to include classified ads as well, a business that has traditionally been operated by newspapers. The Internet has also lowered the costs for customer service, market research, subscription sales and helped magazines to differentiate their brand from competitors' offerings. Virtual communities also support innovation as they allow magazines to find out more about their readers' interests. Publishers have described virtual communities as 'continuous online focus groups' and 'ideapools' for their product development.

In most cases, the Internet is no longer a venue for republishing print copy, but an opportunity to fulfil a range of new services such as to update content, to engage consumers in interactive experiences (games, polls, contests, etc.) and to manage their customer relationships. A successful website may well complement rather than substitute the print magazine, and add a new dimension to the magazine concept – and to the corresponding business model. Thus, the Internet may support the revenue logic, product development, marketing and sales and servicing and implementation dimensions of the magazine business model (Rajala et al., 2001).

Book publishing

The Internet has affected the book publishing sector profoundly but in less dramatic and more subtle ways than once envisaged. As with other sectors, the changes that can be observed have arisen in large part from the confluence of the Internet and digital technologies, although the various very individual segments that together make up the sector have been affected in different ways.

Most attention on the impact of the Internet on book publishing has centred on the digital delivery of consumer books and the associated concept of the e-book – books that could be downloaded as files to be read on special devices. Despite optimistic prognoses during the dotcom era, this field of activity has yet to take off. A range of inter-related problems have plagued initiatives: portable e-readers have not sold well; standards concerning file formats, reader software, hardware platforms, DRM and protection have failed to emerge; there are relatively few products; consumer response has been muted; and probably, as a result, there is currently not enough market potential to justify the effort and expense of e-publishing. The industry continues to be sceptical about whether reading on a screen will ever replace reading on paper and they doubt consumers would be happy to print off entire books. But others suggest that as soon as an accessibly priced, ultra-light, portable e-paper device emerges, there will be a shift towards downloading titles from the Internet, and compelling digital content will emerge. They further predict that specific pockets of the market might migrate to an e-book basis – the oft-quoted example is of male readers of science fiction.

Thus, while there were once concerns that the consumer book market would be damaged by illegal digital file sharing as the recording industry has been, this problem has failed to materialise. Indeed, the most significant impact of the Internet on book publishing to date concerns online retailing, and this is a positive development. The Internet has established itself as a permanent additional sales channel for the industry and book publishing has gained overall as a result. This reflects the fact that books are ideally-suited to online sales: they are relatively low-risk, low-cost products and their characteristics lend themselves well to online description. From a consumer perspective better information (reviews and customer ratings, for example) on a wider range of individual titles – particularly the backlist titles that are increasingly neglected by mainstream retailing chains – can be found on the Internet rather than in traditional sales environments. A further benefit for publishers is that returns are negligible from online sales. The Internet has also boosted the sales of second hand books. This is a mixed blessing for publishers. It brings out-of-print titles back into circulation but also competes with new book sales. The evidence is that this trend is most damaging for college textbooks.

The digital delivery of books is taking place in the STM (scientific, technical and medical) sector of publishing where players such as Elsevier, John Wiley and McGraw Hill are delivering an increasing amount of content through e-publishing, and in the educational arena, where e-books offer advantages for distance learning, a growing segment of the market. Taking a broader perspective, these developments are part of a fundamental reshaping of educational book publishing arising as a result of digital technologies in general. Not only are more and more educational and academic publishers selling their titles directly from their own websites, but as more and more teaching shifts onto digital platforms, demand for digital content and online learning grows. The result is an extension in terms of the basic product offered from book publishing into service provision, such as assessment services and lesson planning.

Television

The impact of the Internet on television has been strong but indirect. Since the spread of the Web as a new medium, several voices have sounded an alarm about how devastating its effects would be on traditional media, including television. But most of these warnings have been silenced by time. Television is still the strongest mass medium all over the world, and although the Internet is modifying it in some ways, and these processes are speeding up, it will continue being an essential element of contemporary society for a long time.

The most immediate influence is the potential displacement effect on television advertising revenues. Television takes the biggest share of advertising expenditures in most markets, based on its high audience penetration across every age range, gender and socio-economic background.

This displacement effect on media use has been identified as one of the challenges that the Internet poses for television. It works at two levels: as users spend more time on the Internet, time is 'stolen' from television viewing, and this leads to a transfer of advertising spend from traditional to new screens. The bulk of the literature suggests that new communication media would have their greatest displacement effects on older communications media because of their functional similarity (McDonald, Dimmick, 2003:30).

The displacement hypothesis has several conceptual problems. It does not consider multi-tasking (Perse, 2000), which is a common consequence of the arrival of new technologies at home and certainly occurs with television and the Internet. Further, it is clear that the activities that were most affected by the arrival of the Internet are 'doing nothing' or 'sleeping', rather than watching television (McDonald, Dimmick, 2003:30). In fact, what happened at the beginning was that the popularisation of the Internet had little or an insignificant effect on television viewing. This was mainly because heavy Internet users never were heavy television viewers.

But this could happen in the near future, because young people, who are heavy Internet users, appear not to be adopting their parents' media consumption patterns. Television could be replaced by the Internet, mobile phone or another new technology activity: according to a recent study, young people are leading the way in the use of other devices than television, such as iPods and cell phones, to access video content.[2] Certainly Spring 2007 was the worst season ever for American networks, which lost 2.5 million viewers in two months.[3] Among the reasons for this fall in audiences is that users are downloading and recording content and consuming it in a personalised manner.

Whether a displacement effect has influenced television advertising incomes is not clear. Over the last few years advertising expenditure on television did not decrease. Rather, because of digitalisation and the arrival of new channels it has grown. However, television channels are certainly looking for new revenue streams to reduce their dependance on advertising money.

Two other effects of the Internet on television could be attributed to its increasing popularity. The first is the speeding up of digitisation processes. Because content needs to be digitalised to be used online, media companies have invested in digitising the whole process, from content production to distribution and reception. Digital television initiatives fall into this category.

Most countries have advanced plans for such services and fixed dates for analogue switch-off. These systems will open the door to new possibilities for television as interactive services.

Digitalisation poses a new and broad challenge to television. It allows content to be distributed through the Internet which is a new and competitive distribution channel that is not limited by geography or reception problems. It opens other new channels also. Mobile phones are clearly a platform for future television consumption. These new distribution channels mean new competitors also. YouTube, for example, allows users to upload their personal or favourite videos to be shown to everyone accessing their page. Thus accessing content of a traditional channel does not depend on residing in a particular geographic region or paying for its services.

Traditional television channels have reacted in two different ways to these competitors. One response is allowing websites to show their content – examples include the UK's BBC or Spain's Antena 3TV, which opened a branded channel on the popular video portal. The other reaction has been to sue those companies for 'massive international copyright infringement',[4] as the Fox Network and Viacom have done. Since YouTube was acquired by Google Inc.[5] for $1.65 billion, its position has changed from a website developed for a couple of friends; to a potential enemy for anyone that sees the Internet as a strategic asset. 'YouTube looked like the end of commercial TV, but really it has opened the door to a much bigger contest: the battle for the control of TV' (Hare, E., 2007). The second effect concerns how the Internet is changing the concept of television itself. Until recently television involved consuming content in a linear pre-packaged way. Once such content is available in digital format, it can be accessed through several devices, channels can be broken down into constituent parts, advertising can be avoided and programmes can be consumed on demand, and in different locations, according to consumers' individual preferences.

Sociologist Zygmunt Bauman (2000) has developed a concept of 'liquid television', which views the medium as a fluid entity that is changing its shape in order to adapt to market conditions and, therefore, survive. The concept of television is changing and the Internet has much influence on how it will develop in the future.

Radio

The Internet is having a far more direct impact on radio broadcasting than on many other sectors of the media industries. The growing presence of broadband Internet access in the home and advances in audio coding systems mean that streaming or downloading audio across the Internet is straightforward (and allows for high audio quality given its relatively low bandwidth in comparison with video content). Hence Internet users are readily listening to radio over the Internet and the proliferation of personal digital audio players has meant that mobile listening to Internet-based content is now becoming commonplace. Broadband Internet connection is key to Internet radio: in 2006, for example, 5.5 per cent of the US population listen to Internet radio at least once per week, but of those who had broadband Internet access at home the figure was 27 per cent (Screen Digest et al. 2006: 135; Ofcom, 2006b: 149). Elsewhere, when broadband access was available, 52 per cent of Chinese and 40 per cent of Italians listened at least once per week (Ofcom, 2006b: 149).

The broadcast radio industry faces challenges from the Internet in a number of ways. 'Conventional', terrestrial radio stations are simulcasting Internet-based streams in increasing numbers, while other Internet-only radio stations also stream content 24 hours per day. Hence, there are simply more stations available to listeners. Internet radio also includes new formats and practices, such as time-shifted radio and programme downloading. While in many cases these new formats have not been originated by existing radio stations, many have subsequently begun to incorporate them into their Internet-based activities. Four different categories of Internet radio formats can be identified:

- Internet-streamed radio: linear, 'live' streaming, where the content is heard as it is transferred from station to the listener's computer.
- Time-shifted streamed radio: the listener instigates the streaming of an archived programme but, once started, the programme is streamed as above (though may be paused or rewound). This is frequently referred to as 'on-demand' audio.
- Time-shifted, downloaded radio: the listener instigates the downloading of the entire audio file to her computer, to be listened to later (or transferred to a portable player). This includes podcasting, in which download can be automated using 'feeder' software.
- Hybrid: a combination of juke-box style linear programming but with a facility for the listener to select the content or favour a particular type of content.

While some radio stations tried streaming in the early 1990s, the launch of the Real Audio software in 1995 helped audio streaming grow dramatically (Priestman, 2002). By 1999, it was estimated that in the US, the world's largest radio market, around one-third of existing radio stations were streaming content to some extent; now, most stations in America and in Europe (certainly the public service stations) stream over the Internet. With concern amongst some radio broadcasters that audiences may be lost to the Internet, radio stations are appropriating the full range of opportunities offered by Internet radio. For example, in the UK the BBC runs a 'Radio Player' on its website that allows most of its broadcast output to be streamed via the Internet at any time during the following seven days. An increasing number of its programmes are available as downloads or as podcasts.

In 2007, the BBC claimed that 7.1 million hours of time-shifted listening had been streamed during the single month of January, while the two most popular podcasts, a daily 'news pod' and highlights of music presenter Chris Moyles's show, recorded 1 million and 750,000 downloads respectively (BBC, 2007).

For existing radio stations, then, Internet radio offers an additional platform for its existing broadcast output and allows that content to be presented in new ways. Furthermore, the same broadcasters can provide additional audio content: the UK's Virgin radio, for example, offers three additional music stations as largely automated audio streams on its website alongside a streamed simulcast of its over-the-air station. Thus although, in general, increasing use of the Internet is correlated with a reduction in the use of other media, for the radio industry this is not such a threat compared with, say, television. Most Internet users report a reduction in use of all 'offline' media, but the reduction in radio listening is less than the reduction in television and in newspaper reading. Even in the 15–24-year-old group, where radio listening (and TV watching) is in general decline, print media consumption is reduced more than radio listening (Ofcom, 2006a: 43). Given the numbers reporting listening to radio over the Internet, the consequences of Internet usage for *overall* radio listening may be minimal (Ofcom, 2006b: 150).

As well as exploiting the Internet for its audio capabilities, existing broadcasters also use the Internet to add a visual aspect to their radio brands and to increase interaction with the audience. Indeed, in the earlier days of radio station websites, other than content streaming this latter aspect was the main reason cited for establishing an Internet presence (Lind and Medoff, 1999: 217). Visual content frequently includes presenter profiles, webcam links to studios, discussion forums, competitions and advertising in addition to programme-related content such as playlists, background information and links to resources relevant to the programme.

For new radio stations, the Internet offers, possibly, the only realistic platform for 'transmission'. In most countries, terrestrial markets are full with all spectrum allocated while the costs of carriage on a digital platform such as satellite or terrestrial digital television are high. However, start up costs for an Internet-only radio station are comparatively low. Ting and Wildman estimate initial costs for a typical Internet station could be just five per cent of those for a comparable broadcast, over-the-air station (cited in Wall, 2004). In other respects, the 'broadcast' model of over-the-air transmission offers considerable advantages over Internet radio. While the initial costs of establishing a transmission network (or contracting with a third party for carriage) are high, the ongoing costs are minimal – broadcasting to 10,000 listeners costs no more perhaps than broadcasting to 100 (for example, in an urban environment). To put this another way, the incremental cost of adding listeners to a broadcast station's audience is practically zero and costs per listener fall. In contrast, the capacity of the Internet to deliver data is finite, and the capacity, or bandwidth, required to serve 1000 audio streams is significantly greater, and thus more expensive, than that needed to serve 100. So, as an Internet station begins to succeed in attracting listeners, it must pay for additional bandwidth and costs increase accordingly, with cost per additional listener being more-or-less the same, or even increasing if additional listeners force an upgrade in a station's equipment. Ting and Wildman's estimates for the running costs of radio stations are the reverse of startup costs, with Internet radio costing around four times as much as broadcast radio per year to run (Ting and Wildman, 2002). These costs are further increased by the payment of music royalties. In most parts of the world both broadcast and Internet radio music stations pay royalties both for performers as well as composers and songwriters (although in the US broadcast radio stations are exempt from performers' royalty payments, but Internet stations are not). Furthermore, if a broadcast station starts to simulcast over the Internet, it pays separate royalties for streaming and, in general these rates have been higher than for broadcasting. Thus many UK commercial broadcasters have restricted their Internet streams to domestic consumption only, while Finnish stations have shut down their Internet radio operations altogether (Grossman, 2006; Anon, 2003). In March 2007, increased royalty fees for music streaming threatened to put a number of US Internet stations out of business (Kharif, 2007).

Hence the business model for an Internet-only radio station is quite different from that for broadcast radio. For a broadcast radio company, the aim is to serve the maximum audience with the minimum number of stations, thus seeking greater revenue from advertising while reducing overheads. So in many markets, radio groups employ a high degree of networking, sharing content between the group's stations while, in seeking the biggest possible audience, content tends towards mainstream formats. However, a typical Internet-only station may target only a small audience (figures in the region of just a few hundred simultaneous streams are common) and thus adopt different strategies to raise revenue (Wall, 2004). This might include niche programming and subscription-based radio. If an audience is expected to remain small, niche content might make sense, particularly if the on-demand facility of Internet radio means a programme is not made as a one-off, but has a life longer than its transmission date. A niche audience can be sold more precisely to potential advertisers, particularly so given that Internet tracking can determine where and when listeners are online and precisely what they are listening to. Niche content, and the ease with which Internet content may be encrypted, also makes subscription radio viable, particularly if it is promoted as advertisement-free.

Thus we see here two different models of 'radio', models which might be seen more as complementary rather than in competition. While radio streamed over the Internet might be an exemplary instance of convergence, Internet radio and broadcast radio remain in many ways distinct. Sitting in front of a computer, it might be that streaming radio stations over the Internet and listening to them on a nearby terrestrial receiver amount to the same thing. But away from a computer, radio's ubiquity, its cheapness, portability and mobility set it apart and help explain why in most countries radio listening overall is either steady or increasing. In-car listening is still, in the main, to terrestrial radio (augmented by satellite services in the US) and Internet radio is, for now, unable to replicate this flexibility in reception: mobile phone IP services remain expensive and wireless Internet coverage remains patchy and not designed for mobile reception; the few WiFi Internet radio receivers on the market are aimed at fixed reception within the home. Interviews with radio industry figures in Europe and Canada suggest that radio is expected to retain its importance for the audience, while seeking to enhance its functionality and branding by using the facilities offered by the Internet (Ala-Fossi et al., 2007).

Where the Internet is perceived to have had an impact on radio is in advertising. Radio's share of all advertising in a number of European countries has declined while Internet advertising has increased, although this varies greatly from country to country, with radio revenues growing substantially in some (Ofcom 2006b: 152–3). However, this transfer to the Internet has not been to Internet *radio stations*, but to other areas of the Internet. There remains little evidence of widespread success by Internet radio stations in generating revenue through advertising (Ting and Wildman, 2002; *Screen Digest* et al., 2006: 124–5). Instead, it would appear that the broadcast radio industry has identified the Internet as a technology naturally allied with radio and, rather more than other media sectors, has sought to appropriate its capabilities to enhance brands and diversify its output, while continuing to see radio as consisting principally as streams (whether over the Internet or the airwaves) of linear, live content. For now, there is little evidence that Internet-only radio and podcasting are able to become mainstream mechanisms for audio consumption. While Black's (2001) question: 'Why should an audio signal delivered through the Internet be called "radio" in the first place?' – invites a range of responses, radio as it is currently understood will be with us for some time.

Music

Although downloading music from the Internet was in theory possible from the start of that medium – music can be converted into digital formats like any other content and can be distributed accordingly – it was not until the end of the nineties that four major technological developments changed downloading music and sound from a possibility to a reality. The first was the development of compression technologies, with mp3 as the most well-known, that converted sound files into smaller sizes without losing too much quality. A normal 128 bits mp3 version of a CD track is 10 to 12 times as small as the original file. The second development was the introduction of high-speed, flat-rate Internet connections. First ISDN, and after that cable and ADSL connections reduced download time to a fraction of what it used to be. An mp3 track would take 24 minutes to be downloaded with the traditional 14.4 Kb modem while a modern T1 connection can do the same thing within 20 seconds. The third development was the introduction of multi-media computers with more storage capacities and sound playback capabilities such as soundcards and speakers. Hard disc capacity moved from 10 to 20 Mb – suitable for storing only two to five tracks – to 60 or 80 Gb. The last and most visible development was the introduction of free and easy-to-use software to rip CD tracks into mp3 files, to play mp3 tracks and most of all to download music files from the Internet.

These developments together divide the history of music on the Internet in four periods. The first is the mp3.com era from 1997 until 1999 when music could be downloaded as files from websites, mostly with mp3.com. Users could not search for their favourite tracks – supply was limited. This all changed dramatically when Napster was introduced in 1999 – ushering in the second period. Suddenly millions of files became available and users could search, download and play tracks without being limited to the supply of a website. Napster used a centralised database that was soon targeted by the music industry and within two years Napster was closed down. The third period proved to be much more damaging to the music industry: instead of one system with one centralised database dozens of new file-exchange networks emerged, many of them with decentralised databases, so it was almost impossible to find out where a file was coming from. The fourth period started in April 2003 when Apple introduced their iTunes software and their iPod music player. At first, the system was only usable for Apple users but later that year a Windows version was introduced which resulted in a huge increase in legally bought music files. Before the introduction of iTunes, the music industry launched their own legal download systems but all were hard to use, contained a limited amount of music that also came with a punitive DRM system, which meant that users rented music and if they ended their subscription or got a new computer the chances were that their music disappeared (Bakker, 2005).

The Internet has been a fundamental force for change for the music industry – whether this is constructive or destructive depends in large part on the response of the established players. The Internet and digitalisation mean that entire value chain of the music industry can be supported by digital platforms that are widely available at lower costs (although the actual costs for digital music and CDs are converging – digital distribution might be less expensive, but the expenses associated with DRM systems, handling, billing and maintaining digital shops tend to increase costs). It offers new ways to reach consumers and promote music. It also creates new format for music delivery: streaming, downloading and burning. Young consumers represent the most important customer group and this is the group that has embraced the Internet most energetically.

While it is clear that the Internet is significantly affecting the core business model of the music industry, it is far from clear what the ultimate impact of the Internet will be. The market for legitimate downloading of music is expanding rapidly and could become a key driver for future industry growth, expanding markets and invigorating the sector. In 2005, the value of sales from digital downloads in the US was almost 5 per cent of that of physical CDs and CD singles, while growth of digital download were over 75 per cent in 2005 compared to 2004 (RIAA 2005 Year end statistics). Legal downloads offer a new income stream and an opportunity to make marketing more dynamic and to connect better with artists' fans. Mobile music sales for ring tones are also a platform for growth. The Internet is also recreating the singles market (because the majority of sales is from single downloaded tracks), which in the 1970s formed 20 per cent of record company revenues. Some research suggests some tracks are being bought by people who would not have bought the album, and that people who buy music online tend to buy more music overall. The Internet has also led to the emergence of niche audiences for specific types of music products, and global networks allow these to be aggregated into global niches that offer significant market potential.

However, the Internet also threatens the industry with continued disruption. Digital distribution bypasses processes that have traditionally yielded the most value for record companies, pressing CDs and digital distribution. Also, new non-traditional players have entered the market, the computer firm Apple being the most clear example, but also credit card companies. ISPs take substantial shares of the revenues generated, thereby marginalising the role of the traditional 'record' company. Broadband Internet connections will accelerate this trend, making downloading faster and easier. It also could ultimately marginalise the music companies, since it is now possible for musicians to bypass the music majors: to load tracks directly on to the Internet, and to market using that medium also. New business models along these lines are emerging, for example, record companies that use the Internet to discover and distribute artists' work, or create online markets for touring artists with an established fan base or using the Internet to build a fan base for as yet unsigned bands.

Such moves address the dissatisfaction consumers might have with the sector's current practices: bundling tracks together when buyers in reality only want one song and the high prices currently charged by the industry. While successful examples of musicians bypassing the music industry in favour of the Internet are still rare in popular music (although classical musicians and orchestras are increasingly establishing their own record labels), the opportunities are substantial and relatively straightforward in comparison to the complexities of signing a deal with a major music label. However, since it is still problematic to secure an income for digitally distributed music, a hybrid model seems to be appearing, whereby the Internet is used to gain exposure and a following, at which point artists shift to more conventional arrangements.

What happened to the music industry in the beginning of the last century – losing their grip on the total value chain when sheet music was replaced by records that could be played on machines manufactured by third parties – is now happening again. Other parties – online retailers like the iTunes Store, credit card firms, DRM companies, ISPs, concert venues, booking agencies, merchandising firms – have taken a substantial share of the money that is now spent in music. Also the unbundling of music (single tracks downloaded instead of whole CDs bought) is causing a substantial dent in the music industry's revenues. In addition, CD prices have dropped almost everywhere to keep prices competitive with digital downloads. The reaction from the music industry has included consolidation, downsizing and closing down local operations. But all-in-all the quantity of music on offer does not seem to have declined. Where the traditional labels have retreated, other players – in some cases even musicians – have moved in.

Summary

These industry analyses demonstrate the range of responses in the various media industries to the threats and opportunities offered by the presence and growth of Internet use. The business models that have been adopted and that are being modified show that the industries are adapting to the new environment and responding to consumers' readiness to embrace the Internet. It is also clear that for both producers and users, change is ongoing.

Notes

1. A fourth option, syndication, is not discussed here. Syndication revenues do not come directly from users, but from other companies, in particular online news

providers that want to republish newspaper content. Syndication is not new, but the Internet has obviously increased opportunities for providers than want to syndicate their news (Werbach, 2000).

2. E-Poll, 'Multi-Platform Viewing of Video Content', via http://publications. mediapost.com/index.cfm?fuseaction=Articles.showArticleHomePage&art_ aid=59875

3. 'Where have all these viewers gone?', accessed at http://www.cnn.com/2007/ SHOWBIZ/TV/05/09/tv.missingviewers.ap/index.html, May 1st 2007.

4. http://www.internetnews.com/bus-news/article.php/3665256

5. http://www.google.com/press/pressrel/google_youtube.html

References

Ala-Fossi, M., Lax, S., O'Neill, B., Jauert, P. and Shaw H. (2007). 'The future of radio is still digital – but which one? Expert perspectives and future scenarios for the radio media in 2015'.

Anon. (2003). 'YLE to end streaming of radio programmes', *Helsingin Sanomat (International Edition)* 19 December.

Bakker, P. (2005). File-sharing – fight, ignore or compete; paid download services vs. P2P-networks. *Telematics and Informatics* 22, 41–55.

BBC (2007). 'BBC radio websites set standard for weekly users'. Press release, 8 March 2007.

Black, D. (2001). 'Internet radio: a case study in medium specificity'. *Media, Culture and Society* 23(3) 397–408.

Brook, S. (2006, February 27). 'One newspaper reader worth up to 100 online users in ad revenue'. *The Guardian*. Retrieved November 13, 2006, from: LexisNexisAcademic database.

Bauman, Zygmunt (2000). *Liquid Modernity*, Cambridge: Polity Press.

Chyi, H.I., & Sylvie, G. (2000). 'Online newspapers in the US Perceptions of markets, products, revenue, and competition'. *International Journal on Media Management,* 2(2), 69–77.

Evans, P., & Wurster, T.S. (2000). *Blown to bits*. Boston, MA: Harvard Business School Press.

FIPP (2003). Routes to success for consumer magazine websites. A survey by the International Federation of the Periodical Press. Compiled by Guy Consterdine. Retrieved 30.12.2004 from: http://www.fipp.com/assets/ downloads/fippconsumersurvey.pdf

FIPP (2005). 'Routes to success for consumer magazine websites. A survey by the International Federation of the Periodical Press'. Compiled by Guy Consterdine. Retrieved 10.10.2005 at http://www.fipp.com/assets/ downloads/ConsumerMagWeb.pdf

Gallaugher, J.M., Auger, P., & BarNir, A. (2001). Revenue streams and digital content providers: an empirical investigation. *Information & Management,* 38(7), 473–485.

Grossman, W. (2006). 'Will licensing kill the radio star?' *The Guardian* 4 May.

Hare, E. (2007). 'The Revolution Will be Televised', *Contagious Magazine*, Inform March 2007.

Harvey, F. (2004, April 20). 'Screen presence. Online versions of newspapers can stretch brands but publishers are cagey about showing they have repaid their investments'. *The Financial Times*, p. 12. Retrieved November 13, 2006, from: LexisNexisAcademic database.

Hayward, D. (2002, June 19). 'Curtain falls on "longest free trial in history": online newspapers'. *The Financial Times*, p. 2. Retrieved November 13, 2006, from: LexisNexisAcademic database.

Ihlström, C., & Palmer, J. (2002). 'Revenues for online newspapers: owner and user perceptions'. *Electronic Markets, 12*(4), 228–236.

INMA (2006). *INMA Brand Extension Seminar*. Retrieved November 13, 2006, from http://www.inma.org/2006-barcelona-line-extensions.cfm

Kharif, O. (2007). 'The last days of Internet radio? A decision by the copyright royalty board to raise royalty fees could put some small online radio stations out of business'. *Business Week online* 7 March. www.businessweek.com. Accessed 26 March 2007.

Lasica, J.D. (1996). Net gain. *American Journalism Review, 18*(9), 20–33.

Lauf, E. (2001). 'The vanishing young reader – Sociodemographic determinants of newspaper use as a source of political information in Europe, 1980–98'. *European Journal of Communication, 16*(2), 233–243.

Lind, R.A. and Medoff, N. J. (1999) 'Radio stations and the World Wide Web'. *Journal of Radio Studies 6*(2) 203–221.

Mcdonald, Daniel G. and Dimmick, John W. (2003). 'Time as a niche dimension: competition between the internet and television', in Albarran, Alan and Arrese, Angel, *Time and Media Markets,* pp. 29–48.

Newspaper Association of America (2006). *The source. Newspapers by the numbers*. Retrieved November 13, 2006, from Newspaper Association of America website: http://www.naa.org/thesource/the_source_newspapers_by_the_numbers.pdf

Ofcom (2006a). *The Communications Market 2006*. London: Ofcom.

Ofcom (2006b). *The International Communications Market 2006* (London: Ofcom).

Perse, Elizabeth M. (2001). *Media Effect and Society*, NetLibrary, Inc.

Picard, R.G. (2000). 'Changing business models of online content services; their implications for multimedia and other content producers'. *The International Journal on Media Management, 2*(2), 60–68.

Picard, R.G. (2003). 'Cash cows or entrecôte: publishing companies and disruptive technologies'. *Trends in Communication, 11*(2), 127–136.

Porter, M.E. (1985). *Competitive Strategy*. New York: Free Press.

Porter, M.E. (2001). *Strategy and the Internet*. Harward Business Review, March, 63–78.

PPA (2004). '*Lines of Engagement: The opportunities for magazines in a changing media context*'. A report for PPA by the Henley Centre. 5.4.2004. Retrieved 9.2.2006 from http://www.ppa.co.uk/mags2004/conference/downloads/day2/round_table/henley.pdf

Priestman, C. (2002). *Web Radio: Radio Production for Internet Streaming*. Oxford: Focal.

Rajala, R., Rossi, M., Tuunainen, V. and Korri, S. (2001). 'Software Business Models: A Framework for Analyzing Software Industry'. *Technology Review* 108, TEKES, Helsinki Paper presented at *BEA Annual Convention*, Las Vegas, 18–21 April.

RIAA (2005). Year-end statistics. Downloaded from www.riaa.com. Accessed 24 February 2006.

Schiff, F. (2006). 'Trends emerging more clearly: business models of news web sites'. *First Monday, 11*(7), Special Issue #6 on Commercial applications of the Internet. Retrieved March 6, 2007, from http://firstmonday.org/issues/special11_7/schiff/index.html

Screen Digest, CMS Hasche Sigle, Goldmedia Gmbh and Rightscom Ltd (2006). *Interactive Content and Convergence: Implications for the Information Society,* London: Screen Digest.

Silk, A.J., Klein, L.R., & Berndt, E.R. (2001). 'The emerging position of the Internet as an advertising medium'. *Netnomics, 3*(2), 129–148.

Ting, C. and Wildman, S. (2002). 'The economics of internet radio'. paper presented at the *30th Research Conference on Information, Communication, and Internet Policy*. Alexandria, VA, 28–30 September. http://www.si.umich.edu/tprc/papers/2002/89/InternetRadio.pdf. Accessed 22 March 2007.

Wall, T. (2004). 'The political economy of internet music radio'. *The Radio Journal* 2(1) 27–44.

Weber, J. (2006, October 3). Newspapers grapple with an unbundled world. *Times Online*. Retrieved November 13, 2006, from: http://technology.timesonline.co.uk/article/0,,20411-2386875,00.html

Werbach, K. (2000, May–June). 'Syndication; the emerging model for business in the Internet era'. *The Harvard Business Review*, pp. 86–93.

9

CONCLUSIONS

Lucy Küng, Robert G. Picard and Ruth Towse

This chapter explores the conclusions that can be drawn from this book concerning the impact of the Internet on the mass media industries. As explained at the outset, the focus is that of social science and the lenses through which we have analyzed the Internet's development over the last ten years or so – the period of the expansion of Internet use and its establishment as a mass medium – are those of a range of social science disciplines that have been used to investigate the media, as well as other industrial sectors and technological developments.

The Internet clearly involves far more than simply the production and consumption of mass media products and has wrought far-reaching changes for a broad range of fields. Some of these other developments may well impinge on the media industries, but this book has as its starting point the 'traditional' mass media industries and has concentrated on print, sound recording, broadcasting: the means through which content (knowledge and information, news, entertainment and so on) were being delivered to mass audiences or users (readers, viewers, listeners, etc.) in the last half of the twentieth century.

How revolutionary was/is the Internet?

One clear conclusion is that in terms of its current status the Internet so far represents little more than a new medium for delivering what appears to be very familiar old media content. The problem, however, is that there are clearly strong signs of very different kinds of content-related activity emerging – social networking sites, Wikipedia and blogs to name but a few. Further, the business models of the 'old' media businesses most affected by these developments are suffering as a result. So how significant a change is the Internet for the mass media industries?

In order to answer this question we need to turn to the distinction drawn in this book between the two eras of the Internet. The initial 'bubble' phase and the later less newsworthy era that brought real and profound change to the media industries.

During the first Internet era, which began around 1996 (this research began in 2000) the new medium was considered very significant indeed. The so-called 'dotcom boom' was engendered by combination of what Alan Greenspan termed 'irrationally exuberant' financial markets, a stream of innovations by high-tech organisations, enthusiasm on the part of the business press, and extraordinary stock option grants to key executives in dotcom companies. It led to a sense of panic in established firms in certain sectors, and quickly enmeshed the political process in the excitement so that governmental bodies (supranational and national) felt the need to react strongly to the promise or threat of the Internet. It is clear in retrospect that much of this early stage was indeed hype: for the majority of the mass media the Internet was not as immediately destructive as initially supposed. Established products were not immediately cannibalised. Traditional media firms did not head towards extinction.

Since the dotcom collapse, the Internet has entered a second, calmer era. Interestingly, while the Internet has fallen out of the headlines, and is no longer destination of choice for ambitious job seekers (that spot has probably gone to the hedge and private equity funds), its ultimate significance may well be exactly that prophesied during the first Internet era. Over the past decade the Internet has continued to inexorably gain strength and a central position in the life of increasing numbers of people. And the Internet has brought irrevocable change for the mass media – some of the dire warnings of the first Internet era are actually coming to pass, but through a series of modest incremental changes that somehow cloak their actual import. Recorded music, film and newspaper segments in particular face uncertain futures, and that uncertainty is attributable in large part to the advent of the Internet, although there are other contributory factors at work. Further, some 'old' media businesses are investing at almost dotcom boom levels in Internet businesses – News Corporation's acquisition of MySpace and the BBC's MyBBCPlayer project, which will let users download its TV and radio programming and allow the corporation to compete with Google and Yahoo are just two examples. The incremental and adaptive nature of these organisations' strategic responses (the BBC is, for example, launching its project on the back of a decade's successful Internet engagement and a position as the UK's fifth most popular Internet site) are perhaps the critical differences between the first and the second Internet eras. In the absence of hysteria, incumbents can adapt gradually and critically with the benefit of the revenues from existing products that analysts of the first Internet era predicted would disappear.

Which technological advances are driving change?

In terms of technological development, the authors of Chapter 3 argue that the Internet is essentially another stage in a stream of innovation that started with radio, and that this stream will continue to flow. The Internet, therefore, is itself continuing to evolve. They also caution that what is generally termed 'the Internet' in fact involves the coming together of several distinct technologies. These include digitalisation, the Web, streaming technologies and the IP. IP technologies and digitalisation have been as significant change drivers as the Internet. These points should be sufficient to warn policy-makers and analysts that regulatory and other policy measures need to be flexible and adaptable. Rigid intervention that does not recognise the emergent and unstable nature of the technological developments could do more harm than good.

The really difficult problem in interpreting the impact of the Internet, however, is disentangling its effects from those of associated technological changes, particularly that of digitalisation, which took place more or less simultaneously.

Digitalisation and the Internet are two developments that are distinct but tightly interwoven and this makes the cause of changes to media industries very difficult to disentangle. It can be argued that digitalisation is equivalent to or perhaps even more important for the media industries than the emergence of the Internet. Many of the threats and opportunities in the current strategic environment can be traced back to this single development. Digitalisation has transformed the delivery system of virtually all media products. The Internet would not have been able to offer songs to download or newspapers if those products had not already been transformed into binary code. With digitalisation combined with the Internet, the potential for upheaval became tremendous. It has altered industry structure – for example, creating new strategic interdependencies between organisations – for example, the BBC's Freeview value system, compromised the business models of industry participants – for example, peer-to-peer file sharing of digital products threatens music and movie companies. At the same time, it is creating new products and markets, and forcing incumbents to confront out-of-date products, practices and business models. It is enlarging potential revenues by increasing opportunities for cross-media strategies, and allowing products and brands to be leveraged across more platforms.

Digitalisation is also increasing consumer choice. Without digitalisation, sound recordings would still be being played on record players and only listeners within a household would typically have access to the recording, which would have had to be purchased; the only exception would have been recorded music played on the radio or television. That contrasts strikingly with digitalised music data that can be shared over the Internet by millions of people without limit and burned on to home-based devices without authorisation or payment. Moreover, unlike a vinyl disc that would eventually wear with use, there is no loss of quality with digitalised material and indeed, the more people are downloading an item at any one time, the easier it is for others to do so simultaneously.

In addition to digitalisation, the spread of the use of the Internet for downloading material has been greatly assisted by the growth of access to broadband and by reductions in the price of devices that use it, such as computers. The increased possibility of much faster downloading of images is expected to encourage access to digitally made films in the same way that digitalisation enabled access to digitally recorded music and this challenges the film industry to offer workable legal methods of paid delivery.

The role of the consumer

Thus, it is no easy task to disentangle the causes of change that new technologies have permitted. As social scientists, we see change as the outcome of choices that individuals and groups in society make as responses to social and economic forces. Those choices are determined by the products and services that businesses offer but in turn, the success of the business depends upon the acceptance of their products by the public as consumers. Entrepreneurial ability and managerial organisation are needed to read their response; that response depends upon consumers' tastes and preferences and their willingness to adapt to new technologies and upon economic factors, such as prices and incomes. In a situation of ongoing technological change, the pace of product adoption is greater and that leads to greater uncertainty for businesses. As the authors of Chapter 4 suggest, users have been well able to handle new devices and adapt them to their own needs: many households use the Internet actively in interaction with other technological devices, like mobile phones, camcorders, cameras. Interactivity is clearly one of the leading changes connected with the Internet.

Moreover, consumers do not passively consume content. Use of the Internet has shown that much of the new content on the Internet has come from consumer generated material. This has given rise to a new phenomenon of mass media – far more content and *un*mediated content. The gate-keeping role of the 'traditional' media firms is diminished, which on the one hand, gives rise to greater freedom of choice, and on the other, to greater confusion about quality and veracity as suppliers compete for attention. Without guidance from some source, Internet users can waste time searching. It is an interesting question whether a 'free marketplace for ideas' will lead to spontaneous developments and institutions that assist users. The experience of *Wikipedia* suggests this can happen.

Moreover, consumers also influence each other and that tendency has been reinforced by the Internet; it seems that the Internet has emphasised an effect that was previously present but more limited in scope – the influence of networks. Being in a network increases the satisfaction or enjoyment a consumer gets from a product or service, though this may be subject to diminishing returns if the size gets too large. File sharing of music and movies seems not only to be physically facilitated by a network but also is psychologically more satisfying to know others share your tastes. Sociological factors play a role here in forming tastes and identities and therefore in consumption and patterns of use. Network effects can act as a positive reinforcement mechanism and may play a role also in the choice of business models by producers: if a critical network size can be achieved that snowballs consumer choices in favour of a product or brand, free access may be a good way of setting the ball rolling. This might mean giving the product away and/or waiving copyright or other restrictions to free use. This is an issue that economists among others have begun to consider.

However, as against this, though connected to it, consumer freedom may be effectively limited by a market phenomenon known as lock-in. If, for whatever reason, the market focusses on one product – even one that may not be the most technologically efficient – economies of scale may well cause that to become dominant to the point where it would be very difficult and costly to switch to another system. Many of us are locked into our ISPs because of the inconvenience that is involved in changing an email address.

Policy questions

These points raise questions about the ability of a government that is concerned with lack of competition to regulate markets. In Chapter 6, it was noted that the general economic policy shift towards freer markets coincided with development of Internet and also that economists are wary of regulation in times of considerable technological change. Even so, the question of regulating the Internet is frequently raised. In Chapter 7 the question whether the Internet will lead to greater market concentration was raised. One issue is whether 'traditional' policies, such as competition policy and media policies, can be adapted to the 'Internet economy'. The authors conclude that indeed competition policy could be used more in the media industries but that traditional media policies concerned with cross-media ownership rules are not necessarily appropriate. Other means of regulation, specifically copyright law, have clearly been adapted to the Internet, though the problem of enforcement is still an outstanding one. The globalised nature of the Internet is a limitation on the efficacy of national policies and pressure for stronger copyright law and its enforcement (a whole question in itself) seems likely increasingly to be targeted at and coordinated by international bodies. In this and other ways (making interference with technologies of rights management illegal in copyright law, for example), the Internet has had a fundamental impact on copyright law and other regulatory policy, a trend that is likely to increase with ever greater Internet use and its power with broadband.

Relationship between the media industries and technology

One message of this book may be that the media and technologies industries are growing closer. The media industry has always to some extent been a parasite on the body of technological progress: historically, each sector has come into being as a result of technical or technological advance, be that the invention of sound recording, broadcasting, the printing press, book binding, offset printing, cinematography. But this interdependency is seldom referred to by those working in the media, who often prefer to focus rather on the industries links to the cultural and artistic fields.

The Internet and associated technological developments do appear to have strengthened and made more apparent the relationship between the media and technology, and the present-day media industries' fate seems to be more closely entwined with technological developments than it once was. This is evident particularly in terms of the strategies, structures and processes used by the industries, which as has already been noted are increasingly influenced by the behaviour of the high-tech and IT sectors. Competition strategies, alliance structures, value chain analysis, which have long been a feature in the technology field, are increasingly commonplace in the media also. This shift, whereby the influence of technology and of the technology industry grows, and that of the arts and cultural sectors declines, may need addressing in media management education.

Convergence revisited

During the first Internet era the concept of convergence was accompanied by hype and hyperbole on the part of industry practitioners and consultants, and strident claims and counter-claims on the part of theorists. Despite the volume of attention devoted to the subject, a commonly accepted definition never emerged. The media industries arrived at a 'default one', involving the technologically driven blurring of the media/communications, telecommunications and information technology sectors (the telecoms and information technology sectors tended to use different definitions).

A decade into the process it is clear that while the definition that the media industries arrived at prior to events was not wrong, it does not really capture the reality of actual developments. It cannot be said that the IT, telecoms and media sectors have substantially merged. The various sectors are intact, and most observers would still baulk at describing Yahoo! or Google as media firms – rather they are Internet players with designs on aspects of the media industry's revenues and value chains.

There are, however, businesses that have adopted what could be described as 'converged business models'. Endemol is a case in point: it develops programme formats that generate revenue from traditional media sources (sale of formats, advertising and sponsorship), but also from telecoms and PC platforms via telephone voting and Internet sites. This example shows that a form of convergence is taking place, but that it is more subtle than once envisaged. One important type of convergence is between products and services. For instance, university textbooks still exist in printed, bound form, but have evolved into Internet-enabled support systems for academic faculty that include the provision of lecture plans, assessment and grading, as well as the provision of texts. Another type of convergence is evident in the content field: the websites of established media organisations, such as the BBC's News Online or News Corporation's MySpace, blend amateur and professional content.

There is also an intriguing type of convergence of strategies and structural options between sectors whereby media firms are adopting business strategies and structures from adjoining sectors, but particularly the IT industries. This was evident during the first Internet era when the media industries flirted with venture capital funds, initial public offerings and spin-offs. But the trend persists, for example, in the continuing high level of alliance and partnership activity, and in the trend towards outsourcing an increasing number of functions.

Theoretical preferences

This book has, by design, applied a wide range of theoretical approaches to the subject of the Internet and its impact on the mass media industries. In line with the multi-lens approach adopted, researchers were encouraged to apply whatever theoretical lenses they felt appropriate for analysis of their subject. As a result, a heterogeneous range of theories are used. But it is interesting that a handful of theories that have been applied by researchers from different disciplines – that, to stretch a metaphor, a convergence in terms of theories has taken place.

One body of theory frequently mentioned is that concerning network economics and network effects. This holds relevance for technology specialists, and also for strategists working in the new media field. The theory of incumbent disruption arising from technological discontinuity developed by Christensen (a management theorist with a background in engineering) is referred to by economists, technologists and strategists (Christensen, 1997). Riepl's theory concerning the (non) replacement but adjustment of the part of established media when technologically more advanced media appear is applied by strategists and communication scientists interested in user behaviour (Riepl, 1913). Finally, Schumpeter's theories of innovation and creative destruction are applied by economists, technologists and strategists (Schumpeter, 1934; 1942). Echoing a point made earlier in this chapter, each of these deals with dynamics associated with technological change. This conclusion has implications for the design of a range of academic courses in media fields.

The research that led to this book stretches back over the last five years or so. The authors are a disparate group of academics from all over Europe. The experience of collaboration between social scientists and media specialists over this period has produced an outlook and insights that do not rest on one discipline or another but instead reflect the benefits of an open-minded multi-disciplinary approach. That has much to recommend it for future research in this fast moving arena, work that is bound to be ongoing as the Internet's impact changes our society, our economy and our media industries.

References

Christensen, C. M. (1997). *The Innovator's Dilemma: When New Technologies Cause Great Firms to Fail.* Boston, MA: Harvard Business School Press.

Riepl, W. (1913). *Das Nachrichtenwesen des Altertums mit besonderer Rücksicht auf die Römer.* Leipzig: Teubner.

Schumpeter, J. A. (1934). *The Theory of Economic Development.* Cambridge, MA: Harvard University Press.

Schumpeter, J. A. (1942). *Capitalism, Socialism, and Democracy.* Harper: New York.

INDEX

Note: Page numbers for tables appear in italics.

Abernathy, W.J. 33
academic books 157
acquisitions 138–9
advanced research projects agency
    network 49–50
advertising 7, 151–4, 158
    radio 162–3
age of users 90, 92–4
alliances 135–7
anti-trust law 28–31
anti-trust policy 109
AOL/Time Warner 110–11, 130, 139
architectural innovations 33–4
ARPANET 49–50
attention economy 23
audio files 72
audio technologies 60–1
author's rights 116–7

Baldwin, T.F. 36
bandwidth capacity 38
*Bangemann Report, Europe and the Global
    Information Society* (EC) 104–5, 109
Bauman, Zygmunt 159
Being Digital (Negroponte) 115
Bertelsmann 111–3, 128–9
Black, D. 163
blogs 62, 81
BMG Publishing 113
books 156–7
    comparison with bytes 72–3
    electronic 1, 156–7
bouquet providers 58
British government and ownership
    rules 115
broadband 6, 48, 93, 160
broadcasting 48
    see also radio; television
bundling 22
    see also unbundling
Burgelman, J.C. 106
business economics 21–3

CA systems 59–60
cameras, digital 89
Carlaw et al. 26
Castells, M. 138, 145
Caves, R.E. 24
Chen, Y. 96
children 90, 92, 94, 158
Clark, K.B. 33
class divide 93–4
Coase theorem 24
collective rights management 111, 152–3
communications
    and media applications/technologies 45–6
    networks 20
    one-way/two-way 45–6
    social 68–9, 94
communities, virtual 69–70, 156
competition law 28–31, 109–16
competition policy 109
computer games 89
Congdon, Tim 107
*Consultation on Media Ownership Rules
    (DTI/DCMS)* 115
consumers 173–4
    see also users
content 13–4, 42, 65–83
    policy 107–9
    rights 59–60
    sharing 55
    using single platform 90
content industries 7
contract theory 24–5
controversial information 77–8
convergence 4, 36–9, 90, 105–6,
    138, 175–6
Coonan, Helen 107
coopetition 131–2
Copyright Directive 119
copyright law 1, 11–2, 29–31,
    116–20, 175
copyright, protection systems 59–60
corporate convergence, definition 4

countries
    content type 73
    newspapers 98
    by penetration 5, 6, 90, 92–3
    by use 5, 94, 96
creative destruction 25–6
CRM 111, 152–3
cross media 7–8, 132–5
crossmedia narrowcasting
        model 153
customisation 21–2

DAB 60
Danish TV 58
debundling 22, 143–4, 150
decentralised control and distributed
        design 53
Deevey, S. 74, 76
deregulation 38–9, 109–10
digital audio broadcast 60
digital cameras 89
digital, definition 3
digitalisation 3, 158–9, 172–3
digital music player 89
digital radio 60–1
digital radio mondiale 60–1
digital rights management 59–60, 119
digital TV 56–7
digital video broadcast–terrestrial
        standard 58–9
Dimmick, J. 96
discontinuous innovations 33–4
disintermediation 143–4
Disney 129
displacement effect 158
distributed design and decentralised
        control 53
distribution 67–8
distribution economics 22
domain names 71
dominant design theory 32, 35
dotcom boom 171
downloading 117–8, 165, 173
DRM 59–61, 119
DVB-H 58–9
DVB-T 58–9
dynamic competition 18, 25

e-books 1, 156–7
e-commerce 6
EC 103–4, 110–3, 121
    Rental Directive (1992) 118
    see also EU
e-commerce 6
economic theories 9–10, 17–27

economies of scale and scope 19–20
educational books 157
education, as predictor 93–4
electronic books 1, 156–7
EMI 110–1, 113–4
employees, categories 145–6
endogenous innovation 26
endometriosis 74, 76
end-to-end architecture 52
entrepreneurship 10–11
EU
    copyright 30, 119
    directives 107–9, 118–9
European Commission 103–4, 110–3, 121
European online newspapers 80–1
evolutionary economics 25–7
extension 144

fair use 30
file sharing 54–5
FIPP 155
first Internet era 15, 126–30, 171
fragmentation 144
front pages, newspapers 79–80

games, computer 89
Garino, J. 141
Garnham, N. 102
gender 93
general purpose technology 26–7
Gerhart, S.L. 78
Gibbons, T. 122
Gilbert, C.G. 141
globalisation 8–9, 39
Gnutella 55
goods, information 42
Google 114
Gore, Al 104
government policies 174–5
GPT 26–7
Graham, Andrew 121–2
Green Paper on Convergence
        (EC, 1997) 106
Guardian blog 81
Gulati, R. 141

Hagen, L.M. 95
Hare, E. 159
horizontal integration 110, 134
hosts 6, 70–1
hyperlinks 51, 66, 82

IBOC (in band on channel) 60
IMPALA 112–3
incremental innovations 33–4

incumbents 125–30, 134–5,
   140–1
InfoPen 86
information, definition 8
information economy 41–2
information goods 42
Information Rules (Shapiro and Varian) 18
innovations
   architectural 33–4
   discontinuous 33–4
   endogenous 26
   incremental 33–4
   market-based 34–5
innovative reporting 81
Innovator's Dilemma, The (Christensen) 34
insurgents 125–6, 134
integration 141–2
   horizontal 110, 134
   vertical 110–1, 114, 134
intellectual property law 11–2, 30
   see also copyright law
intellectual property rights 30
interactivity 87–9, 97, 151, 155
International Federation of the Periodical
   Press 155
Internet audio 61
Internet, definition 3–4
Internet economy 39–40
Internet eras
   first 15, 126–30, 171
   second 130–5, 171
Internet Protocol 46, 47, 51–4, 57, 62–4
Internet radio 160–3
Internet resource surveys 74, 76–7
Internet service providers 92–3
inter-organisational partnerships 136
invention-innovation-diffusion 47
investment funds 140
IP 46–7, 51–4, 57, 62–4
IP law 11–2, 30
   see also copyright law
iPods 61, 89
IPRs 30
IPTV 57–8
IPv4 53
IPv6 54
IP-VoD 57–8
ISPs 92–3

Jensen, J.F. 88
Johnson, T.J. 95
journalists 145–6, 150–1

Kaye, B.K. 95
knowledge, definition 8

knowledge economy 40–1
knowledge workers 41–2

languages 73
Li, Z. 96
Lipsey et al. 26
locking in customers 20–1, 174

magazines 154–6
management theories 12, 31–5
market-based innovations 34–5
McChesney, Robert 122
McVoy, D. 36
media 7, 95–7
   convergence 4, 36–9, 90, 105–6,
      138, 175–6
media and communication applications/
   technologies 45–6
media firms 22, 34, 78–81
   distribution of content 67–8, 82
   processes 142–6
   structure 135–42
media industries 7, 63–4, 134
   contract theory 24–5
   public policies 102–22
   and regulation 11–2, 27–31
   and technology 31–5, 175
media-use hypothesis 88–9
mergers 110–5, 138–9
mobile phones 90–1, 93
mobile TV 58–9
Monti, Mario 111–2
mp3 164
MP3 player 89
Murdoch, James 109
music industry 1, 97, 110–5, 163–6
music player, digital 89
music sharing 55
MySpace 69

names, domain 71
Napster 55, 164
narrowcasting model 153
Negroponte, Nicholas 115
neighbouring rights 116–7
neoclassical economics 18–9
   see also non-neoclassical economics
network architecture, standards 38
network economy 39–40, 145–6
networking sites, social 68–9
networks 20, 38, 137–8, 174
news 79–81, 95, 97–8, 152
news.nl 86
newspapers 35, 62, 79–81, 95–8,
   144, 149–54

non-neoclassical economics 23–5
    see also neoclassical economics

Ofcom 121
OMA 59
one-way communications 45–6
online advertising 151–4
online communities 69–70, 156
online newspapers 79–81, 150–3
open mobile alliance 59
organisational technology 31–2
ownership rules 115–6

P2P networking 54–5
packet switching technology 49–50
partnerships 135–7
Pathfinder 129–30
pathology of sustained success
    syndrome 35
Pavlik, J. 146
peer-to-peer networking 54–5
penetration level 90, 92–4
personalisation 22
Peterson, I. 77
phones, mobile, use 90–91, 93
platforms 90, 105, 106
Podcasting services 61
Porter, M.E. 155
Powell, Michael 115
price discrimination 21
print front pages 79–80
print newspapers 150, 152
property rights 23–5, 29–30
public choice theory 28

radio 60–1, 78, 95, 159–63
Rafaeli, Sheizaf 87–8
reading 96
record companies 110–5
recorded music 97
regulation 11–2, 27–31
    see also competition law; copyright law
regulatory capture 28
reintegration 141–2
Rental Directive (EC, 1992) 118
reporting, innovative 81
revenues 151–3
Riepls law 88
royalties 162
rural areas 94

Salaverría, R. 81
scalability 53
Schumpeter, J. 18
search engines 77–8, 82

second hand books 157
second Internet era 130–5, 171
servers, web 71
service providers 58
Shapiro, C. 18
size of the Internet 70–1
social class 93–4
social networking sites 68–9
Sony 111–3
spin-offs 139–41
static competition 25
Steinfeld, C. 36
Steuer, J. 88
STM books 157
strategy processes 142–6
streaming technologies 47, 61,
    160–3
sunk investment 24–5
supply chain management 40
surveys 74, 76–7
switching costs 20–1

TCP/IP 46, 50, 63
technological protection measures
    119–20
technology transitions 32–5
television 4–5, 78–9, 95–7, 157–9
    digital 56–7
*Television without Frontiers Directive
    (EC)* 107–9
text media 61–2
time constraints 22
time-shifted radio 160–1
time spent on Internet 88, 94
Time Warner 129–30
Time Warner/AOL 110–1, 130, 139
Ting, C. 161–2
TPMs 119–20
transaction cost economics 23–4
Transmission Control Protocol/Internet
    Protocol 46, 50, 63
TRIPS Treaty 30
trust 98–9
TV *see* television
TV2 Sputnik 58
TVF 107–9
two-way communications 45–6

unbundling 22, 143–4, 150
Universal Publishing 113
USENET 69
use of Internet 94
users 87–8, 173–4
    age 90, 92–4
    by country 90, 92–4

users (*continued*)
  number 5–6
  time spent 88, 94
US ownership rules 115

value chains 142–5
VAoD 48
Varian, H. 18
versatility 89
vertical integration 110–1, 114, 134
video and audio on demand 48
video technologies 55–60
virtual communities 69–70, 156
Vivendi Universal 130

Waldvogel, J. 95
Warner music group 113–4

wealth, as predictor 93–4
weblogs 81
web pages 71–3
web servers 71
websites 71–6, 78–9
Wikipedia 70
Wildman, S. 162
WIPO (World Intellectual Property
  Organisation) 30
WIPO Internet Treaties 118–9
WMG 113–4
workers, knowledge 41–2
World Wide Web, definition 4
WTO (World Trade Organization) 30

Yoffie, D.B. 37
YouTube 114, 159